THE SUDAN UNDER WINGATE

Sir F. Reginald Wingate and Karl von Slatin Pasha

THE SUDAN UNDER WINGATE

Administration in the Anglo-Egyptian Sudan 1899-1916

Gabriel Warburg
Haifa University, Israel

FRANK CASS & CO LTD
1971

First published in 1971 by
FRANK CASS AND COMPANY LIMITED
67 Great Russell Street, London WC1B 3BT

ISBN 0 7146 2612 0

Printed in Great Britain by
Clarke, Doble & Brendon, Ltd., Plymouth

Preface

THE purpose of this book is to describe and to analyse the administrative policies in the Anglo-Egyptian Sudan during the formative years of the Condominium. The period chosen for this purpose corresponds with the governor-generalship of Sir Reginald Wingate, whose seventeen years as governor-general of the Sudan, had a lasting effect on later developments. This book is therefore primarily about Wingate, Slatin Pasha and a handful of British officials who formulated and executed the Sudan's administrative policy. It also tries to assess the role played by the Egyptian government and its representatives in the Sudan, in shaping the government of a country, of which they were supposed to be co-rulers. Finally, the book attempts to estimate the effects of administration on the population of the Sudan and to find out whether certain groups within the population influenced the development of government policies as time went on.

I have tried to evaluate the impact of the British and Egyptian governments in formulating policies in the Sudan. However, I limited myself to administrative aspects without trying to assess the political implications of the reconquest. Certain spheres of administration have been dealt with quite briefly. The development of education in the Northern Sudan has been covered adequately by Mr. Mohammed Omar Beshir, while Dr. L. M. Sanderson has devoted her research to education in the South. In view of these works, and also the fascinating autobiography of Shaykh Bābikr Badrī, the founder of girls' education in the Sudan, I have decided to limit myself only to those aspects of education which had a direct bearing on other fields of administration. Similarly, the development of communications and transport has been described by Mr. R. L. Hill and Dr. O. M. O. Abdu, while the beginnings of a medical service were dealt with by Dr. H. C. Squires. Finally, the economic financial and agricultural policies during the early years of the Condominium, have been admirably dealt with by Mr. J. Stone, Dr. A. W. Abdel Rahim and Mr. A. Gaitskell.[1]

The source materials used in writing this book are primarily the official and private papers of the Sudan government officials who worked in the Sudan until the end of the First World War. Most of these papers have been stored at the Sudan Archive in the School of Oriental Studies, University of Durham. Other collections are those of the Church Missionary Society in London, the Anti-Slavery Society at Oxford, private and official records at the Public Record Office, London, and the *Sudan Intelligence Reports* at the War Office Library, London. This brings me to a major shortcoming, namely the lack of adequate source material of Egyptian or Sudanese origin. Ample use has been made of the few existing autobiographies written by inhabitants of the Sudan. Nonetheless, in the absence of adequate sources, I tried to assess the reactions of the Sudanese to their new rulers through the reflection of their views in the private papers of the administrators. I can only hope that further evidence will emerge and enable historians to shed some light on this problem.

For the spelling of Arabic names and terms I have followed the accepted system of transliteration which will enable readers to find these terms in Arabic publications and dictionaries. The only exception is in regard to names of larger towns which are spelt in the conventional form, e.g. El Obeid, Khartoum, Suakin.

Acknowledgements

My thanks are due to many who assisted me in writing this book and in preparing the thesis, on which it is largely based. In the first place I acknowledge my gratitude to Professor P. M. Holt, who guided me throughout my research and made many suggestions with regard to the final form of this book. I owe many thanks to Professor G. Baer, whose initial encouragement prompted me to undertake this research, and who offered me invaluable advice. Professor G. N. Sanderson, Dr. H. Shaked and Dr. N. Rose read the manuscript and offered many recommendations regarding its structure and contents; numerous suggestions have been included in the book and improved its final form. However, none of the above hold any responsibility for any errors or shortcomings the book may still hold.

I express my gratitude to Mr. I. J. C. Foster, keeper of Oriental books at the University Library, Durham, who enabled me to pursue my research at the Sudan Archive. I am also grateful to the librarians of the War Office, the Public Record Office, the Church Missionary Society, and the keeper of the Anti-Slavery archive, for allowing me to use their valuable collections.

For valuable assistance I would like to express appreciation to the late Sir Harold A. MacMichael who placed his vast experience of the Sudan at my disposal. Also Lady C. Bonham Carter, who answered my inquisitive questions regarding the work of the late Sir Edgar Bonham Carter, first legal secretary of the Anglo-Egyptian Sudan.

Quotations taken from Crown Copyright records in the Public Record Office and other archives appear by permission of the Controller of H. M. Stationery Office. I would like to thank the editors of *Asian and African Studies* and *Middle Eastern Studies* for allowing me to include parts of two of my papers, which had previously been published in their journals, in the present volume.

My thanks are extended to the Central Research Fund of the University of London, the Friends of the Hebrew University of Jerusalem in London, and the Haifa University College, whose financial generosity enabled me to pursue my research in the most favourable conditions.

I am gratefully indebted to Mrs. J. Reinhold who prepared the book for print and assisted me in eliminating many remaining mistakes. Finally, I would like to thank my wife Rachel without whose constant encouragement and immeasurable help this book could never have been written.

GABRIEL WARBURG

Haifa University.
November 1969.

Abbreviations

CAO *Sudan Government Civil Administration Orders.*

CMSA Church Missionary Society Archive.

DNBS *Dictionary of National Biography, Supplement.*

GGC Governor-General's Council, minutes of meetings.

GGR *Reports on the Finances, Administration, and Conditions of the Sudan, (Confidential).*

FO Foreign Office Archives.

Hill, *BD* R. Hill, *A Biographical Dictionary of the Sudan* (2nd ed.) London 1967. Reprinted by Frank Cass & Co. Ltd.

SAD Sudan Archive, at the School of Oriental Studies, University of Durham.

SG *Sudan Gazette.*

SIR *Sudan Intelligence Report.*

SNR *Sudan Notes and Records.*

SPS *Sudan Political Service, 1899–1929,* Khartoum 1930.

Contents

CHAPTER I

The Governors-General, Kitchener and Wingate

The reconquest of the Sudan and the Condominium Agreement

'. . . ON 4th September [1898] the British and Egyptian flags were hoisted with due ceremony on the walls of the ruined palace at Khartoum . . .' and the Mahdist state came to an end.[1] The overthrow of Mahdism had been propagated for many years by some of the senior British officers of the Egyptian army. Most notable among them was Major Wingate,[2] head of the intelligence department, whose book *Mahdiism and the Egyptian Sudan* was the beginning of a concerted effort to revive British interest in the reconquest of the Sudan. When on 13 March 1898, the British government ordered Kitchener[3] to advance into the Sudan, public opinion in Britain was well prepared for the forthcoming campaign. Britain was furnished with a pretext for the expedition by the defeat of the Italian forces at Adowa on 1 March 1896. However, subsequent evidence has proved that the British decision of 11–12 March was prompted by European reasons connected with the Triple Alliance. Egyptian interests in the Upper Nile played no role in the government's considerations, nor did the struggle for the control of the Nile, which became a dominating factor only in the later stages of the reconquest.[4] The military campaign which brought about the collapse of the Mahdist state started on 18 March 1896 and came to its successful conclusion on 24 November 1899. It was planned and executed by Kitchener, the sirdar of the Egyptian army, assisted by the information supplied by Wingate, Slatin,[5] and the intelligence department. However, the crushing defeat of the Khalifa's army in the battles of the Atbara, Karari, and Umm Diwaykarāt, was first and foremost the result of the technological superiority of the advancing conquerors.

The overthrow of the Mahdist state forced the British government to determine the status of the reconquered Sudan as well as its future administration. Until June 1898 there was every indication that the British government intended to restore Egyptian rule in the Sudan. In June 1898 Cromer pointed out to Salisbury that after the conquest of Omdurman the French might be encountered in the Upper Nile. In that case the Anglo-Egyptian commander would have to lay claim to the territory in the name either of the Egyptian government or of the British government, or of both. Thus, in July 1898 the 'two flags' policy was adopted which marked the beginning of Anglo-Egyptian rule in the Sudan. The Condominium Agreement which came into being as a result of this policy excluded Egyptian and international authority from the Sudan and vested the supreme civil and military command in the British-nominated governor-general. On 19 January 1899 Lord Cromer and Buṭrus Ghālī Pasha signed the 'Agreement for the Administration of the Sudan', and on the same day Lord Kitchener of Khartoum was appointed as the first sirdar and governor-general of the Anglo-Egyptian Sudan.[6]

Kitchener's governor-generalship

The relationship between the governor-general of the Sudan and the British agent and consul-general in Egypt was largely determined during the short period of Kitchener's governor-generalship. Following the battle of Kararī, the relations between Cromer and Kitchener reached a crisis. Cromer had just completed the first draft of the Sudan agreement. Included in it were two articles relating to the control of the consul-general over Sudanese affairs. Kitchener strongly objected and during his visit to England persuaded Salisbury to alter the proposed constitution. In a letter to Cromer, Salisbury summed up Kitchener's arguments:

> . . . the Governor General of the Soudan is to govern and is to spend the money he has. In both cases he is, of course, to obey orders received from you . . . but he shall not by a formal document be forbidden to pass an Ordinance or to spend 100 £ without preliminary approval . . .[7]

As a result of this letter the original draft of the proposed Condominium Agreement was amended. This draft had contained, under article IV, a passage stating that the governor-general of the Sudan could not promulgate laws or regulations without the prior consent of the Khedive and the British consul-general in Cairo. Article VI stated that in all financial matters the Sudan would be controlled by the Egyptian ministry of finance. Both these articles were deleted from the final text of the agreement. The financial regulation of the Sudan government thus became a separate document. This gave a much greater latitude to the governor-general of the Sudan who was empowered to make appointments of personnel and changes in the budget, with the only proviso that, should such changes entail any increase in the liability of Egypt, they must be approved by the ministry of finance and the Egyptian council of ministers.[8] The signed agreement, as amended, contained no mention of the control exercised by the British consul-general in Cairo over the governor-general. Salisbury, therefore, suggested that '. . . it will be necessary to take an acknowledgement from each new Governor-General, on his appointment, of his subordination to the British Agency . . .'[9] In the absence of any clearly defined regulations, it was left to Cromer and Kitchener to find a workable *modus vivendi* for the future relationship. On 19 January 1899 Cromer wrote to Kitchener stating the principles of his relations with the Sudan: '. . . Generally what I want is to control the big questions, but to leave all the detail and execution to be managed locally . . .'[10] However, it was soon apparent that these general regulations were open to misinterpretation.

Kitchener's aims were clear when he became governor-general. He had avenged the murder of Gordon and proved that the Egyptian army could fight. Now, his first priority was to re-establish the seat of government in Khartoum, in the palace where Gordon had ruled, and to transfer the remnants of the population of Omdurman back to the former capital. The rebuilding of Khartoum was ordered by Kitchener in November 1898, while enjoying a hero's welcome in England. Inadequate sums had been set aside for this project in the Sudan budget, and Kitchener set out to find the necessary funds through less conventional methods. On 26 January 1899, he directed Wingate to '. . . loot like blazes. I want any quantity of marble stairs, marble pavings, iron railings, looking glasses and fittings; doors, windows, furniture of all sorts . . .'[11] Again he ordered Wingate not to send any of the Sudan accounts to Gorst, the financial adviser of the Egyptian government. Even Maxwell,[12] the new governor of Khartoum province, was left in the dark and complained to Wingate that everything was sacrificed in order to facilitate the rebuilding of Khartoum. Cromer attempted to interfere, but to no avail. On two occasions Kitchener's obstinacy had far-reaching consequences. First, he decided to stop the field allowance granted to the Egyptian army serving in the Sudan; Cromer's order to renew this allowance went unheeded. Secondly, Kitchener adamantly refused to cancel some of the trainloads of building materials destined for Khartoum which were needed to supply grain for the famine stricken provinces. *The Times* correspondent who wrote in April 1900 that the building of Khartoum was executed '. . . by the autocratic will of a single man . . .' was therefore not far from the mark. But he made the following criticisms. Firstly, owing to hasty legislation, most of the town's lands had passed into the hands of a few speculators. Secondly, Kitchener's assumption that the population of Omdurman would move to Khartoum proved fallacious. Khartoum remained an empty city, while the inhabitants of Omdurman were completely neglected.[13]

The Anglo-Egyptian administration of the Sudan started before Kitchener became governor-general. The reconquest had taken more than two years, during which period the new administration was slowly extended, first to Ḥalfā and then to Dongola and Berber. By April 1899, the reconquered territories of the country had been divided into five provinces and three districts, each under the governorship of a British officer, with Egyptian officers acting as *ma'mūrs*.[14] A number of ordinances were promulgated, dealing mainly with tenure of property, taxation, the licensing of firearms, and the sale of alcoholic liquors. Kitchener also sent a set of instructions to all governors, inspectors, and *ma'mūrs* laying down his principles of government.[15] The main premise of these instructions was that '. . . The absolute uprootal by the Dervishes of the old system of government has afforded an opportunity for initiating a new administration more in harmony with the requirements of the Soudan . . .' The new administration was to be built by '. . . individual action of British officers, working independently, but with a common purpose, on the individual natives whose confidence they have gained . . .'. Kitchener warned his governors that this could be achieved only through the '. . . better class of native, through whom we may hope gradually to influence the whole population . . .'. Furthermore, the governors were warned against trusting the people of the Sudan who make things appear as pleasant to their superiors as possible. The treatment of the inhabitants was to be just but severe: '. . . The Government should do nothing which could be interpreted as a sign of weakness, and all insubordination must be promptly and severely suppressed . . .' The memorandum included also detailed instructions to the Egyptian *ma'mūrs* who were warned against accepting bribes, and were ordered '. . . to make the government of your district as great a contrast as possible to that of the Dervishes . . .' Lastly, the memorandum mentioned the three main principles to be observed by the Sudan government in the coming years. These were: the toleration of domestic slavery, low taxation and the encouragement of Orthodox Islam as opposed to Sufism.

Having laid down these general principles, Kitchener left his new governors to use their own initiative. He was not concerned with central administrative measures, and even refused to consider the *Sudan Annual Report*, which he ordered Wingate to compile in his name.[16] In general, this system of decentralization might have been acceptable in a country like the Sudan, devoid of effective communications and hampered by immense distances, provided that the governor-general enjoyed the respect and trust of his provincial governors. Unfortunately, Kitchener's relations with the British officers were predominantly based on fear. Hence the criticisms they offered never reached his ear, but were received by Wingate, who could only offer his sympathy.[17] Cromer, who knew Kitchener well, attempted to change the latter's attitude to his subordinates. In a private letter sent on the day of his appointment as governor-general, Cromer warned Kitchener, '. . . In the first place, pray encourage your subordinates to speak up and tell you when they do not agree with you. They are all far too much inclined to be frightened of you . . .'[18] It was not only fear which disturbed the relationship between Kitchener and his subordinates. They also lost faith in his ability to construct a civil administration and were concerned over his absolute absorption in the rebuilding of Khartoum to the exclusion of everything else.

When in 1899 famine broke out in the Sudan, conditions were still unchanged. Kitchener had received ample warning as to the coming plight. Towards the end of 1898, over seventy Sudan notables presented him with a petition in which they complained that the people of the Sudan had been robbed of all they possessed. Moreover, they claimed that owing to the compulsory recruitment of agricultural slaves into the army, cultivation was at a standstill, and hence famine was imminent.[19] As early as April 1898, Talbot[20] wrote to Wingate : '. . . I fancy we've skimmed the people pretty well. I hope they will have enough left for seed . . .'[21] By April 1899, Talbot reported that on the White Nile '. . . people live upon water and nuts and are dying in large numbers . . .'[22] Yet, despite these warnings and Cromer's repeated demands, Kitchener refused to take any measures to alleviate the people's plight. He maintained that the famine aided his policy of depriving the Khalifa of local support, and left for a two months' vacation in England. This same attitude prevailed in Kitchener's treatment of the Egyptian army. The army was employed in constructing the Sudan railways and in the works' department, without receiving additional remuneration. But it was not only in the financial sphere that Kitchener's attitude manifested itself. He also regarded the Egyptian officers with profound distrust, as expressed in his *Memorandum to Mudirs*. Before leaving the Sudan, he reiterated this distrust to Maxwell, who duly reported it to Wingate :

> . . . the last thing he said to me was to keep this in mind. The fact is they [the Egyptian officers] are not to be trusted and he always said

even a British officer with no experience whatever would be better than a discontented intriguing Egyptian . . .[23]

Kitchener's treatment of his officers, and his administrative measures, had won him the fear and mistrust of most of his subordinates. The destruction of the Mahdi's tomb, and the treatment of his remains, turned certain sections of public opinion in Britain against him. The Mahdi's tomb was erected in Omdurman, according to the Khalifa's orders, on the spot where he had died and was buried. It became a centre of worship and of pilgrimage, thus replacing the pilgrimage to Mecca, which had been discontinued during the Mahdia. The order issued by Kitchener to raze the tomb to the ground and to cast the Mahdi's bones into the Nile, caused widespread resentment in Britain. Throughout the crisis, Cromer and the British officials in the Sudan fully backed Kitchener's order to destroy the Mahdi's tomb. Kitchener argued that the destruction was dictated by political considerations, and that it was fully backed by the orthodox Muslim leaders.[24] This attitude prevailed when a few months later a Mahdist insurrection was reported from the Blue Nile. On 27 August, Muḥammad Sharīf (one of the Mahdi's Khalīfas) and two of the Mahdi's sons were killed, and fifty-five prisoners taken. The insurrection seems to have been a minor affair, only three men of the Egyptian army force being slightly wounded. Yet Kitchener, fearing that any leniency might be interpreted as weakness, decided to execute all the prisoners and to arrest all those implicated in the revolt. Rodd, who was acting consul-general in Cromer's absence, refused to comply with Kitchener's demand, because '. . . of the effect on public opinion in England of a wholesale execution . . .'[25]

Kitchener's term of office as governor-general should probably be regarded as an extension of his work as sirdar, rather than as a new venture of a civil administrator. His desire to leave the Sudan was first expressed in September 1898, and persisted throughout his governor-generalship. Hence, it could hardly be expected that he would devote his time and his talents to the tedious details of long term government. The glory of rebuilding Khartoum and the governor-general's palace, and the foundation of Gordon College, were bound to appeal more to Kitchener who regarded his sojourn in the Sudan as purely temporary. Cromer, who originally proposed Kitchener's appointment as governor-general, soon changed his mind. He realized that the details of civilian government were beyond Kitchener's comprehension and hence did not insist that he should remain in the Sudan. On 18 December 1899 Kitchener was appointed as Lord Roberts's Chief of Staff in the Boer War, and a week later he sailed for South Africa. To his successor he left a skeleton staff, a famine-stricken country and an army rife with discontent. It is no wonder, therefore, that when he expressed his wish to return to the Sudan after the Boer War, Cromer objected strongly and wrote : '. . . He would not be able to hold the Soudan without a large British force . . .'[26]

Wingate's governor-generalship

Wingate was appointed governor-general of the Sudan and sirdar of the Egyptian army on 23 December 1899. Up to the battle of Kararī, Wingate had been in charge of military intelligence and so had played an important role in preparing the reconquest. He had established close relations with many of the Sudanese shaykhs and with the help of Slatin and Na'ūm Shuqayr[27] had succeeded in providing valuable information for the advancing Anglo-Egyptian forces. With the battle nearing its end, Wingate knew that the importance of military intelligence was bound to decline. He, therefore, decided to seek a post which would secure his future in case Kitchener decided to leave. In a letter to Kitchener, Wingate explained his views about the reorganization of the intelligence department and its division into quite distinct military and civil branches. He suggested that he should head the civil branch in Cairo, and coordinate policies with the British agency.[28] Wingate was at this stage next to Kitchener on the Egyptian army seniority list. His presence in Cairo in close proximity to Lord Cromer and at the head of the Sudan office, could therefore place him in a better position when the next governor-general was appointed. In a letter to Rodd, Cromer's first secretary at the agency, Wingate stated his views as to his future prospects :

> . . . The departure of Hunter has placed me in the position of second in command of the Egyptian Army; I do not say for a moment that in the event of the departure of the present Sirdar, I should be selected to succeed him; at the same time I should not submit to any other officer now in the Egyptian Army being given the preference over me to succeed the present Sirdar. It seems to me quite possible that some senior general from outside the E.A. [Egyptian Army] may succeed, but under any circumstances I should, as head of the Sudan Office, be in a better position to have my claims considered . . . if I were an Anglo-Egyptian than if I were a purely British official . . .[29]

Cromer had mentioned the possibility of Wingate's appointment to the governor-generalship as early as May 1899. He had known Wingate for fifteen years and held his achievements in the intelligence department in high esteem. Moreover, Cromer knew that Wingate would be easier to control than a general nominated by the war office, whose appointments Cromer regarded with complete mistrust. The appointment of a civilian governor-general was not considered at that time, as the whole country was ruled by military officers. For these reasons, when Kitchener was ordered to leave for the Boer War, Wingate's nomination for the governor-generalship seems to have been unopposed.

Wingate's appointment was greeted with satisfaction by many of the Egyptian army officers, who had suffered from Kitchener's autocratic methods.[30] *The Times* correspondent in Khartoum described the atmosphere which was created by the appointment as '. . . a general expectation as of something springlike and mild . . .'[31] Even *al-Ahrām* accepted Wingate as the best possible choice, though commenting that it would have been better to appoint an Egyptian.[32] For Wingate himself, the initiation into the long-cherished post of governor-general could hardly have been more difficult. Many of the veteran officers who had been administering the provinces had left to take part in the Boer War, and before Wingate could wind up his affairs in Cairo, a mutiny of a Sudanese battalion broke out in Omdurman. Furthermore, the country was impoverished by continuous wars culminating in the famine of 1899. Cultivation and trade were practically at a standstill owing to the decline in population, the tribal policy of the Khalifa 'Abdallāhi, and the trade and agricultural policy adopted by Kitchener. These were some of the difficulties faced by Wingate when, with a handful of British officers inexperienced in administration and with little knowledge of local languages, aided by Egyptian officers and officials whom he did not trust, he set about to build up the civil administration of the Sudan.

Wingate's powers as governor-general and sirdar were the same as those of his predecessor. The following definition which appeared in *The Times* is a fairly accurate summary :

> . . . Everything derives from the will of the Governor General . . . He unites in himself, and delegates from himself, all legislative, executive and judicial powers . . . He 'notifies' his ordinances to the joint Sovereigns, but he is under no obligation to attend to their advice . . .[33]

The governor-general was, to a certain extent, controlled by the British consul-general in Egypt, but apart from that his authority was not limited either by representative bodies or by public opinion. The consultations which did take place on an executive level, were undertaken by Wingate voluntarily, at least until 1910 when the governor-general's council was instituted. During the seventeen years of Wingate's governor-generalship, the underlying principle emerging was one of reconstruction. Development was slow, and consistent, but lacking in outstanding episodes. The Sudan emerged from a state of near famine and of financial dependence on Egypt, to a fairly stable economy which could support its growing population. An administrative structure was built up in the provinces and the centre, and though military rule prevailed, an ever-increasing number of civilians was recruited into the service and slowly affected its character.[34] The extension of communications by rail and river, and the building of Port Sudan were some of the important achievements of this period which greatly contributed to economic development. Economic expansion culminated in the Gezira development project, sanctioned in 1913, which enabled the Sudan to become a major cotton-producing country. Thus the country, which was reconquered for strategical and political reasons only and was regarded as a financial liability, emerged as a potential economic asset for Britain before the Wingate era was over.

The routine of a governor-general[35]

A survey of Wingate's routine of office is essential in order to understand how his government functioned. The 'Sudan year' started in Cairo. The governor-general, accompanied by Slatin and by his private secretaries, used to arrive in Cairo from their annual leave towards the end of October. During the following two weeks the biggest annual meeting of Sudan officials took place. The directors of all the departments and most of the provincial governors were gathered in Cairo to discuss the Sudan budget for the following year. The budget had already been hammered out during the summer months in England in endless meetings, in many of which Wingate had participated. The purpose of the meeting in Cairo was to enable the governors and directors of departments to voice their objections, with the hope that some minor changes could still be effected. The Cairo gathering was Wingate's only opportunity of meeting all his provincial governors personally. Therefore, there was as much activity behind the scenes of the budget discussions, as in the meetings themselves. Matters ranging from personnel and promotions to tribal policy and military expeditions were discussed, and in many cases decided upon. There are numerous letters from Wingate to his governors insisting on their attending the Cairo gathering, so as to conclude arrangements regarding their provinces. During the month he stayed in Cairo, Wingate was a regular guest at the British agency where discussion with the consul-general took place regarding matters on which the latter's approval was necessary. In his capacity as sirdar, Wingate had also certain functions to perform in Cairo. A courtesy visit to the Khedive and the Egyptian minister of war, followed by a review of the troops and barracks, formed the official part of the sirdar's visit. More important, however, were the discussions with the financial adviser to the war office and with the British staff officers in Cairo. These were usually attended by the adjutant-general, and all matters concerning finance, recruiting and army personnel were decided upon.

Wingate arrived in Khartoum towards the middle of November and took up his residence at the governor-general's palace. The following extract from the diary of Butler, of the intelligence department, affords a glimpse of the palace routine.

> . . . Sir Reginald Wingate, Governor General and Sirdar, was a most kind, pleasant little man . . . He loved pomp and state and his early morning rides round Khartoum were rather a joke with British Bimbashis, as the cavalcade was so glittering and immense, black cavalry men with lances, ADCs, P.S.s. and a herd of all grades of officials . . .[36]

The rest of the morning was spent in dealing with correspondence. Wingate kept up a regular correspondence, with nearly all his provincial governors, in which matters concerning their respective provinces were discussed. Most of their requests were then sent by Wingate to the heads of departments enclosing his own recommendations. Wingate's letters to the British consul-general and the Sudan agent in Cairo formed the most voluminous part of his correspondence. A lot of time was also devoted to dealing with petitions from inhabitants of the Sudan. The direct appeal to the governor-general had been an accepted procedure of government during the Turco-Egyptian regime, and had been carried on by the Mahdi and the Khalifa. The number of petitions presented during the year was regarded by Wingate as indicating the extent of public contentment. Many of the petitions were forwarded by Wingate to Slatin and to the intelligence department. Others found their way to the provincial governor or the departmental director concerned. Wingate's Arabic secretary sorted out the petitions, translated them, and presented them to Wingate. The number of petitions presented to Wingate in 1900 was 4,074, and he soon realized that many petitioners were repeating requests which had already been decided upon. Hence in 1902 Wingate published an order to the effect that his decisions were final, and by 1905 the number of petitions had decreased to 1,108.[37] Most of these dealt with problems of land ownership and taxation, while the number dealing with slavery cases decreased rapidly over the years.

During the winter Wingate entertained a host of distinguished guests, and compiled his annual report on the administration of the Sudan. This consisted of detailed reports by provincial governors and heads of departments, as well as a memorandum by Wingate himself. It was from these reports that the British consuls-general compiled their annual reports on the Sudan, which were published as command papers. As for Wingate's guests, there were constant complaints in his correspondence with the consuls-general, about the time and money he had to spend on entertainment. Yet judging by the many invitations he sent, he was by no means eager to put an end to these visits. It was Cromer who tried to limit his enthusiasm for guests when he wrote in 1905, '. . . I am all for entertaining the officials and local people. But I do not think you are at all called upon to do much for tourists. I do mighty little for them . . .'[38]

Until 1912, the governor-general's palace was the only place for Anglican services in Khartoum, and Wingate never failed to attend. Wingate's deep religious feelings were described by Gwynne, the first Anglican Bishop of the Sudan : '. . . The holiness of life is most marked by all who come in contact with him . . . He never moves in the morning without prayer and Bible reading . . .'[39] But apart from his duties as a Christian, Wingate was also a keen Freemason, and soon after his appointment to the governor-generalship, he was approached to establish a district lodge in the Sudan. In 1903 he founded the Reginald Wingate Lodge, which held its regular meetings at the palace. Wingate played an active part in all its activities which were often mentioned in the Sudan correspondence.[40]

Wingate undertook at least one big tour of inspection each year. The official reports on these tours which were published in the *Sudan Intelligence Reports*, give little information. Fortunately, detailed accounts of some of them were written by the inspectors who accompanied Wingate or by Slatin who kept a regular diary of events. In 1902 Wingate himself kept a diary of his tour of the White Nile up to Gondokoro. On these tours the governor-general was usually accompanied by over twenty officers and officials of the Sudan government in addition to his military escort. Before arriving at any government post or village the governor-general was met by all government officials and army officers as well as by the shaykhs of the various tribes. Following a parade of the army and an inspection of its magazines, Wingate met the assembled shaykhs and religious notables to whom he distributed presents of beads or money and gave robes of honour or religious robes. During his stay at each station, Wingate received and settled petitions, appointed new shaykhs wherever necessary and attended various races and sporting events organized in his honour. Wingate's intention in these inspections was to keep in direct touch with his officers and officials as well as with the people of the Sudan. During the First World War, Wingate's tours covered the length and breadth of the country. As a strong advocate of the value of direct contact, he believed that the loyalty of the Sudanese people to British rule was in fact a personal loyalty to the British governor-general who had ruled them for fifteen years. Wingate elaborated on this when he wrote: '. . . I feel that were I to leave the Sudan, even for a day . . . I should seriously risk an upset of the present tranquil state of affairs here . . .'[41] Commenting on his tours of Kordofan and the Gezira he noted: '. . . I have spent several hours daily talking to important natives . . . and I am confident that the sympathetic touch which these conversations produce is very helpful . . .'[42]

During the hot summer months of April–June the governor-general and his staff moved to Erkowit, a hill station not far from Suakin, which was established in 1902. During his stay there Wingate had more time to deal with correspondence and to prepare the confidential reports on the British officers for the war office. While at Erkowit, Wingate usually undertook a tour of inspection of the Red Sea province.

In June Wingate left the Sudan for his annual leave in England, where he stayed until October. During the summer the Sudan was practically deserted by its British officials. A skeleton staff was kept in various government departments, but very little work was done and practically no decisions were taken. The acting sirdar and governor-general had to be an officer of the rank of colonel, and consequently was not too well acquainted with the problems of administration. During Wingate's long absence in England at least two acting governor-generals filled his position every year and apart from the adjutant-general, Colonel Asser,[43] most of them never did it for more than one year. As a result, the acting governor-general had very little authority and had to consult Wingate on any matter of importance. During these four summer months, the Sudan government continued to function in England. Wingate spent most of his time in his country house in Dunbar from where all the Sudan correspondence was conducted by his private secretary. Many senior government officials visited Dunbar to discuss their departments or provinces between rounds of golf, and Slatin was a constant visitor. The stay in England usually culminated in a visit to Balmoral, where both Wingate and Slatin were regular summer guests, and in October the whole retinue started on its way back to Egypt.

CHAPTER II

The Sudan, Egypt and Britain

THE Condominium Agreement provided for a joint administration of the Sudan by the British and Egyptian governments. Yet it was clear from the outset that Egypt's part of this administration was to be purely nominal. The supreme civil and military command of the Sudan was vested in the governor-general, who was nominated by the British government. Thus his appointment by Khedivial decree had few practical implications. It is, therefore, no wonder that during the whole period of the Condominium, all the governors-general were British, and owed allegiance to the British government. Furthermore, Egypt had lost her own autonomy as a result of the British occupation in 1882. Hence her share of the Sudan administration was in reality carried out by the British consul-general and the British advisers in the Egyptian ministries.

Wingate's attitude towards Egyptian rule in the Sudan crystallized during the Mahdia. He regarded Egyptian misgovernment of the Sudan as one of the principal reasons for the Mahdi's revolt. Consequently he aimed at minimizing Egyptian influence in the new administration. To pursue this policy he had to overcome not only Egyptian opposition, but also the reluctance of the British consuls-general who had to face its consequences in Cairo. The main difficulty was in finance. Until 1913, the Sudan budget was balanced by an annual subvention granted by the Egyptian government and its development projects were financed by the Egyptian reserve fund. Under these circumstances both Cromer and Gorst had adopted the attitude that '. . . those who pay the piper have a right to call the tune . . .'[1] This was challenged by Wingate who aimed at increasing Egyptian financial aid to the Sudan, while diminishing Egyptian influence in the country. In spite of the obvious difficulties, he managed to pursue successfully this policy throughout his governor-generalship.

Financial relations

The Sudan's financial relations with Egypt were laid down in the 'Regulations for the Financial Administration of the Soudan' approved by the Council of Ministers, which were appended to the Condominium Agreement. But whereas the signatories of the Condominium Agreement were Britain and Egypt, the financial regulations were set down by the Egyptian council of ministers, without formal British participation, the reason being that Britain did not intend to assume any financial responsibility for the Sudan. The regulations stated that the Sudan's annual budget was to be approved by the council of ministers. Any special or unforeseen expenditure had to be applied for by the governor-general. Even appointments or minor administrative changes, if they affected the budget, had to be passed by the Egyptian ministry of finance. Article 10 of the regulations stipulated that the annual Egyptian grant to the Sudan would remain for the following two years the same as in 1899, after which it would gradually decrease.[2] In May 1901 a new set of regulations was signed by Wingate and Gorst, then financial adviser to the Egyptian ministry of finance. The Sudan was forbidden to impose any new taxes or to increase existing ones. No new appointments affecting the budget were allowed during the financial year. These regulations were in fact stricter than the ones they superseded. Supervision was removed from the council of ministers and entrusted to the Egyptian ministry of finance. In reality, it was executed by the British financial adviser.[3]

Egypt thus became a supplier without any adequate means of control. The amount of the annual subvention, as well as Egyptian aid to Sudanese development, were determined according to the Sudan's needs as assessed by the British financial adviser and the consul-general. The moral justification for this procedure was enunciated by Cromer in 1904. He claimed that Britain would never have undertaken the reconquest had Egypt not been prepared to pay. Secondly, he stated that Egypt was morally obliged to help the Sudanese following their long maltreatment by Egyptian administration. Lastly, he regarded the Sudan investments as being of benefit to the Egyptian economy. Bernard,[4] the Sudan's financial secretary, went even further by claiming that '. . . possession of the Sudan is necessary, nay more necessary to Egypt, than the possession of Alexandria . . .'[5] Consequently, Egypt had to pay. Its loans for the Sudan development in the years 1901–1914, amounted to £E 5,414,525. Egypt's annual contributions, which according to the financial regulations, should have gradually decreased, in fact grew from the original grant of £E 134,317 in 1899 to a sum of £E 335,000 in 1912. In 1913 the grants were finally abolished.

The Egyptian annual contribution 1899–1913 (in £E)[6]

1899	134,317	1901	194,545
1900	134,317	1902	267,173

1903	196,063	1908	379,763
1904	193,850	1909	335,000
1905	379,763	1910	325,000
1906	379,763	1911	360,000
1907	379,763	1912	335,000

This policy evoked a large measure of criticism in Egypt, voiced mainly by the Egyptian nationalist press, as the government, under British control, was not in a position to interfere. The main points of criticism were:[7]

(a) Egypt had no control over the way the money it contributed was spent.

(b) Many of the investments undertaken in the Sudan were detrimental to Egyptian interests.

(c) Egypt was financing a British administration in the Sudan.

(d) The Egyptian contribution increased while it was supposed to diminish.

(e) As a result of the annual grant, the Sudan was enabled to pursue a policy of low taxation, and did not need to seek any additional sources of revenue.

Most of the points raised in this critique were, in fact, true, the one exception being that concerning Sudanese investments. Apart from Port Sudan, whose customs revenue proved detrimental to Egypt's income, practically all major investments in the Sudan during these years were connected with communication and irrigation, and were, in the long run, beneficial to Egypt.

The Sudan government claimed that Egyptian grants were much smaller than the official figures suggested, as Egyptian customs gained by Sudanese transit goods. Furthermore, Egypt would have had to spend far more on its defence had the Sudan not been reconquered. The Sudan government was far from satisfied with the extent of Egyptian aid, but even more was it exasperated by the limitations which evolved from these grants. The Sudan was forbidden from growing tobacco north of Khartoum. Agricultural development was limited to crops which did not compete with Egyptian products. Irrigation was strictly limited, and only 10,000 feddans could be irrigated during low Nile. Lastly, the Sudan was forbidden to levy customs on any goods it exported to Egypt. These conditions prevailed until the First World War, and it is hardly surprising that the Sudan government was as anxious to find alternative financial resources as the Egyptians were anxious to stop their aid.

Wingate's relations with the Khedive and the Egyptian government

In his relations with the Khedive and the Egyptian council of ministers, Wingate observed certain rules derived from the Condominium Agreement. As sirdar and governor-general he owed his official appointment to the Khedive, and was supposed to report to him on developments in the Egyptian army and the Sudan administration. In fact, this was not fully observed. Wingate visited the Khedive whenever he passed through Cairo, but reported to him only when the Egyptian army embarked on a major campaign. The one field which was actually controlled by the Khedive, was Egyption decorations, but even in this sphere he only bestowed or refused decorations recommended by Wingate. When the Khedive's control over decorations was restricted by Kitchener in 1913, Wingate wrote: '. . . I am much amused at the subterfuges to which our "ruler" is reduced owing to stoppage of funds from graves and decorations . . .'[8] In order not to inflate Egyptian influence, Wingate never recommended Sudanese for Egyptian decorations, as he feared it '. . . would transfer the patronage from the British governing authorities to the Khedive . . .'.[9] If Wingate observed certain formalities with regard to the Egyptian army, there was certainly no pretence of doing this as far as the Sudan administration was concerned. Wingate did not report to the Khedive regarding administrative measures, and strongly objected when a more cooperative attitude was advocated by Gorst.[10] The Khedive's role was thus purely nominal. The anniversary of his accession was marked by an official exchange of letters and by a levée of officers and senior officials held by Wingate in Khartoum. The day was observed as a general holiday throughout the Sudan, and marked the occasion for a bestowal of decorations granted by the Khedive.

Throughout his reign 'Abbās Ḥilmī II visited the Sudan only three times. His first visit in 1894 ended in a fiasco when, on criticizing the Egyptian army, he was forced to render an apology to Kitchener. His second visit took place in 1901, and was reported by Cromer to have been a failure. Gorst's period of reconciliation brought 'Abbās once again to the Sudan, for the official opening of Port Sudan. Yet it did little to affect 'Abbās's relations with the country. Thus, when he was deposed in December 1914, the reports '. . . were received with equal apathy by the natives both in Khartoum and in the provinces . . .'[11] Ḥusayn Kāmil, the new Sultan,[12] had no more influence over the Sudan than his predecessor. Wingate was already bent on detaching the Sudan from Egypt, and his relations with the Sultan were cordial but of little consequence.

The control exercised by the Egyptian council of ministers over Sudan affairs was practically non-existent. As sirdar, Wingate had to report to the Egyptian minister of war about all expeditions undertaken by the Egyptian army. But he was not required to consult him beforehand; even the reporting was not always carried out, and in certain cases the Egyptian minister of war only learnt of a military engagement from the Egyptian press. In Wingate's reports to his Egyptian superiors, he was extremely careful not to supply them with any confidential information. His attitude to the minister of war was clearly expressed in a secret letter to Cecil,[13] the financial adviser, where he asked him to raise the salary of Najīb 'Azūrī, the war minister's private secretary. '. . . Azuri is no more worth his salary than my boot, but it suits our policy to have a purely nominal War Minister and a still more nominal Private Secretary to that War Minister . . .' He ended by hoping that his request will not be refused '. . . as such an attitude would only emphasize the fact that the War Minister and his Secretaries are practically nobodies . . .'[14] Wingate's attitude to other Egyptian ministers was even worse, and he did not acknowledge their right to interfere in any matters concerning the Sudan. Sudan ordinances which, according to the first draft of the Condominium Agreement, had to be submitted to the council of ministers for its approval, were later only submitted as a matter of form and the council of ministers had no right to amend them.[15]

Co-operation between the Sudan authorities and the Egyptian government was only limited to those spheres where the Sudan could benefit. According to the Condominium Agreement the Egyptian courts had no legal power in the Sudan. But the Sudan government as well as Egypt were, for practical reasons, interested in coming to an arrangement whereby judgements given in one country would have legal power in the other. This was necessary in order to deal with Egyptians residing in the Sudan and vice versa. Consequently, arrangements were made which enabled sentences passed in one country to be executed in the other, as well as mutual extradition rights. A certain amount of co-operation was also necessary in the religious sphere. Although Wingate did not tolerate Egyptian interference in the Sudan's religious affairs, he had no option but to rely on Egyption *qāḍīs* for the *Sharīʿa* courts and for teachers at the *qāḍīs* training course at Gordon College. However to minimize the danger of pan-Islamic propaganda, the *qāḍīs* were first vetted by Slatin and Bonham Carter, the legal secretary,[16] and only then were appointed by the grand *qāḍī* of Egypt. Wingate's attitude to the latter was clearly demonstrated when he refused to grant him permission to visit the Sudan.[17] A policy of educating young Sudanese *qāḍīs*, was followed from the early days of the Condominium, and as soon as these graduated, the Egyptian *qāḍīs* were replaced.[18]

The only other exception Wingate made to his rule of non-interference by Cairo's religious authorities was when he needed £E 20,000 for the Khartoum Mosque from the Egyptian *Waqf* administration. The latter was quick to seize this opportunity and asked in return for lands in the Sudan and for the right to supervise all Sudanese mosques.[19] Wingate withdrew his request and wrote to Gorst explaining the reasons for his refusal to let the Egyptian *Waqf* administration into the Sudan :

> . . . I know of no subject (except perhaps the slavery question) which is of so thorny a nature as this, owing principally to the racial hatred between Egyptians and Sudanese. Egyptian maladministration, especially in Wakfs matters, had a great deal to do with the original revolt and it has been an essential part in our reorganization of the Sudan to keep out of the country any interference on the part of the Egyptian Wakfs administration . . .[20]

Apart from these fields there was hardly any interference by Egyptian ministers in the administration of the Sudan. The Sudan irrigation schemes were run by the Egyptian ministry of public works, but as they were entrusted to a British official, they could hardly be regarded as under Egyptian control.

The Egyptian Legislative assembly had little occasion to intervene in Sudan affairs. During Wingate's governor-generalship its members were only invited twice to the Sudan; once in 1906, for the opening of the Nile–Red Sea railway, and again in 1909, at Gorst's insistence, for the opening of Port Sudan. Following their first visit, the legislators made certain suggestions with regard to Sudan administration. These were openly disregarded by Wingate who wrote to Cromer : '. . . I will not bother you with the replies I gave . . . They will find our answers quite identical . . .'[21] After the second visit, Wingate reported to Gorst that the visit was a failure, and wrote to Phipps, the civil secretary :[22] '. . . God help the country that is governed by such rubbish . . .'[23] When a new Legislative Assembly was elected in 1913, its members decided to play a more active role in Sudan affairs, and ventured to discuss the legality of the importation of Egyptian convicts into the Sudan. Kitchener had insisted on the employment of these convicts on the Blue Nile dam, for reasons of economy, much to Wingate's dismay and against the express wish of the governor-general's council. There was little doubt that the sending of Egyptian convicts to the Sudan was illegal, and could, therefore, have caused a vote of censure against the Egyptian council of ministers. Kitchener, however, warned Sa'd Zaghlūl that the convicts would be brought back to Egypt '. . . but that of course this would settle the question once and for all of the Sudan being in any way part of Egypt . . .'[24] Thus everything was settled. The convicts stayed in the Sudan, and the legislative assembly refrained from interfering. Consequently the legislative assembly as well as the Khedive and his ministers did not represent a major obstacle to Wingate's policy of excluding Egyptian interference from the Sudan. Wingate sincerely believed that Sudanese hatred of Egyptian rule was deeply rooted. Furthermore, he did not underestimate the power of Egyptian nationalism, and wanted to secure the Sudan for Britain, should Egypt turn restive.

The impact of pan-Islamic ideas and Egyptian nationalism

One may assume, as there is no evidence to the contrary, that the majority of the older generation of Sudanese mistrusted the Egyptians, and even regarded them with contempt. Wingate quoted the following from an interview he had with Sayyid 'Alī al-Mīrghanī, head of the Khatmīya *Ṣūfī* order :

> . . . "Why should you English people be surprised at the thoroughly disloyal attitude of the Egyptians?—They are a race of slaves and never will be anything better; their character is contemptible and, after all, you are to blame for having given them an education altogether beyond their capacity and put them upon a pedestal, and you now find your idol has feet of clay" . . .

Whereupon Wingate commented :

> . . . This opinion is really representative of the bulk of the better class Sudanese, who are in every respect superior in character to the Egyptians and look down upon them with contempt . . .[25]

However, it is equally probable that many of the younger generation of Sudanese did not share this view. They had not lived under the Turco-Egyptian regime, and had not been influenced by the anti-Egyptian propaganda of the Mahdi. Hence they found more in common with their fellow Muslim Egyptians than with their British Christian rulers. With this in mind, Wingate employed all the means at his disposal to stem the infiltration of Egyptian nationalist and pan-Islamic ideas into the Sudan. A special system of intelligence was devised in order to deal with this subtle penetration. The intelligence department, whose headquarters were in Cairo, kept a close watch on developments in the Egyptian capital and warned its branch in Khartoum to take any necessary action. Special agents were employed '. . . to ascertain how and to what extent native feeling in the Sudan was influenced from Cairo . . .' They were instructed to keep in close contact with those Egyptian officers who were most likely to introduce nationalist ideas in the Sudan.[26] To cut down the hazards of Egyptian influence, the Sudanese were discouraged from travelling to Egypt for any length of time. When a Sudanese unit of the Egyptian army, was stationed in Egypt in 1908, Wingate asked his adjutant-general to replace it by Egyptians as, '. . . they may imbibe all sorts of undesirable ideas . . .'[27] A suggestion made by Sudanese *'ulamā'* to send young Sudanese to study at al-Azhar was rejected by Wingate on similar grounds, '. . . I have always had a strong feeling against Sudanese coming to Cairo where they undoubtedly imbibe ideas which are prejudicial to our system of Government in the Sudan . . .'[28] After the murder of Buṭrus Ghālī Pasha, Egypt's Coptic Prime Minister, Wingate was concerned about its effects in the Sudan. The intelligence department at Khartoum reported that the majority of the Egyptian army officers sympathized with the assassin. Clayton, then Wingate's private secretary, wrote shortly afterwards: '. . . there is little doubt that there is widespread feeling of pleasure at the news among the Egyptians both military and civil . . .' He added, however, that the Sudanese were quite indifferent.[29] Slatin regarded these rumours as grossly exaggerated. He wrote to Wingate: '. . . It is a mistake to make a Copt Prime Minister over a Mohammedan population . . . this will only strengthen the so-called Nationalist party . . .'[30]

Wingate was convinced that in order to decrease the dangers of Egyptian nationalism in the Sudan, he had to bar the Egyptian press from the Sudan. The attacks on the Sudan government in the Egyptian nationalist press encompassed a large area of subjects. First and foremost they attacked the Condominium Agreement, and the fact that the British flag flew in the Sudan. Then came Egypt's financial liability, which had been enforced against her will. Heavy attacks were launched against the sirdar himself, whose rule in the Sudan was described as similar to that of the Russian Czar. He was accused of not promoting Egyptian officers whose honour was degraded by having to kiss the sirdar's hand. A popular and frequent demand was that the governor-general of the Sudan and his *mudīrs* should be Egyptian and not British officers. The most bitter criticism, however, was directed against the government's religious policy, both as regards missionary activities and Islam in the Sudan.[31] Wingate would have preferred to see all these papers suspended. Like many a military man of his era, he regarded the press in general as a nuisance which had to be firmly dealt with. Yet owing to the reluctance of the British consuls-general to act as severely as he advocated, Wingate had to devise his own methods for dealing with the press. He was allowed to stop any hostile Egyptian paper from entering the Sudan, and the Sudan agent in

Cairo was given full powers to this effect. Wingate also made use of the pro-government papers, *al-Muqaṭṭam* in Egypt and the *Sudan Times* in Khartoum, in order to counteract nationalist propaganda. Naʿūm Shuqayr (Shoucair) of the intelligence department, was well suited to undertake this task. He used his wide circle of local acquaintances to sponsor pro-government articles in *al-Muqaṭṭam*.[32] When Muṣṭafā Kāmil, leader of the nationalist party, died in 1908, Wingate expressed his hopes that the nationalist press would die with him. These hopes were, however, not realized. *Al-Liwāʾ*, *L'Étendard Égyptien* and *The Standard* launched a bitter attack against the Sudan government following the Wad Ḥabūba rebellion in 1908, and accused it of executing seventy of the rebels.[33] The growing vehemence of the nationalist press led to Gorst's decision to revive the 1881 Egyptian press law. Wingate was not satisfied and decided to promulgate a more comprehensive press law for the Sudan.[34]

Egyptian officials and officers both in the army and in the Sudan administration were probably Wingate's major worry. Apart from his general mistrust of Egyptians, he regarded them as the most likely bearers of nationalist and pan-Islamic ideas. Yet he could not dispense with their services while no alternative source of manpower existed. He therefore followed a line of policy whereby the Egyptians were relegated to positions of minor importance, both in the army and the administration. The mutiny of the Egyptian army in Omdurman in 1900, was a convenient peg upon which to hang his policy. All the accounts of the mutiny indicated that its major cause was to be found in Kitchener's maltreatment of the Egyptian army. Wingate, however, was convinced that the centre of the trouble lay in Cairo and was supported by the Khedive. Hence both he and Cromer concluded that the size of the Egyptian army as well as its composition presented a major threat to the security of the Sudan.[35] The policy pursued was to reduce the Egyptian army by recruiting territorial units in the Nuba Mountains and the southern provinces and placing them under British command. Furthermore, Wingate dispersed the Egyptian battalions over the Sudan and entrusted the security of Khartoum to a British detachment.[36] Senior Egyptian officers, both in the army and the civil service, were passed over for promotion or retired prematurely in order to make way for British personnel. Lastly, a military school was opened in Khartoum in 1905, and an ever increasing number of Sudanese replaced the lower rank Egyptians. In executing this policy Wingate enjoyed the full support of the majority of his British subordinates who wished to purge the Sudan civil service of its Egyptian element. These views were most adequately expressed by the civil secretary when he wrote :

> . . . The wording *'British Influence'* is a mistake, but it of course means the influence of *honest* administration as opposed to Egyptian. Later on our part of the pink of the African map must be effectively British as well as honest . . .[37]

Of the senior British officials only Currie,[38] the director of education, regarded this policy as unrealistic. However, his was a lone voice and government policy remained unchanged throughout Wingate's governor-generalship.

The Sudan and the British government

There were few direct links between the Sudan and the British government during Wingate's governor-generalship. Control was maintained through the British consuls-general in Cairo who reported to Whitehall whenever necessary. The prior consent of the British government was only necessary in the case of major policy decisions; these included border disputes, large scale military expeditions, and treaties with neighbouring states. In all other spheres the Sudan government, acting under the guidance of the British consul-general, was free to act and only had to report to London afterwards. The reports sent to London included an annual report on the administration of the Sudan prepared by the consul-general, reports on military expeditions, and Sudan laws and ordinances following their publication in the *Sudan Gazette*. British decorations were granted mainly to British military and civilian officials. Wingate sent his recommendations to the consul-general who forwarded them to London. Whereas in his capacity as governor-general Wingate had no direct dealings with the British government, as sirdar he communicated directly with the war office. These communications included confidential reports on military expeditions, recommendations for military decorations, the command of British troops in Khartoum, and the service of British officers in the Sudan.

Wingate tried to make up for what he regarded as insufficient British influence by increasing the impact of British royalty in the Sudan. This he hoped to achieve by personally cultivating the Royal family. Both he and Slatin were regular guests at Balmoral during their summer vacation and attended many of the special functions at Windsor. His major aim was to project the image of British royalty in the Sudan by all the means at his disposal. Coronation day was observed as a holiday throughout the Sudan. A levée and garden party were held at the governor-general's palace, the Royal standard was hoisted, and money was distributed by the governor-general to the poor of Omdurman and Khartoum.

A one-day visit by King George V to Port Sudan in 1912 became the occasion of yet another national holiday. Apart from sporadic visits by the Duke of Connaught, the most important official Royal visitor was the Prince of Wales, who came to the Sudan in 1916. Wingate, who since the beginning of the First World War had openly sought the complete separation of the Sudan from Egypt, tried to exploit to the utmost the Prince's visit '. . . Tell it not in Gath, but I am distributing two or three hundred pounds to the poor . . . which they will, I hope, think came from the Imperial Treasury . . .'[39] Hence it is clear that although official ties between the Sudan and Britain were few and of little significance, Wingate tried to increase their impact to the best of his ability.

Britain had no financial responsibilities in the Sudan. The financial regulations of the Sudan stipulated no British participation in the country's expenses. Hence, despite repeated efforts by Wingate, the British government maintained its policy of regarding the Sudan's finances as a purely Egyptian obligation. The very few occasions on which Whitehall deviated from this line deserve to be mentioned, if only for their pettiness. Britain refused to pay the additional cost for keeping a British detachment in Khartoum. It was only sanctioned after a protracted correspondence, in which Cromer adamantly refused to charge Egypt with this expense.[40] The cost of the British flags in the Sudan was borne by Egypt until May 1900. The British war-office refused to pay a gratuity to British soldiers who participated in the reconquest, and it was charged against the Egyptian budget.[41] In 1911 Wingate asked the war office to contribute towards the repair of British graves in the Sudan, and to undertake their upkeep. Out of the £438 Wingate demanded for the repair, he received £300, and the annual upkeep had to be paid by the Sudan as before.[42] On the two occasions on which Wingate demanded a more substantial contribution from Britain, he was rebuffed. In 1910, when the Sudan assumed responsibility for the Lado Enclave, Wingate urged Gorst to demand British aid for the extra expenditure involved.[43] The reasons enumerated by Gorst, in his appeal to the foreign office, reiterated many of the Egyptian nationalists' arguments against Egyptian contributions for the Sudan. He argued that payment for the Sudan was generally unpopular in Egypt. Moreover, Egypt was not consulted when the Lado Enclave was originally leased to King Leopold, and had no direct interest in its return to the Sudan. He further claimed that from an Egyptian viewpoint the East Bank of the Nile, which had been ceded to Uganda, because of British imperial interests, would have enabled Egypt to control the Nile. Hence, he concluded that the money should be contributed by Britain. The necessary money for administering the Lado Enclave was ultimately included in the

Egyptian budget, without waiting for Whitehall's reply.[44] The second time Wingate requested help was during the World War. In a letter to McMahon he described the increasing expenditure incurred in the Sudan as a direct consequence of the British war effort. The British treasury refused Wingate's request and wrote that '. . . Even if the expenditure cannot be met from Soudan Government balances . . .' Britain would not come to its aid.[45]

Britain's and Egypt's financial liabilities in the Sudan, were described by a correspondent of *The Times* as follows :

> . . . England contributed one third to the cost of the conquest; she contributes nothing to the cost of governing the conquered country. On the other hand, the Governor-General, the Governors of Provinces and their assistants, and all the officers in the Egyptian army in the Sudan are exclusively Englishmen; the lower officials are almost exclusively Egyptians. Two men have jointly bought a horse, A contributing one third, B two thirds of the price. A rides the horse, B grooms it and pays its upkeep. That is approximately the situation in the Sudan . . .[46]

By 1910, Wingate who was exasperated by the Sudan's slow rate of progress, devised a plan by which he hoped to achieve a more rapid development. Basically his plan was to prove that the cotton-growing prospects of the Sudan were second to none, following which, he would be able, with the help of the Lancashire cotton manufacturers, to force the British government to assume direct responsibility for the country. Wingate, with his senior British officials embarked on a propaganda campaign amongst British capitalists and politicians based on the following assumptions :

> . . . It is quite clear that the present attitude of the Nationalists and the Legislative Council is to prevent any Egyptian money being expended in the Sudan; the attitude of the Home Government is also one of 'hands off' in regard to their Sudan responsibilities . . . therefore it is a matter of the most vital importance . . . to induce British Capital and thus the British Capitalist to have a vested interest in the country . . . This is the only sound and practical way of developing the Sudan and keeping the British flag flying, when it is now so seriously threatened by the political attitude of both British and Egyptian Governments . . .[47]

It soon became clear that capital would not be forthcoming unless Britain declared its intention to remain in the Sudan. Following a meeting with several leading British capitalists and politicians, Clayton reported that they hoped to get a satisfactory assurance as to the permanent character of British occupation of the Sudan. Wingate himself approached the Prime Minister, while at Balmoral, and gained his full support.[48] In 1912, Kitchener finally decided to ask for a British guaranteed loan for cotton growing in the Gezira. His official request was forwarded by Grey, then foreign secretary, to the treasury, with a warm recommendation, in which the following words stand out as proof of Wingate's success: '. . . We have been strongly pressed from Lancashire to facilitate the development of cotton growing in the Soudan . . .'[49] On 19 November 1912 the first draft of The Soudan Loan Act, 1912 was laid before the Cabinet; and on 2 January 1913 the final draft of the bill was accepted.[50]

Following the declaration of a British Protectorate over Egypt on 18 December 1914, Wingate advocated the complete separation of the Sudan from Egypt. In many of his private letters, written during and after the war, Wingate argued the case for British control over the Sudan. His main premise was that the inherent hatred of the Sudanese for the Egyptians, based on a long history of oppression, made Cairo's control, in whatever form, distasteful to the majority of the people. Secondly, he argued that by assuming direct control of the Sudan, Britain would hold the key to Egypt through its control of the Nile. Lastly, he maintained that the future cotton-growing prospects of the Sudan, '. . . are sufficiently good to justify the assumption of complete political and administrative control of the country by H.M.G. . . .'[51] These arguments were not a departure from Wingate's prior attitude. He had advocated a similar policy for many years. Yet as long as the Sudan depended upon Egypt financially, there was little chance of achieving these aims. With the end of Egyptian subventions in 1913, and the declaration of a British protectorate over Egypt, conditions altered substantially. Even then Britain was not prepared to embark on this new venture, and only after the Egyptian revolt of 1919 was a policy more in line with Wingate's ideas advocated for the Sudan. The Milner Mission, though primarily concerned with Egypt, suggested: '. . . the independent development of the Sudan, while safeguarding the vital interests of Egypt in the waters of the Nile . . .'[52]

Wingate's relations with the British consuls-general in Egypt

While direct interference in the administration of the Sudan by the Egyptian and British governments was kept to a minimum, supervision was maintained by the British consuls-general in Cairo. During Wingate's term of office in the Sudan, four British consuls-general filled the post in Cairo. In order to assess the extent of their control, it will be necessary to analyse their respective policies in some detail.

Cromer and Wingate

Throughout Cromer's tenure of office his relations with Wingate were strict but cordial. Wingate trusted Cromer and relied on his greater experience. On Wingate's arrival in Egypt in 1883, as a junior officer in the Egyptian army, Cromer was already British consul-general in Cairo. Hence his supreme authority was never questioned by Wingate. Cromer regarded Wingate as an able administrator, but without any real grasp of the principles of government. '. . . Wingate and his military officers are in their own way excellent, but I am very decidedly of the opinion that they require control . . .'[53] These were the personal attributes upon which the Cromer-Wingate relationship was to be based. Regarding practical applications, Wingate had been witness to the uneasy relations between Cromer and Kitchener. He knew that, although from a constitutional point of view he was under no obligation to obey the consul-general, he had in fact little alternative but to follow his directives. Many years later he explained to Clayton, then the Sudan agent,

> . . . in the 1896–8 campaign, Kitchener happened to be Cromer's nominee and naturally the former could not 'bite the hand that fed him'—but no sooner had K. been appointed Governor-General of the Sudan, than he began to assert his independence and, had he not been called off to South Africa, there would have been an unholy row between them . . . Of course Cromer's personality and his strong character resulted in his being considered by our Government as the supreme authority both civil and military in Egypt and the Sudan, although if one hunted up chapter and verse for his constitutional right of this, one would not find it . . .[54]

Under these circumstances it is no wonder that, despite minor incidents, relations between Cromer and Wingate remained cordial. It was Cromer who formulated government policy and advised on all administrative measures, while details of execution were left in Wingate's hands.

The principles of policy were enunciated by Cromer on 4 January 1899, when he addressed the shaykhs and notables of the Sudan at Omdurman. They included non-interference in the people's religion, low taxation, and a toleration of domestic slavery. Cromer's belief in these principles was based on his concept of the Arab people which he expressed in a letter to Wingate many years later: '. . . so far as I know, the ordinary Arab cares only for two things, namely 1. his religion 2. his piastres, and I am not at all sure that he does not care for his piastres more than he does for his religion . . .'[55] The 'piastres' were taken care of by Cromer's insistence on low taxation and toleration of slavery; religion was safeguarded by the principle of non-interference in Islamic affairs and the prohibition of missionary activities in the northern Sudan. Although these principles were never questioned by Wingate, the insistence on low taxation meant, in effect, a very slow rate of development for the Sudan. Cromer further insisted that as long as the Sudan was dependent on Egyptian financial aid, expenditure should be reduced to an absolute minimum. Theoretically, there were two other alternatives to pay for development in the Sudan, namely, British aid and private enterprise. Cromer, however, objected to both. His reluctance to encourage the latter was expressed in a letter to Wingate in 1901 : '. . . I do not much believe in private enterprise in the Soudan except on terms which throw all the risk on the Gov. and give all the profits to private individuals . . .'[56] Consequently very few concessions were granted and even some of these were withdrawn at Cromer's request. Cromer himself toyed for a short while with the idea of British aid. In January 1901 he approached the British government for a guaranteed loan of £1m. for the Sudan to facilitate the development of railways and irrigation. Cromer's appeal was, however, rejected and a year later he revised his opinion and wrote to Lansdowne :

> . . . Not only am I altogether opposed to any idea of imposing further burdens on the British tax payers on Soudanese or Egyptian accounts, but I hold that, if we move at all it should be in the opposite direction, that is to say, we should relieve the British tax payer of what he now pays . . .[57]

Cromer's opposition to British financial aid for the Sudan increased after his retirement. In 1908 Wingate attempted to secure a yearly grant from the British government for Gordon College. Cromer, who was the Chairman of Board of Governors of Gordon College, opposed the grant, and consequently it was refused. In a private letter to Malet, Cromer explained the reason for his opposition :

> . . . I think the continued occupation of Egypt and the Soudan is most desirable, and that if the democracy were to be conciliated to that occupation, the main thing was not to ask them to put their hands in their pockets . . .[58]

The one remaining way for Wingate was to insist on an increase in the Egyptian annual grant to the Sudan. In this he succeeded, but only in a limited way, and not without opposition. Cromer's refusal to increase taxation in Egypt for the benefit of the Sudan, was not merely because of his own convictions, but also because he had to reckon with strong opposition from the Egyptian nationalist party and its outspoken press.[59] Cromer had devoted most of his active life to his work in Egypt and considered the Sudan of minor importance. All economic measures undertaken by the Sudan had to be examined according to their relative importance to Egypt. When in 1904 Wingate proposed to impose an export duty on cattle destined for Egypt, Cromer rejected the proposal arguing that the Sudan was an Egyptian province and could not impose separate export duties: '. . . The only reason why the British flag is flying, and why the Soudan has a Governor-General and special laws, is to avoid the capitulations and the rest of international paraphernalia . . .'[60] This same attitude was demonstrated again in 1905, when Cromer contemplated withdrawing from the Baḥr al-Ghazāl, the administration of which proved to be expensive: '. . . I daresay that the real point is how far is its possession necessary in order to secure the Egyptian water supply . . .'[61] Cecil, then the Sudan agent-general in Cairo, reported Cromer's views to Wingate following a conversation they had on the Baḥr al-Ghazāl: '. . . He thinks I believe genuinely that some minor alteration in the capitulations is of more importance than the whole Sudan . . .'[62] In this instance Cromer modified his views, and the threat of abandoning the Baḥr al-Ghazāl was averted. It was the principle of relegating the Sudan to a position of minor dependency on Egypt which dismayed Wingate. During Cromer's period as consul-general there was little he could do, for he knew that Cromer's prestige would outweigh all his arguments. But once Cromer left Wingate tried his best to relieve the Sudan from what he termed excessive Cairo control.

Cromer did not limit himself to determining the broad principles of administrative policy. He played an active role in the actual details of administration by means of his extensive correspondence with Wingate, and through his control over Sudanese ordinances and annual reports. The volume of correspondence between the Sudan and Cairo increased considerably following Wingate's appointment. It included not only direct communications between Cromer and Wingate, but also letters from Cromer to heads of departments and governors of provinces, to whom he offered advice. Wingate exploited the Sudan agent in Cairo as his confidant and in many delicate situations it was the Sudan agent who acted as his go-between with the consul-general. Broadly speaking, this correspondence covered every field of policy and administration. Among the more important subjects dealt with, were finance, border disputes, land settlement, concessions, slavery, education, missionary activities, and problems of personnel. According to Cromer's instructions to Kitchener, every Sudan government ordinance had to be approved by the British consul-general and the Egyptian council of ministers, prior to its publication in the *Sudan Gazette*. This procedure was, however, overlooked on several occasions, and only after Cromer called Wingate's attention to it was the mistake rectified. Thereafter, every ordinance, however trivial, was laid before Cromer, who in many cases asked for amendments to be made prior to publication. The procedure to be followed in approving ordinances was finally laid down in 1905. The draft prepared by the Sudan government was submitted to the consul-general by the Sudan agent. Following the consul-general's approval, it was translated into Arabic and put to the Egyptian council of ministers. This last stage was a mere formality, as the council of ministers had no right to amend the approved text. The ordinance was then printed in the *Sudan Gazette* and only afterwards sent to the British foreign office.[63]

Apart from an occasional visit to the Sudan and his correspondence with Wingate, Cromer's most effective method of controlling the Sudan was through its annual reports. These contained detailed reports by heads of departments and provincial governors which were summarized by Wingate in his yearly memorandum. The reports, which ran into 700–800 printed pages, were then summarized by Cromer in his annual report of Egypt and the Sudan. Cromer used his red pencil freely and struck out whatever was, in his opinion, non-essential or might cause embarrassment to the British government. Commenting on Wingate's first annual report, Cromer wrote, '. . . You will see some slavery passages are struck out. They frighten the F.O. . . .'[64] A year later Cromer wrote :

> . . . Your report is very interesting but it is *much* too long and detailed for publication . . . I leave out 'prisons' for other reasons. The employment of Egyptian convicts in the Soudan is wholly illegal . . . The less we say on the subject the better . . .[65]

On another occasion Cromer insisted that a punitive raid undertaken by the governor of Kordofan in the Nuba Mountains should be mentioned in the report, though Wingate suggested leaving it out.

> . . . I shall have to mention this last raid . . . The worst one can do is to say nothing of these incidents. They are sure to leak out sooner or later, and then the fact of our silence will be considered as positive proof that we have something to hide . . .[66]

Hence it is clear that, despite the lack of official rules for control, Cromer managed to keep close watch over Sudan affairs.

Cromer's control over Sudan policies and administrative measures was so extensive that it is hard to discover any area unaffected by it. Egyptian penetration into the Sudan was regarded by Cromer as a necessary evil which was unavoidable as a result of the Condominium Agreement and the fact that Egypt had to foot the Sudan bill. Nevertheless, Cromer was the first to propose reducing the Egyptian army following the Omdurman mutiny in 1900. He also warned the British government against the Egyptian officials, who were, '. . . almost without exception, lazy, corrupt and tyrannical . . .' The main trouble was that although '. . . the people [of the Sudan] trust us . . . they complain that between them and the Englishman there is always some Egyptian underling . . .'[67] The same views were expressed in a letter to Jackson[68] who was acting governor-general during Wingate's absence : '. . . the success of our rule in the Soudan will depend on the power displayed in controlling the Egyptian "Mamurs" and such like. I have not the slightest confidence in any of them . . .'[69] As for the Egyptian traders and press, Cromer, as a free trader and liberal, could not bring himself to suppress either of them. He advocated free trade even during Kitchener's governor–generalship, and under Wingate this was to become government policy. But Wingate was given enough latitude in dealing with the dangers of traders in the pagan provinces propagating Islam. Cromer's reasons for advocating a free press were two-fold. He believed in freedom of expression, and did not regard the Egyptian press as powerful enough to cause any real damage. He allowed Wingate to stop certain Egyptian newspapers from entering the Sudan but refused to take any action against the nationalist press in Egypt.[70]

Missionary activities in the northern Sudan were strictly forbidden by Cromer. There was, however, one field where he had to give way, namely in missionary education. As there was a fairly large Christian community in Khartoum, the Catholic and the Presbyterian missionary societies were allowed to open schools for their co-worshippers. The Church Missionary Society (CMS) could not then be stopped from opening a school too, though there were no children belonging to the Anglican denomination. All these schools, ostensibly set up for Christian children, in fact accepted Muslims too. Cromer's basic belief was that missionary activities were the concern of private institutions and should not in any way be supported by the government. Furthermore, he believed that the Muslims would regard any activity undertaken by Europeans, let alone English missionaries, as a government-sponsored movement. These views were fully shared by Wingate, and remained government policy throughout his governor-generalship.[71]

Education was a subject on which Cromer had very definite views. He insisted that educational policy should aim at providing a basic elementary education for the general masses. As for higher education, this was to be developed only as far as was necessary to supply manpower for government and private-sector jobs, while the primary aim was to extend technical training to as many youths as possible.[72] Commenting on the education department's report for 1903, Cromer criticized Currie, then director of education, on three points. Firstly, he objected to the fact that out of a total of 577 pupils in government schools, there were only 180 *bona fide* Sudanese; the remainder were Egyptians and *muwalladīn*. Secondly, he commented that Sudanese textbooks were largely designed to encourage Muslim feelings and, therefore, should be changed. Finally, Cromer rejected Currie's reliance on Indian experience. Cromer believed that by government supervision Egyptian nationalism could be kept out of Sudanese educational institutions.[73] Currie considered this assumption to be fallacious :

> . . . the progress made along the lines of Lord Cromer's policy goes on so fast . . . that one is nearly choked by the dust. One thing I do know that it must all react on the Sudan, it's vain to suppose it won't. TO SUPPOSE THAT AN ENGLISH COMMUNITY can *rule* in Khartoum . . . is to imagine a vain thing. And for better or for worse it is the *Anglo-Egyptian* Sudan . . .[74]

Major appointments, such as heads of departments and provincial governors, required Cromer's authorization. When a head for the department of agriculture was required, Wingate had first to ask Cromer's permission before advertising in the press and, later, when the appointment was made. It was Cromer who insisted on the civilian element being introduced into the Sudan civil service and, as a result, 21 civilians were incorporated into the service as early as 1901.[75] Official British visitors to the Sudan were regarded by Cromer as an unnecessary evil, to be avoided whenever possible. In July 1905, he wrote to Wingate that he would try his best to discourage the Prince of Wales from visiting the Sudan : '. . . We have had quite enough royalties at Khartoum. They cause no end of trouble and expense. They interfere with the work, and their visits certainly do no good and may do harm . . .'[76] As for British Members of Parliament, Cromer asked the British government to keep them away whenever possible. His mistrust of M.P.s expressed itself most strongly when he warned Wingate against suppressing information from the British government about a punitive expedition against one of the *makks* (leaders) of the Nuba Mountains. '. . . I wish to impress very strongly on you that the Mek of Shabsafia[?] is a far less dangerous enemy to the Soudan and to Egypt than the Meks in the House of Commons. . .'[77] In this sphere, as noted above, Wingate disregarded Cromer's advice. He cultivated the friendship of both royalty and politicians, for he hoped in this way to bring the Sudan to the notice of British political opinion.

Before leaving Egypt, following his resignation, Cromer wrote to Grey, then foreign secretary, stating his opinion of Wingate and of the extent of control under which the Sudan should be kept:

> . . . Wingate has done very well in the Soudan . . . But I cannot conceal from myself the fact that he is very local, and has not got any firm grip of the main principles on which the Government of the Soudan, or indeed of any other country, has to be conducted. Also, he is ignorant as a child of everything connected with financial affairs . . . I conceive that no Government in the world has been so little controlled as that of the Soudan. I have practically confined myself to an annual review of the reports . . . and also to exercising some financial control . . . Wingate will have to choose between the very light control exercised from here, or a much more stringent control exercised from a London Office. If he is wise, he will not resist the former, in order that he may not incur the very serious evils of the latter . . .'[78]

Whereas in his letter to Grey, Cromer stressed his lack of control over Sudan affairs, he wrote in an entirely different strain to his nephew Lord Revelstoke, '. . . My policy when I was in Egypt was to put Wingate to the front as much as possible before the public, but behind the scenes, . . . to exercise a thorough control over the whole administration . . .'[79] This admission was probably nearer the truth. Cromer's correspondence with Wingate over the years clearly proved that he influenced even minor administrative decisions in the Sudan. Wingate was, of course, well aware of the true relationship, and regarded Cromer as the supreme authority, whose control he never questioned. When Cromer left Cairo in 1907 the situation radically changed. Cromer believed that with a weaker consul-general in Cairo, control of the Sudan would have to be strengthened. Wingate held exactly the opposite view, since he regarded his own experience as second only to that of Cromer. With a lesser man in Cairo, control should, therefore, be relaxed. It was left to Sir Eldon Gorst, the new consul-general, to overcome this difficulty.

Gorst institutionalizes Sudan supervision

Gorst was nominated by Cromer to succeed him and arrived in Egypt in October 1907. His previous experience as financial adviser to the Egyptian government might have implied that his would be a policy of continuation rather than of change. Cromer clearly thought so when he wrote to Grey: '. . . If, as I hope will be the case, Gorst succeeds me, you could lay stress on the fact inasmuch as he may almost be called a pupil of mine, his nomination is of itself an adequate guarantee that no change of policy is in contemplation . . .'[80] These hopes were not realised. Gorst decided to implement new policies some of which had been advocated by Cromer but never carried out. As a result, his Egyptian policy became a new venture in Britain's relations with Egypt, which was cut short only by his untimely death in 1911. As regards the Sudan, Gorst intended to leave things as they were, and limit himself to the necessary supervision. Following his first visit to the Sudan in January 1908, Gorst was convinced that Wingate could be trusted to administer the country without undue interference: '. . . He [Wingate] has known how to surround himself with capable and zealous heads of departments, and . . . has been able to make them work harmoniously together with a minimum of frictional jealousy . . .'[81]

Wingate was however uneasy. Gorst's previous relations with the Sudan had not been too cordial. When he was financial adviser during the Sudan's formative years, there had been several clashes between Gorst and Kitchener. Wingate had borne the brunt of these as head of the Sudan office in Cairo. It was, therefore, not surprising that rumours about Wingate's forthcoming dismissal became current as soon as Gorst's appointment was officially announced. These rumours persisted until 1909, when Gorst finally convinced Wingate that he had no intention of replacing him. Although relations remained cordial, Wingate soon became convinced of Gorst's failure in Egypt. In 1908, Owen, then Sudan agent, wrote to Wingate about the rumours that Gorst was leaving Egypt: '. . . I am perfectly convinced he is a failure and there will be trouble if he stays on . . .'[82] In a letter to Slatin, Wingate commented that Gorst had no confidence in his advice with regard to Egyptian affairs, which were in an utter mess: '. . . I am only too anxious to help him all in my power—more especially when I do feel that the honour of our country is at stake . . .'[83] Wingate was, however, quite satisfied with Gorst's attitude to the Sudan. In 1911, when Gorst was already seriously ill, he wrote to Slatin, '. . . I hope he will soon get well again—he has been a good friend to the Sudan and I don't fancy beginning all over again with a new man . . .'[84] The same view was expressed in a letter to Stack,[85] then Sudan agent in Cairo, about Gorst's annual report for 1910: '. . . So far as the Sudan is concerned . . . all he [Gorst] has said is both kind and complimentary . . . I can honestly say that his report is distinctly satisfactory . . .'[86] Wingate's reason for wanting Gorst to stay was not that he trusted his advice as he had trusted Cromer's, but that they had established a *modus operandi* and Wingate was afraid of a new man. The relations between Wingate and Gorst were never as harmonious as those between Wingate and Cromer. After eight years as governor-general of the Sudan, Wingate probably felt that he could manage the country's affairs without interference. Hence he asked for Gorst's advice only in those cases where he felt that it was absolutely necessary. The striking decrease in correspondence between Khartoum and Cairo, following Gorst's appointment, was only one manifestation of Wingate's increased independence.

The foundation of the governor-general's council, in November 1909, was a natural result of this development. It placed the relations between Wingate and Gorst on a more formal basis and thus relaxed the previous tension.[87] Gorst's next move was to define the subjects on which he expected to be consulted by the governor-general.

> . . . Hitherto this duty had been carried out by the maintenance of close unofficial relations between the Governor-General and the Consul-General in matters of general interest to the welfare of the country . . . The creation of a council with definite functions . . . renders it desirable to lay down in general terms the matters on which the Consul-General expects to be consulted . . .[88]

These matters included: major policy decisions, laws, ordinances, military or punitive expeditions, new services, concessions, loans or grants from public funds, appointment of new members to the council, and the appointment of an acting-governor-general. On all matters of day-to-day administration, the governor-general was to report regularly to the consul-general. Differences of opinion between the Sudan government and the Egyptian ministries had to be referred to the consul-general for arbitration. A close look at this list will prove that on all these matters Wingate would have consulted Cromer in any case. The reason that Gorst found it necessary to express these relations in a set of written regulations was due to the broader scope of activities undertaken by the Sudan government, and to Gorst's feeling that Wingate did not consult him as much as he had consulted his predecessor.

During Cromer's period, there were differences of opinion regarding finance, but it never came to an open clash with the financial adviser, as Cromer preferred to deal with the Sudan himself. Gorst apparently decided to act differently; financial matters were discussed and decided with his new financial adviser, Harvey, and Gorst was called in only if arbitration became necessary. The first clash between Wingate and Harvey occurred in 1907, when the latter refused to grant any of the increased salaries suggested by Wingate. Less than a month later Harvey cut the Egyptian army budget by over £150,000. Wingate protested and warned Harvey that unless supplementary credits were granted the government would lose its authority. Relations went from bad to worse. In March 1908, Harvey refused to agree to promotions in the education department, an action which according to the director of education, would have brought about the collapse of the educational system.[89] Wingate was exasperated with the new adviser:

> . . . It is quite clear that Harvey does not realize that in strongly combating the views of Heads of Technical Departments in the Sudan . . . he is running the risk of a very serious row in which in spite of the position he holds in Egypt he might come off second best . . .[90]

It was at the same time that a controversy about the land of Port Sudan came to a head. The Sudan government had decided on a leasehold system in order not to lose its control of the new port's lands. Harvey objected and demanded that the lands be sold outright, so as to reimburse Egypt for the capital invested in Port Sudan.[91] Shortly afterwards, Harvey objected to the *Sudan Pensions Ordinance*, and demanded that pensions in the Sudan should be lower than in Egypt. Wingate reacted bitterly: '. . . I presume that the argument is this: The Sudan is a poor country and therefore cannot afford to give pensions which a rich country like Egypt can . . . we must be content with the "crumbs which fall from the rich man's table" . . .'[92] Wingate's understanding of finance was not very highly regarded by either Gorst or Harvey. Commenting on the Sudan budget for 1909, Gorst wrote to Harvey, '. . . it would be as well to bring home to the Sirdar what the financial situation of the Soudan really is . . .', to which Harvey replied, '. . . I am somewhat sceptical as to this argument having very much weight with Sir Reginald . . .'[93] Gorst nevertheless decided to write to Wingate and warned him that future budgets would have to be on a sounder basis: '. . . there must be no increase of administrative expenditure, or further development . . . until such time as the Budget can be drawn up on sound financial lines . . .'[94] When Bernard, the financial secretary of the Sudan government, suggested not decreasing the Egyptian subvention for 1909 by the minimum sum of £E 25,000, which had been agreed to in 1907, Harvey insisted on the reduction, owing to '. . . the very strong feelings prevailing in this country on the subject of the Sudan debt . . .'[95] The brunt of financial relations was thus borne by Harvey. Financial policy remained unchanged since Cromer's consul-generalship, yet relations deteriorated. The reason was probably twofold. Firstly, there was a difference between what Wingate was willing to accept from Cromer, and what he was prepared to take from Harvey, who was a newcomer, and who had never visited the Sudan. Secondly, Gorst tried to conciliate the Khedive and the Egyptian legislators, and one of their main grievances was the ever-increasing demands made by the Sudan on the Egyptian government.

The relationship between the Sudan and Egypt caused friction between Wingate and Gorst, not only on the financial level. Wingate assumed that Britain would eventually have to evacuate Egypt, as a result of internal or external pressures. He therefore advocated that the Sudan should become a separate political entity. These views, as noted, were not fully shared by Cromer who regarded the Sudan as an Egyptian province. Yet he agreed with Wingate regarding the hazards of Egyptian penetration and helped him to minimize their effects. Following Cromer's retirement, Wingate tried to force his views on the new consul-general. In July 1908, Wingate suggested to Gorst that the military command of the Sudan be separated from that of Egypt, but Gorst refused. In analysing Gorst's attitude Wingate wrote :

> . . . He has evidently not quite understood the desirability of separating Egypt and the Sudan from a Military and political point of view. I can fully understand his mental attitude in this respect . . . he, as British Consul General in Egypt, would naturally foresee in such a separation, a possible diminution of his own control . . .[96]

The opening ceremony of Port Sudan in 1909 illustrated Gorst's views. Gorst had decided not to accompany the Khedive to the opening ceremony and stated his reasons as follows :

> . . . I am anxious that the show should be made as Egyptian as possible . . . I should keep H.M.G. and the Union Jack as much as possible in the background . . . My reason for all this is as follows. The Soudan cannot possibly make any further progress without capital, and, as Great Britain cannot or will not find this, you have only Egypt to look to . . . Therefore we must try and reconcile the Egyptians to spending some of their money on the Soudan, and the only way to do this is to make them feel that the Soudan is part of Egypt . . .[97]

Wingate was not convinced and wrote to Stack :

> . . . I am rather inclined to think that the more malevolent amongst them [the Egyptians] will argue that this is only another attempt of perfidious Albion to throw dust in their eyes and to force the Egyptian tax payer to provide for British Colonization purposes . . .[98]

Following this visit, Wingate wrote to Gorst that most of the legislators would have preferred the money spent on Port Sudan to have been spent in Egypt, and the senior positions in the Sudan to be filled by Egyptians instead of British officers.[99] Wingate persisted in these views. In 1910, Ismā'īl Sirry Pasha, the Egyptian minister of public works, paid a visit to the Sudan. He then prepared a critical memorandum for the Egyptian government. Wingate was indignant and protested against this interference to Gorst :

. . . Such controversial matters as the status of Slavery in the Sudan, the position of Christian Missionaries, the inadequate representation of Egyptian officers and officials in the higher Government appointments, etc. etc., are freely commented on . . . I am at a loss to know in what capacity Sirry Pasha is reporting on the Sudan . . .[100]

Gorst's reply was brief:

. . . you may be sure that I shall not pass anything which is likely to embarrass your work. At the same time we cannot object to Egyptian Ministers taking an interest in Soudan affairs, if we are continually asking the Council of Ministers to provide money for the development of the country . . .[101]

Gorst's views on the relations between Egypt and the Sudan differed from those of Cromer. He sought a reconciliation with the Khedive and the Egyptian ruling class, so as to drive a wedge between them and the nationalists. The Sudan was one of the most thorny issues used by the nationalists in their anti-government propaganda. Gorst, therefore, aimed at neutralizing this problem by encouraging the Khedive and the Egyptian legislators to play a more active role in the Sudan, and sought to dissuade Wingate from making additional financial demands. Thus Wingate's hope for increased independence from Egypt clearly suffered a set-back during Gorst's consul-generalship.

The Egyptian nationalist press was another source of dispute. Wingate had advocated a tougher line than the one followed by Lord Cromer. Gorst, to begin with, followed Cromer's tolerant approach. He promised Grey not to take any drastic measures against the press unless forced to do so. Wingate tried to force through his views and asked the Sudan agent to stop *al-Jawā'ib al-Miṣrīya* from entering the Sudan. Gorst refused: '. . . He appeared to regret that the Moayad and Minbar had been stopped and thought we should only stop papers that are absolutely offensive and personal like El Lewa . . .'[102] The turning point in Gorst's policy was the Gezira rebellion in 1908. The attacks against the Sudan government in the nationalist press following the rebellion, and the subsequent acquittal of Shaykh Shāwīsh, the editor of *al-Liwā'*, by the Court of Appeal, led to Gorst taking a tougher line and reviving the Egyptian press law. Wingate was glad to help. He wrote to Stack that the constant attacks on the sirdar in *al-Liwā'*, and *al-Quṭr al-Miṣrī* '. . . might serve Sir Eldon's purpose . . . as a peg on which to hang the contemplated modification of the Press Law . . .' A month later, he added, '. . . I am glad you keep on rubbing it in at the Agency about the "Kotr el Masri". I am certain that something will have to be done . . .'[103] On 27 February 1909, the modified press law was approved by the British government, and on 13 March by the Egyptian legislative council. It soon became clear, however, that the law was inadequate, as newspapers owned by foreigners could not be suppressed without the sanction of their respective governments. Wingate, therefore, decided not to introduce the Egyptian press law into the Sudan, but to promulgate a new law. On 29 March 1910, he wrote to Clayton about the inadequacy of the Egyptian press law, '. . . why we should copy one of the worst systems which probably exist in the whole world is a mystery to me and makes me tremble for the sanity of my advisers . . .'[104] The Sudan press law was promulgated finally only after Gorst had left Egypt.

The 'Adb al-Qādir Wad Ḥabūba revolt in Gezira in 1908 was the occasion of yet another clash between Wingate and Gorst. A Sudan court had found twenty of the rebels guilty of waging war against the government, and had condemned twelve of them to death. Wingate decided to confirm the sentences as all his advisers were '. . . strongly of the opinion that greater leniency would be misunderstood in the country . . .' Gorst asked Wingate to postpone the execution until he had confirmation from the British government. '. . . I quite accept your view that greater leniency might be misunderstood in the Soudan, but we also have to take into account the effect in England . . .' On 30 May, Gorst received the foreign secretary's instructions to commute the sentences.[105] Gorst's attitude throughout this crisis was rather ambiguous. He had expressed his full understanding of the Sudan government's point of view. Yet three days later, after receiving the British government's instruction to commute the sentences, he wrote to Grey that he quite agreed with the British government's decision as '. . . the real reason that they [the rebels] were convicted on the charge of waging war was that it would not have been possible to prove direct complicity . . .'[106] Gorst did not express his own views until after the decision was reached and preferred throughout the crisis to act as a neutral intermediary between Wingate and Whitehall. The aftermath of the revolt was in the financial sphere. On 9 August 1908, Wingate sent Gorst a memorandum in which he stressed the insecurity of the Sudan as proved by the recent rebellion, and demanded an extension of its railways to the outlying provinces, or alternatively an increase of the British military forces in the Sudan. Wingate's demand was fully supported by both Harvey and Gorst in their official letters to London,[107] yet privately Gorst took a rather different view and wrote to Grey:

> . . . Wingate will no doubt draw you a very gloomy picture of the military situation in the Soudan. He is by nature an alarmist and I do not think, that from the point of view of security, the country is in a worse position than at any time since the reconquest . . .[108]

Gorst's subsequent support of Wingate's demands must have sounded rather half-hearted. When the loan for a railway was finally turned down Wingate demanded instead an additional British battalion. Gorst, once again, promised his full support to Wingate but in a letter to Grey, he stated: '. . . if the Soudan garrison be suddenly increased . . . an unsettling effect will be produced upon the native mind in Egypt and the Soudan . . . The lesser of the two evils is to leave matters in the present condition . . .'[109] Wingate, drew a different conclusion, and when two rebels of 'Abd al-Qādir's group were caught, he had them executed, without asking for instructions, '. . . I have thought it quite unnecessary to worry either Gorst or the Home Government, and the less said or known about it the better . . .'[110]

Cromer had established a working relationship with the governor-general of the Sudan. Gorst in his turn had formalized these relations. The extent of control remained, however, unchanged. Gorst interfered as much as his predecessor in amending Sudan ordinances, and in problems of taxation, land ownership and other subjects. The major disputes between Wingate and Gorst were the result of Gorst's Egyptian policy, of which Wingate disapproved. It is difficult to judge the success of this policy. Gorst died in 1911 before its effects could be felt, and, under Kitchener, who followed him, the policy was completely reversed.

Wingate's greater independence under Kitchener

Kitchener's appointment as consul-general in July 1911 was greeted with approval by both Cromer and Wingate. Cromer, who was asked by Grey to give his views on the appointment, expressed his full consent and wrote to Wingate that Kitchener was on the right track as far as the situation both in the Sudan and in Egypt were concerned. Kitchener had never forgotten his ambition to become British consul-general in Cairo. He had openly expressed his wish to Wingate as early as 1898, and the subject was never forgotten in his long correspondence with Lady Salisbury. In 1909, he had asked Wingate to inquire at the foreign office whether there was any chance of his getting Egypt, adding in a postscript, '. . . if it came off we should work well together I think . . .'[111] Kitchener visited the Sudan regularly after leaving for South Africa in 1899. In 1910, he undertook a hunting trip in the southern provinces of the Sudan. During these visits, he kept in touch with Sudanese affairs, and, through his intimate relations with some of the British officers, he learnt about the inner workings of the Sudan government. Thus, there was every reason to assume that Kitchener's initiation into Sudan affairs would be easier than his predecessor's.

In Egypt, Kitchener reversed the policy of reconciliation followed by Gorst, and restored autocratic rule. The powers of the Khedive were restricted, and Kitchener even sought his deposition. It is therefore of interest to note Cromer's change of heart towards Kitchener, following his enthusiastic support for his appointment. Hardly two years had passed when Cromer wrote to Strachey, editor of the *Spectator* :

> . . . What has now happened? in the first place we have had Gorst acting under Radical inspiration in England, and controlled by a Foreign Office in which no single individual having any knowledge of Egyptian affairs is employed, going to the extreme in one direction. Now, we have Kitchener, backed up by a section in the English press as foolish in its way as the Doctrinaires on the other side, going to an extreme in the other direction. Both extremes are to be deprecated . . . Both have been loud in their profession of a wish "to carry out Lord Cromer's programme", and both have in fact widely departed from the fundamental principles of that programme . . .[112]

Cromer's disapproval of Kitchener referred mainly to his Egyptian policy. However the Sudan, being under Anglo-Egyptian rule, was also affected by Kitchener's new measures, which were manifested in the diminishing participation of Egyptians in the administration of the Sudan.

Wingate had every reason to be satisfied with Kitchener's policy in Egypt. For years he had argued that the impact of Egyptian nationalism and its very effective press were being underestimated. He had been strongly opposed to Gorst's conciliatory efforts with the Khedive, especially as it implied increased Egyptian influence in the Sudan. Kitchener had as little patience with the nationalist press as he had with the Khedive. The Sudan press law, which had been held up for a long time by Gorst, was sanctioned by Kitchener shortly after his arrival. Wingate was soon to realize that the new law was hardly necessary as Kitchener suspended the publication of Egyptian newspapers at the slightest provocation. Wingate was even more delighted when Kitchener stopped Egyptian ministers from interfering in the Sudan, and expressed his feelings in a letter to Stack.

> . . . This is only a p.s. to say how amused and interested I was with your account of Lord Kitchener's interview with Mohammed Said . . . Within the last year our Ministers have learnt some sad truths, and it was just about time they realized the "hands off" policy as far as the Sudan is concerned . . .[113]

Kitchener hardly interfered in the administration of the Sudan and there were only two fields in which he took a keen interest, namely development projects and military affairs. Kitchener had been Wingate's military superior during his period as sirdar and governor-general. Wingate could therefore hardly refrain from asking his advice on general military problems, or on military expeditions against Sudanese tribes. In April 1912, Kitchener suggested withdrawing the British detachment from Khartoum. The principle of not entrusting the defence of Khartoum to the Egyptian army had been advocated by Wingate, and accepted by Cromer since the Omdurman mutiny in 1900. Kitchener regarded it as absurd and told Stack that '. . . it was quite wrong in principle to base any defence scheme on the idea that troops trained by us were likely to turn against us . . .' Stack was able to persuade Kitchener not to persist in his view.[114] Wingate had always wanted to limit the number of Egyptian officers in the Sudan government service, and he asked Kitchener to do so by an administrative order. Kitchener refused, '. . . as he does not care to face the music . . .', but suggested instead working out new service regulations so that '. . . attractions for continued service in the Sudan will be so small as to almost invariably court refusal . . .'[115]

Military expeditions in the Sudan had to have Kitchener's approval not only in principle, but also in practice since he supervised the details of their execution. When Stack brought to Kitchener the official report on the Anuak patrol in May 1912, he wrote to Wingate that Kitchener was upset by the fact that parts of the reports had been given to the press without his approval: '. . . another thing I notice he does not care for much is mention of burning villages, emphasizing enemy's losses etc. . . .'[116] When Wingate asked Clayton to obtain Kitchener's approval for a patrol against the Garjak-Nuer tribe, Kitchener refused on the grounds that it was better to leave the tribe alone than to risk failure. Wingate had to reconcile himself to '. . . peaceful penetration . . .'[117] Expenditure for all military expeditions had to be sanctioned by Kitchener, who also decided whether they should be charged against the Egyptian army or the Sudan government. Wingate was, of course, anxious that expeditions should be charged against the Egyptian army and subsequently paid by Egypt. When, however, Kitchener decided to charge all the expeditions between 1912–14 against the Sudan government budget, Wingate was unperturbed as '. . . captured cattle etc. from them [the expeditions] will in all likelihood cover the expense. . .'[118]

Development projects and economic problems of the Sudan were Kitchener's major interest. His objectives were to loosen Egypt's financial ties with the Sudan by stopping the annual grants and securing the necessary capital for the Gezira development project from other sources. In order to stop Egypt's yearly grant, Kitchener decided to raise the level of taxation in the Sudan. Wingate was in general agreement with this plan, and the only objection came from Slatin who feared tribal unrest. By 1913, Kitchener had managed to achieve this aim, and the Egyptian yearly grant was stopped. Kitchener's major success was in obtaining a British guaranteed loan of £3m. for the Gezira development. He succeeded in seeing the first stage of the Gezira plan started before he left Egypt in 1914. The details of the Gezira scheme, by which the Sudan government, the Syndicate and the tenants were to be partners were carefully supervised by Kitchener, who also dictated to Clayton, then Wingate's secretary, the terms under which the agreement was to be signed.[119]

In every other sphere, Wingate had all the freedom he wanted. Kitchener was not interested in reading through Sudan government ordinances or other lengthy documents on which he was supposed to decide. A special arrangement had to be evolved whereby Clayton marked all the passages in ordinances or minutes of the governor-general's council's meetings to which Kitchener's attention had to be drawn. Stack, the Sudan agent in Cairo, then supplied Kitchener with verbal explanations. It was also difficult to obtain written decisions from Kitchener. Consequently, Wingate prepared a list of all subjects on which he required Kitchener's approval, in order to discuss it with him in Cairo. Apparently, even this did not bring the desired results, as, in May 1913, Wingate complained to Stack about the undue independence given to the Sudan government by Kitchener :

> . . . it is all very well for him [Kitchener] to say that the Sudan being practically autonomous, it is responsible for safeguarding its own interests . . . but you know as well as I do that . . . if the Governor General of the Sudan and his advisers adopted that attitude there would be inevitable reactions. There can be no manner of doubt that the intention of Lord Cromer and the British Government . . . was that the British Agent in Egypt should be the deciding authority, and I have always loyally played up to that understanding . . .[120]

Thus the roles were at last reversed, and Wingate was pleading for more control from Egypt. Kitchener left Egypt on 18 June 1914, and on 3 August he was appointed secretary for war in Asquith's war cabinet. His Sudan policy had followed the pattern laid down by him in 1899, when he was governor-general. He relaxed his own control over Sudan administration, suppressed the nationalist press, and helped diminish Egyptian influence in the Sudan. His main efforts were concentrated in the economic field. By stopping the Egyptian annual grant, and starting the Gezira scheme, he succeeded both in releasing the Sudan from its dependence on Egypt, and in determining its future economic dependence on the British market.

McMahon and Wingate

Wingate's last two years as governor-general can best be described as a period of frustration. At the outbreak of the First World War, he cut short his annual leave and hurried back to the Sudan. He succeeded in preserving peace in the country with negligible forces and despite pan-Islamic propaganda. Yet he felt that his superior knowledge of Arab affairs was disregarded, and that lesser people were being entrusted with greater responsibility than himself. This feeling was first apparent during the brief period when Sir Milne Cheetham was acting consul-general in Egypt. Wingate complained that he was kept in the dark as to developments outside the Sudan and that his advice was not required.[121] It was, therefore, with great expectations that he greeted Sir Henry McMahon's appointment as high commissioner, expressing his hopes that relations with the residency in Cairo would soon return to normal.[122] These hopes were not to be realized. McMahon's was a temporary appointment, made in order to enable Kitchener to return to Egypt after the war. Hence, as a man of no previous experience in Egypt, he suited this purpose well. Wingate soon heard about the true state of affairs from Stack : '. . . The High Commissioner does nothing, Cheetham is in despair and Storrs runs everything . . .'[123] As a result Wingate decided to communicate directly with Kitchener whenever he needed some backing at the residency : '. . . My difficulty is to write in a sufficiently impersonal spirit to McMahon who naturally suffers from want of knowledge . . .'[124] In the war cabinet, too, Kitchener was regarded as an expert on Egypt and the Sudan, and all matters concerning these countries were referred to him for advice. In a private letter Wingate expressed his feelings more precisely: '. . . When one thinks of the old days with Lord Cromer and Lord Kitchener in the Agency chair . . . you can perhaps appreciate my feelings and what I had to submit to ever since the War began . . .'[125]

A controversy regarding the extent of the high-commissioner's control over Sudan affairs broke out shortly after McMahon's arrival in Egypt. It was instigated by Cecil, the financial adviser of the Egyptian government. Following Kitchener's departure, he suggested to Cheetham, the acting agent, that control over the Sudan be tightened :

> . . . It is necessary . . . for us to know what real control the High Commissioner wishes to keep over Sudan legislation. Lord Kitchener's view was, I believe, that the interference of the Egyptian Government should be stopped, but I do not think he contemplated relaxing the British control as exercised by the highest British authority who is in the country. There has been a certain tendency of recent years to make

it more and more a nominal control. Personally I think this is not wise . . .[126]

Wingate was unable to argue with these proposals openly as Cecil's letter had reached him by mistake.[127] Thus the only action taken by Wingate was to write to Lord Cromer, probably hoping that it would find its way into the right hands :

. . . I note a tendency—I do not say on the part of the High Commissioner—but on the part of some of his British advisers who should know better—to attempt to . . . bring the Sudan into a position of a Province of Egypt, on the assumption that the declaration of a protectorate *over Egypt* has altered the status of the Sudan . . . Any pressure in this direction is both undesirable and dangerous . . .[128]

Cecil's proposal was not accepted by McMahon who decided to postpone his decision until he met Wingate. Such a meeting did not take place as during the two years of McMahon's sojourn in Egypt, Wingate refused to leave the Sudan. For Wingate, the elimination of Egyptian control meant a separate status for the Sudan. Now that a British protectorate had been declared over Egypt, there was a chance of placing the Sudan directly under *British rule* as distinct from *Anglo-Egyptian control.* Wingate hoped, that with Kitchener's help in the Cabinet, he could force through this view, despite Anglo-Egyptian opposition. His first move was to write to McMahon, stating his beliefs on the future policy to be adopted in the Sudan. A copy of this letter was sent to Kitchener, who was asked to secure the cabinet's backing.[129] Finally, Clayton, the Sudan agent, was instructed to enlighten the high-commissioner : '. . . Clearly Sir Henry is new to all these intricacies, and I look to you as my agent, to see that he fully understands the situation . . .'[130] As this was the beginning of what Wingate hoped might be a new venture in British-Sudanese relations, his letter to McMahon deserves to be quoted :

. . . Prior to the declaration of a Protectorate over Egypt, (the Sudan being already a partially British *possession*), the policy of H.B.M's Government had been to make the status of the Sudan as *British* as possible, without making an official declaration which would necessarily have raised the question of the status of the two countries—which they were anxious to avoid. It is important to remember that the Mahdi revolt was a revolt of the Sudanese against Egyptian misgovernment, and for that reason our public and official utterances in the Sudan have always been to the effect that the Sudanese would never again be governed from Egypt; it is the adoption of this policy from the beginning which has resulted in the far greater loyalty of the Sudanese, in the present crisis to H.B.M's Government than the Egyptians—for, in their minds, the Egyptian and Turkish Governments are almost

> identical. The declaration of a British Protectorate over Egypt has left them cold—had Egypt been annexed by England and a purely British rule established, then it is possible that, in time, they might have realized that control from Cairo meant *British* Control—as it stands, and in view of the letter accompanying the Proclamation of Sultan Hussein's Accession foreshadowing Egyptian local self-government, the Sudanese now cling more than ever to the British—as distinct from the Egyptian Government. Moreover, in the Proclamations issued in the Sudan on the occasion of Sultan Hussein's accession this point was very carefully safeguarded—indeed all reference to the Sudan was, in accordance with my express recommendation, studiously avoided . . .[131]

There is no evidence that McMahon or the British government accepted this policy, but it is clear that Wingate started to implement it. In August 1915, Wingate planned the elimination of the Egyptian personnel from Gordon College. He did not, however, refer to McMahon for his advice, but applied directly to Kitchener.[132] Under McMahon, Wingate achieved a greater measure of independence than he had before. Yet despite this relaxation of control, Wingate was not satisfied. What he really wanted was the complete severance of Egypt's ties with the Sudan, and had he remained governor-general, he would in all likelihood have pursued this aim. Following his appointment as high-commissioner of Egypt in 1916, Wingate reversed his own policy, and demanded for the duration of the war, a greater control over Sudanese affairs than that of his predecessors.[133]

CHAPTER III

The Inspector-General, Slatin Pasha

AMONG the inner circle of Wingate's confidants, Slatin Pasha reigned supreme. Slatin resigned from the Egyptian army following the battle of Kararī. As assistant-director of intelligence since March 1895, he had played a significant role in the reconquest, particularly after the capture of Omdurman, when, as the only officer who was familiar with the town and its people, he rendered indispensable advice in establishing the new military administration.[1] Yet, despite this, he decided to retire. He felt that he was disliked by Kitchener and that following the setting up of the Condominium, his position as the only officer who was neither Egyptian nor British would become unbearable.[2] Thus in February 1899 Slatin left Egypt as a private citizen, having served in the Sudan for twenty-two years. However, before sailing, he was recruited by the Sudan Territories Exploration Syndicate to undertake a prospecting tour into the Nuba Mountains and in January 1900 he returned to Cairo in his new capacity as prospecting agent.[3]

Slatin's appointment

In the eleven months which had elapsed since Slatin's departure from the Sudan, the situation had radically changed. Kitchener, whose alleged antipathy was one of Slatin's main reasons for resigning, had himself left the Sudan. The new sirdar and governor-general was Wingate, Slatin's most intimate friend among the British officers. Moreover, following the famine of 1898 and the Omdurman mutiny in January 1900, Wingate felt in need of help as most of the experienced British officers had left the Sudan to take part in the Boer War. It was, therefore, only to be expected that shortly after Slatin's arrival Wingate asked him to rejoin the Sudan government, promising '. . . to "create" any post Slatin would ask for . . .'[4]

Slatin did not accede to this request immediately, as he was still committed to prospecting. Yet his trip into the Nuba Mountains can well be described as the first act of the future inspector-general. Slatin's diary, describing the trip resembles an intelligence officer's report rather than that of a prospecting agent. On 20 February Slatin interrogated 'Alī 'Abd al-Karīm an uncle of the Mahdi who was suspected of instigating a revolt. Though Slatin was convinced that 'Abd al-Karīm and his followers meant no harm he recommended they should be banished to Egypt as an example to others. Slatin wrote a proclamation to the people of the Sudan, signed by Wingate, in which he promised them peace and prosperity and urged them to co-operate with the government. He advised Lady Wingate to give money to the poor women in Omdurman, and chaired a meeting of the *'ulamā'* concerning religious problems. *En route* to Kordofan Slatin received petitions, settled cases and advised British officers on the correct manner of administering their provinces.[5] Thus Slatin, a private citizen on a prospecting tour, became Wingate's travelling emissary even before he was appointed to a government post. On his return to Egypt in June 1900, Slatin had long confabulations with Cromer, Gorst, Muṣṭafā Fahmī, and others, all of whom urged him to return to the Sudan. It seems that when Cromer wrote to Salisbury that he was '. . . suggesting to Wingate that Slatin's services might perhaps be utilized . . .',[6] the appointment was as good as settled.

Slatin received his appointment as inspector-general on 29 September 1900. His duties and the extent of his authority were not clearly defined. He was intended to be a highly mobile officer who would travel over the vast areas of the Sudan and act as the governor-general's eyes and ears. Wingate never regarded Slatin as a run-of-the-mill government official. He viewed his appointment as a personal post which would cease when Slatin left the service. Moreover, he confessed that had he wanted to appoint another inspector-general it would have been impossible to find a man of equal qualifications.[7] Thus following Slatin's resignation on the outbreak of the First World War, the post of inspector-general ceased to exist and the work was divided between Symes,[8] then Wingate's private secretary, and the intelligence department.

Following several incidents between Slatin and British officer-administrators, Wingate decided to define more accurately Slatin's duties. He instructed the civil secretary to prepare a draft proposal to this effect. The duties of the inspector-general as enumerated in this document were as follows :

> . . . To act as adviser generally to H.E. the Gov. Gen. on all matters concerning his duties . . . to acquaint himself with the names and characters of the principal Sheikhs and other persons who either through their wealth, position, or for reasons connected with religion, have influence over the natives . . .[9]

Slatin's supreme authority in connection with religious affairs was emphasized in two articles which empowered him to advise on all legal problems connected with religion, and to be in touch with the 'Board of Ulema' and other religious leaders as Wingate's adviser. Article XI emphasized Slatin's power regarding all tribal affairs, including taxation, and stressed his special responsibility for nomads. Several articles were intended to ensure amicable relations between Slatin and the British personnel. He was instructed to inform governors and inspectors before he undertook an inspection of their provinces. Again he was warned not to '. . . issue direct orders to any employee under a Mudir, except in case of absolute urgency when the Mudir is too far away to issue orders in time . . .' Lastly, Slatin was '. . . to examine and remark upon the Intelligence Report before it is submitted to the Sirdar and Gover. Gen. . . .' These detailed instructions were sent by Wingate to all his provincial governors in the hope that the antagonism stimulated by Slatin's unique position would be reduced to a minimum.

Slatin's policies

The inspector-general's department was a one-man show. With a yearly budget of some £E 2,500, Slatin toured the length and breadth of the Sudan, by foot, camel and train. An example of Slatin's method of work during one of his tours is afforded by the following notes :

> . . . 31 January 1913 . . . reach Singa at 7 a.m., meet on the way Taylor, Tippets, Dupuis, Thompson . . . 1 February . . . Have long meeting with Omdehs Sheikhs, merchants, etc. . . . 2 February . . . Have single interviews with Omdehs and Sheikhs . . . 3 February . . . give Govt. officials my instructions and views on all matters (shows in my notes at the end of this diary) . . .[10]

The observations written by a British inspector during one of Slatin's tours, make an interesting comparison :

> . . . Slatin arrived on 14th and I had no news of him till he was only 7 miles off . . . He spent first day interviewing Ali Dinar's messengers—next day visited the Nazirs—interesting to hear him talk over Dervish times and pre Dervish times—He contrives to be amazingly tactless at times . . . Next morning Savile[11] turned up and had to see the Nazirs etc. too . . . We spent most of the day ciphering F.O. telegrams re. French[12] . . . Following day we had gelsa[13] of the Hamar Sheikhs, at which Slatin told them they would be put on to taxes. He managed to put it very badly, it would have been better to leave it alone and let me and Elwi do it . . .[14]

While Slatin clearly regarded his tours as the only guarantee of a just administration, the recipients of his views regarded them as a necessary evil which they had to endure. It was during these tours that Slatin compiled his lists of recommendations which covered almost every sphere of policy. His suggestions, or rather orders, were given to the men on the spot and later communicated to Wingate. A detailed description of all the spheres covered by Slatin would be beyond the scope of this chapter. Yet a brief résumé of his major activities is clearly required in order to assess his impact on policy making.

Islamic affairs were Slatin's prime responsibility. He lacked religious zeal of any kind and tended to steer clear of any spiritual speculation. Yet, his experience as a Muslim during the Mahdia, had made him familiar with Islamic custom and enabled him to understand the Sudanese Muslims better than did his fellow officers. Slatin's first premise was that no missionary activities should be allowed in Muslim provinces. In this he was at one with most of his British colleagues. But as a foreigner he was better able to speak up. '. . . Slatin Pasha . . . has just administered a heavy rebuke to those silly people who wish to shove the English Bibles down the throats of the African blacks . . .'[15] In an interview with the *Neue Freie Presse*, on 10 October 1900 Slatin stated that missionary proselytization among Muslims was impossible and should be avoided.

His tendency was to reduce the impact of every religion to the best of his ability. In 1901 he prepared a proclamation to the Muslims, aimed at diminishing the influence of their religious leaders. He mistrusted all the *ṣūfī ṭarīqas*, an attitude he probably inherited from his Mahdist overlords. Even Sayyid 'Alī al-Mīrghanī, the head of the Khatmīya order, who was decorated by Cromer and received a monthly pay for his services was refused official recognition by Slatin : '. . . I told him that he cannot be recognized as the head of a Teriga which are only tolerated . . .'[16] When H. C. Jackson, then a junior inspector in Dongola, wanted to appoint Sayyid 'Abd al-Muta'āl as head of the Idrīsīya order, Slatin reminded him '. . . that Terikas are only tolerated but not officially recognized and that we neither appoint nor dismiss "Khalifas" . . .'[17] In dealing with the *ṭarīqas* Slatin observed a great measure of neutrality. He strongly opposed the favoured Khatmīya, when they urged Wingate to expel one of the leaders of the rival Majdhūbīya order from the Sudan. The Khatmīya leaders at Ṭokar had convinced Wingate that the Majdhūbīya were still propagating Mahdism Slatin was able to overcome these instigations by proving to Wingate that the hatred between the two orders dated to pre-Mahdist days.[18] Butler, who on being appointed to the intelligence department was instructed by Slatin as to government policy, described the latter's views :

. . . A busy morning with Slatin . . . He does not approve of Savile's action in appointing a leader of the Morghanieh tarika in El Obeid . . . Says Govt. should have nothing to do with these tarikas as the heads are really only after the monetary profits . . . they are really frauds and Govt. cannot be responsible for their activities . . . The only religion recognized by Govt. is Orthodox Muhamedanism . . .[19]

Consequently, Slatin relied on the 'Board of Ulema' which was instituted by the government in 1901, and on several Muslim leaders whom he regarded as trustworthy. He asked their advice whenever a religious problem occured and they became his sole interpreters of orthodox Islam. Slatin was also responsible for the appointment of *qāḍīs*, many of whom were of Egyptian origin, and thus was in a position to supervise their activities in the Sudan.[20]

In his policy towards Mahdist insurrections Slatin encouraged a cautious attitude. He was sceptical when a Mahdist rising was reported by Count Gleichen, the Sudan agent, in 1901, and advised Wingate that, '. . . it isn't good to tickle religious people or questions . . .' unless the suspicions were proved beyond doubt.[21] Following a report about a new mahdi in the Nuba Mountains in 1903 Slatin wrote : '. . . I suppose *it was more a private affair* then [sic] religious matter . . .'[22] Even after the Gezira rebellion in 1908, which was the most serious religious uprising during this period, Slatin did not join in the general witchhunt. He demanded a death sentence for the rebels, but at the same time warned against mass arrests amongst their followers who, he knew, would be kept out of mischief by the beginning of the rainy season.[23] When a new religious movement was reported in 1911, Slatin wrote : '. . . I got as usual the report on Nabi Alla Isa and as usual he appears at Sennar province—rott [sic] and nonsense . . .'[24]

The intelligence department remained Slatin's second home even after he became inspector-general. He supervised its work and visited it daily when in Khartoum. It was there that his interviews with 'Alī Dīnār's messengers, religious leaders, and other notables took place. His preoccupation with intelligence work can be seen by the lists of 'Trustworthy men' suited for intelligence work, which he compiled in his diaries.[25] Domestic slavery was also within Slatin's spheres of activity and was dealt with by the intelligence department. Slatin's opinions on slavery were formed during his long service in the Sudan, a country whose economy was largely based on slavery. During the reconquest he stated that he regarded slaves as :

. . . godforsaken swine [who] do not deserve to be treated like free and independent men . . . the blacks should be made to remain under the protection of their former masters who were forced to treat them well . . .[26]

This attitude prevailed throughout Slatin's inspector-generalship. When 'Alī Dīnār's messenger came to Omdurman in 1902 and sold fifteen female slaves, with the government's full knowledge, Wingate asserted that it '. . . was based on Slatin's advice . . .'[27] In 1906, Slatin fully supported a claim by Sayyid al-Makkī, head of the Ismā'īlīya order in Kordofan, for the return of his runaway slaves who had been caught in the Nuba Mountains.[28] He was Wingate's champion in his long drawn battle against the Egyptian department for the repression of slavery, until the latter finally became part of the Sudan government.[29] Slatin realized that in order not to embarrass the government he had to refrain from using the term domestic slaves. In warning one of his subordinates he '. . . told him that if in an official document I find again that he calls Sudanese servants "slaves"—a finger from his right hand will be cut off . . .'[30] Despite his excessive freedom of expression Slatin's views did not differ from those of Wingate. He regarded domestic slavery as an essential part of the Sudan's economy and used all his influence to discourage runaway slaves.

Darfur, to all intents and purposes, was independent under Sultan 'Alī Dīnār until its conquest in 1916. Its major problems during that period were its western borders which were threatened by the advancing French.[31] Slatin, as the last general-governor of Darfur in the Turco-Egyptian Sudan, was regarded by Wingate as the greatest living authority on its history and was entrusted with all its administrative problems. The principles underlying the relationship between Sudan and Darfur were laid down by Cromer in March 1900 when he vetoed Wingate's suggestion that the British flag should be hoisted in Darfur. Cromer insisted that the administration of Darfur from Khartoum would be costly, useless and inefficient, and that 'Alī Dīnār should be left in peace. This policy was endorsed by the British government and was duly carried out by Slatin and Wingate.

Slatin's first aim was to establish cordial relations with Darfur which he hoped to achieve by visiting the country. 'Alī Dīnār thought differently, and wrote to Wingate: '. . . not to send Slatin who, owing to his personality, would do more harm in Darfur than the Khalifa did . . .'[32] In fact, no senior official of the Sudan government, was allowed into Darfur during 'Alī Dīnār's reign. Communications with Darfur were carried on by messengers and were conducted by Slatin until his retirement. His basic policy was not to interfere in Darfur's internal affairs. The Arab tribes of Darfur, such as the Ma'ālīya and the Rizayqāt, who were constantly harassed by the Fūr army, were driven back across the borders whenever they sought refuge in the Sudan. Slatin only agreed to write to 'Alī Dīnār advising him to adopt a more lenient tribal policy. Yet, concurrently, he ordered the Darfur tribes to obey their ruler. 'Alī Dīnār was paying a yearly tribute to the Sudan government, and was, in Slatin's view, immune from any interference in his internal affairs. Thus Slatin, who implemented a policy of free immigration into the Sudan from all the neighbouring states, insisted on this very rigid attitude towards the tribes of Darfur.[33] Numerous clashes also occurred between the nomadic tribes of Kordofan and the Baḥr al-Ghazāl, and between tribes from Darfur and its army. In 1903 the Kordofan–Darfur border was agreed upon by Slatin and 'Alī Dīnār's cousin, and although border incidents persisted they were somewhat easier to control.

Several Mahdist *amīrs* who escaped from the Sudan had found refuge in Darfur. Ostensibly the Sudan government had a right to demand their extradition, or at least to be consulted regarding their fate. Slatin, however, urged Wingate not to interfere, and when Karamallāh Kurqusāwī, the first Mahdist *amīr* of Baḥr al-Ghazāl, was executed by 'Alī Dīnār in 1903, he advised Wingate against any official censure. Darfur affairs were, thus, conducted by Slatin without undue interference by Wingate or by other British officials.

Slatin's tribal policy and his relations with non-British personnel

In 1902, all the provincial governors were instructed that matters concerning nomad Arab tribes were to be dealt with by Slatin.[34] Yet the difference between nomad and sedentary tribes was in many cases obscure, so that Slatin in fact assumed full responsibility for almost all tribal affairs, including appointments of shaykhs, tribal justice, land ownership and taxation.

During his first year in office Slatin fixed the tribute of the tribes in Kassala, Dongola, Berber, Khartoum and Fashoda. In 1901 Slatin ruled that all people who had lived in Nahūd for over three years were to keep their lands and a third of their tebeldi trees,[35] even if the previous land owners were to return. Following a tour of Kordofan in 1902, Slatin instructed the Ḥawāzma, one of the Baqqāra tribes, to run a regular post service in the province; he lowered the *'ushr* fixed by the governor and recommended that provincial governors should be enabled to spend a certain amount of money without the prior consent of the financial secretary. In 1903, Slatin forwarded a plan for the complete reorganization of the tribal administration in al-Qaḍārif, where hundreds of villages, scattered over vast areas, were supervised by a single *nāẓir*.[36] A year later, Slatin telegraphed Henry, who was acting governor-general in Wingate's absence, to open the southern provinces to traders. He further objected to Shāyqīya soldiers participating in patrols in the south as they were known to have been slave-raiders and hence were feared by the local tribes.[37]

Slatin's system for dealing with turbulent tribes was by collective punishment. He ordered members of the tribe to be arrested at random and kept in prison until the whole tribe paid the fine. He believed that the best way to deal with rebels was by martial law. He wrote after the Gezira rebellion that '. . . if our rebelles [sic] would have been tried by martial law—I would have hanged them before anybody in Europe would have known that they were under trial . . .'[38]

Slatin was also concerned with the protection of Sudanese land-owners from land speculators and profiteers. He demanded that the government should develop pump irrigation on the Nile as he feared '. . . that "small Greeks" come in with pumps to take the whole profit . . .'[39] These worries were clearly expressed when Slatin pointed out the dangers of the 'Zeidab Concession' in Dongola to local landowners.[40]

> . . . The result . . . will be that the Jaalin will evacuate their Sakiehs[41] and work for the comp. Before long they will sell their lands for which they cannot pay the taxes and instead of land owners they will become tenants . . . it pays a man more to work where water and seed is supplied instead to worry [sic] behind his own Sakieh . . .[42]

Slatin seems to have regarded the pre-Mahdist Sudanese society as an ideal which should serve as a model for the new administration. This did not apply to the old Turco-Egyptian administration which was severely criticized by Slatin and Wingate. Yet in his tribal and religious policies Slatin adopted an approach which can be defined as traditional. He tried to restore the tribes to their position in pre-Mahdist times. This applied to tribal customs as well as to the choice of personnel. Slatin appointed *nāẓirs* and shaykhs whose families had proved loyal and whom he had known personally, rather than the men favoured by the local British officials. Bashīr Kanbāl, was a cause for bitter friction between Slatin and the British officials in Kordofan. Bashīr, of Shāyqī origin, had served with Slatin in Darfur in 1877 and was appointed after the reconquest as a special adjutant *(muʿāwin)* for Arab affairs in Kordofan. Slatin relied on his advice to the exclusion of everyone else, including his British colleagues. The same attitude was adopted towards 'Abd al-Raḥīm Abū-Daqal who, as minor Mahdist *amīr*, received a letter of amnesty from Slatin in September 1898, and was appointed *nāẓir* of the Gharaysīya branch of the Ḥamar. Despite the complaints that were levied against Abū-Daqal by British inspectors, Slatin stood firmly by him.[43] In certain cases he also disregarded the authority of his nominees within their own tribes. He appointed ʿAbbās Raḥmatallāh as shaykh of the Jaʿalīyīn in Omdurman, despite widespread opposition from his tribe.[44]

Slatin's special regard for his fellow-prisoners in Omdurman was clearly proved by the letters of recommendation he gave them. Following their appointments, Slatin regarded their welfare as his responsibility. He insisted that the remuneration of the tribal shaykhs and *ʿumdas*[45] was not adequate. By 1907, shaykhs were paid for assessing *ʿushr*, and in 1912, the general remuneration of all tribal tax collectors was raised. In both cases this was done following demands made by Slatin. He also strongly urged Wingate to abolish the old Ottoman custom which still prevailed in the Sudan, whereby all Sudanese had to dismount when meeting an officer.

> . . . the respectable Sudan merchant, Sheikh and Omdeh—hops like a fly—up and down, because . . . if he rides to the streets of Khart. and Omdurman he is bound to meet officers. If you agree I would find a suitable wording in your name to do away with this old Turkish custom . . .[46]

There was, however, a certain ambiguity in this attitude. Slatin trusted his nominees but mistrusted the Sudanese generally, '. . . Sudanese are always . . . scoundrels—if they are not under control and under Kurbatsh[47] the [sic] go wrong . . .'[48] Hence he insisted that a British officer should be in charge of Sinkāt during the summer months '. . . and not leave thousands of subjects to the mercy of Mohammed Bey Ahmed—although your favourite he is only native . . .'[49] An interesting side-light on Slatin's traditional approach was shown in a memorandum he sent to all provincial governors, warning them against the excessive freedom of the young generation. He instructed the governors to explain to local parents that they were responsible for their children until the age of eighteen, even should it entail '. . . giving a good licking to lazy boys and bad girls . . .'[50]

In his mistrust of the Egyptian personnel, Slatin did not differ largely from his British colleagues. Yet, at the same time he tried to be fair and to support them whenever they had a genuine grievance. This was well expressed in a letter to Wingate, where Slatin complained about a British administrator at Kassala.

> . . . His [the British official] main work was to spy after Egypt[ian] officers and to impress on natives, that we consider all egyptians "scoundrels" . . . I am the last *to trust* a gyppy—but we have to pluck them up as long as nothing is against them . . .[51]

This attitude prevailed when, in 1908, the Egyptian officers wished to open a club in Khartoum. The intelligence department opposed the project as they feared subversive propaganda. Slatin convinced Wingate that there was no harm in the club and that the inherent suspiciousness of the British officials should not be taken too seriously. Slatin also devised a plan encouraging Egyptian officers to settle in the Sudan by selling them land at a special reduced rate. On the other hand Slatin's mistrust of Egyptians led him to oppose their being entrusted with too much responsibility, '. . . I have nothing special against Mah. H. [Maḥmūd Ḥusayn] who is a hard working clever man—but it is my old complaint that *he* runs too much of the show . . .'[52]

Basically, therefore, Slatin regarded both Sudanese and Egyptians as untrustworthy unless kept under strict control. Slatin's mistrust was reciprocated by the Egyptians and Sudanese; perhaps an inevitable repercussion. Wingate, who was aware of this, explained to Cromer that Slatin '. . . is unpopular with native officers whose maladministrative practices he fearlessly discloses . . .'[53] Butler, of the intelligence department, felt that the mistrust of Slatin was of a more general nature: '. . . He was not popular among the Sudanese as he was supposed to show favouritism to his pals among the tribes, and I don't think they trusted him . . .'[54] Sir Harold MacMichael added yet another point saying that many Muslims rejected Slatin as a renegade who had changed his religion twice for reasons of political expediency.[55] This seems to be borne out by a telegram Slatin received from the 'Union of Murder' in Cairo on 9 April 1910, in which they threatened to kill him for becoming a Christian.[56]

While these were Slatin's main spheres of action, he rendered his advice in nearly every other field. In 1906 he advised establishing a separate governorship of the Nuba mountains. In 1910 the reorganization of the department of agriculture and lands was based on Slatin's suggestion. Even speeches by British personalities visiting the Sudan were prepared by Slatin. He suggested the main points for Cromer's speech to the 'Sheikhs and Notables' in 1900,[57] and dictated to Wingate's secretary, his ideas for the King's speech to be delivered during George V's visit to the Sudan in 1912.[58]

Slatin's relations with Wingate and with British officials

Slatin's unique position was largely responsible for his relations with his fellow officials. He was an Austrian exercising:

> . . . the second highest authority in a British Administration. His English was peculiar . . . His practical bent . . . inclined him to be impatient of academic ideas and gave him a very different perspective to that of many of his colleagues . . .[59]

Furthermore, some of the provincial governors regarded their own knowledge of local affairs as superior to Slatin's and therefore objected to his supreme authority which was never questioned by Wingate. They accused Slatin of appointing his cronies from the pre-Anglo-Egyptian period as shaykhs and *nāẓirs*, positions they did not deserve and which they often abused. Some criticized his double talk in dealing with the tribes, claiming that he promised the shaykhs one thing while instructing the local inspector in the opposite sense. Basically the problem was that the men on the spot felt their authority was undermined by Slatin's interference. This feeling was apparently shared by both Cromer and Gorst. Following the 'Jackson affair', Cromer blamed Wingate for the '. . . injudicious manner in which Slatin's services have been utilized . . .'[60] Gorst went even further in asserting, '. . . that it is, of course, quite impossible to get a man of his [Slatin's] character to understand the point of view of the British public . . .'[61]

Slatin was well aware of these views but they did not inhibit him from criticizing his British colleagues, both military and civil, whenever necessary. Following one of the frequent revolts in the Nuba Mountains Slatin complained that the British officers had no inkling as to the real situation in their district. In 1909 he complained that the governor of Kassala '. . . had not seen notables of Berbera awlad Ahmed for two years . . . Never accepts any complaints . . . nobody is allowed to come near him and order is given to drive away natives attempting to talk or to reach him . . .'[62] Even more humiliating were Slatin's charges that some of his British colleagues were acting with undisguised injustice. He denounced them for administering public lashings to local dignitaries without adequate reason, and complained to Wingate that '. . . it isn't pleasant to justify or to defend an action of a comrade publicly which one has to condemn secretly . . .'[63] On another occasion Slatin condemned a military action in the Nuba Mountains insisting that it was undertaken for no better reason than to satisfy the British commandant's dislike of the local shaykh. Even worse was the case near al-Qaḍārif, when the local *nāẓir* was imprisoned, his wives ill-treated, and the whole village evacuated, for no adequate reason whatsoever. Slatin promptly reinstated the *nāẓir* and blamed the British officer for a miscarriage of justice.[64]

Despite these numerous incidents Slatin on the whole preferred the British officers to their fellow civilians with whom he failed to find a common language. He expressed his doubts about civilian employees when the suggestion of their employment was first made. In 1908 he vetoed the suggestion that Kerr[65] should be appointed as the first civilian governor in the Sudan and as a result the appointment was postponed for another year. Slatin constantly clashed with the senior civilian officials. He had no patience for their academic approach or for their insistence on an abstract form of justice which held no meaning whatsoever for Slatin. He criticized them for their 'stand offish' attitude towards the Sudanese, and never failed to mention their shortcomings. In 1910 Slatin wrote: '. . . I have been at the Damer Show [a yearly agricultural display] . . . I was rather sick that not *one* of the Civilians—who are so proud of their "liberal education"— . . . thought it is worth while to go . . .'[66] His opinion of the civilians was expressed concisely when he wrote: '. . . The Red flag for all civilians under C & B [Currie and Bonham Carter] guidance! I wish I would have got a "liberal education" to be able to be useful and improve the situation . . .'[67] Needless to say Slatin regarded his own usefulness as more than adequate and looked upon a 'liberal education' as an obstacle rather than an asset. Wingate, however, hardly relied on Slatin's advice concerning his British personnel, and the volume of Slatin's complaints in this field adequately bears this out. The lack of complaints in other fields proves yet another fact, namely, that apart from personnel and finances, Slatin's advice was generally accepted.

During his fourteen years as inspector-general Slatin contemplated resignation more than once. In 1906 Wingate overcame his threat by sending him on a long holiday and assuring him of his absolute confidence in his advice.[68] In 1908, Slatin sent Wingate an official letter of resignation on the grounds that the clemency extended to the Gezira rebels would endanger the Sudan. Following a strong appeal from Wingate Slatin again withdrew his resignation stressing that he did so for Wingate's sake only.[69]

The high regard in which Wingate held Slatin was expressed when he wrote to Stack '. . . As for Slatin I look upon him as a very privileged person and his value to the Sudan Govt. is so enormous that I am quite ready to sacrifice my "Amour propre", for him . . .'[70] Yet it was Slatin's 'very privileged' position which caused most of the difficulties. Here he was, a single Austrian in an Anglo-Egyptian administration, with a greater impact on policy making than any other official. He was consulted by Wingate on nearly all problems of Sudan administration, and in the majority of cases his opinions became government policy. It is true that Wingate also asked for the advice of his fellow British officials but in most cases they were only consulted regarding their immediate spheres of responsibility. The explanation of Slatin's authority lies in a number of factors. His vast experience of Sudan affairs, his fearless criticism, and his position as inspector-general which enabled him, alone among government officials, to gain an overall view of the country's administration. Yet all this does not explain the unlimited trust

Wingate had in Slatin. To understand it one would have to study the characters of these two men who, above all else, were the closest of friends for nearly four decades. Slatin was first and foremost a man of worldly wisdom and of highly practical bent. He, like Wingate, had little patience for the theoretical manipulations and sophisticated arguments of his fellow civilians. But equally he discarded the purely military approach to administrative problems. Both Slatin and Wingate regarded themselves as the bearers of civilization and progress to the unprivileged people of the Sudan. They treated the penetration of Egyptian nationalism into the country as a great calamity. Even in their personal tastes they were very much alike. Their love of pomp and state and their high esteem for royalty were a standing joke in Sudan government circles. It was as a result of their similarity of views and characters, combined with the high esteem in which they held each other, that Slatin and Wingate worked in close collaboration throughout Slatin's service in the Sudan and remained close friends after his resignation in 1914.

CHAPTER IV

Government Departments and Provinces

THE administration of the Sudan was established during the Wingate era. Some of the central government departments had existed prior to the reconquest, within the Egyptian army, and were later transferred to the Sudan government. Others were established when their services were required and the meagre Sudan budget could support them. Provincial administration also evolved gradually. From 1899 to 1916 the number of provinces increased from eight to fifteen through the extension of territory and the subdivision of existing provinces. At the top of the administrative hierarchy was the governor-general followed by the inspector-general. The Sudan agent in Cairo, who was also head of intelligence, served as a liaison between the Sudan and Egypt and was selected from Wingate's confidants. At the head of the central administration in Khartoum were the financial, legal and civil secretaries, followed by the directors of the other departments and the provincial governors. The following account will be limited to a brief survey of the administrative structure of some of the departments. Only those whose duties had a direct bearing on administrative policy will be more fully discussed in later chapters.[1]

The Sudan Agent and the intelligence department

The intelligence department of the Egyptian army existed many years prior to the reconquest and Wingate acted as D.M.I. from 1889 until he became governor-general. Its major task during these years was to obtain information regarding the Mahdist state, and to transmit it to the British authorities in Egypt and to the war office. After the battle of Kararī in September 1898, the centre of activities was shifted to the Sudan. Hence most of the staff of the intelligence department were transferred to Khartoum, while the head of intelligence remained in Cairo and bore the additional title of Sudan agent. His duties and his relations with other departments were formulated in several circulars during the years 1903–1910. The 1903 circular stated:

> . . . The Sudan agent will broadly be the channel of communication between the outer world and the Civil Administration of the Sudan Government . . . He will be the channel between the Sudan and the various offices of the Egyptian Ministries and the Army of Occupation . . . He will be the sole channel between the Departments of the Sudan Government . . . and the British Agent and Consul General . . .[2]

As for the intelligence department, the Sudan agent was required only to keep in close touch with its work. In November 1904, an additional circular delineated the intelligence duties of the department. It emphasized that it was impossible to divorce military work from political-civil considerations. The duties of Cecil, then agent-general,[3] were further defined, and he was entrusted with the supreme command of all troops in Egypt in the sirdar's absence. Throughout all these years the Sudan agency remained part of the civil secretary's office. Only in 1907, during Owen's tenure of office as agent, were the two finally divorced. It was under Stack and Clayton that the Sudan agent achieved an even greater measure of authority. In 1910, Stack complained that:

> . . . Hitherto many cases have frequently occurred, in which the Sudan Agent, owing to lack of precise information, has been unable to reply at once to enquiries by the British Agency, representatives of the foreign Governments in Cairo, commercial firms and others . . .

Wingate thereupon ordered that the Sudan agency should become an independent office on lines similar to an agency of a colony. He requested his heads of departments to acquaint the agent with all matters of importance so that he might become the sole representative of the Sudan government in Egypt. This order was circulated confidentially to all heads of departments, but was not published for Wingate regarded it '. . . undesirable to . . . draw unnecessary attention to this administrative change . . .' The Sudan agent thus became the major link between his government and the outside world. His duties included commercial negotiations, the sale and registration of Sudan lands, and the recruiting of officials from other Arabic speaking countries. He was also the legal representative of the Sudan in Egypt and in charge of submitting Sudan government ordinances to the consul-general and the Egyptian authorities.

As head of the intelligence department the duties of the Sudan agent were less numerous, as the department's main work was done in Khartoum. Certain functions were, however, performed in Cairo, where secret agents were employed in order to obtain information about foreign missions in Egypt. Others spied on Egyptian officers in Cairo in order to ascertain whether they influenced '. . . native feelings in the Sudan . . .'[4] During the World War, intelligence work in Cairo increased. Clayton, then Sudan agent, collaborated with Storrs, the oriental secretary at the residency, in running the Arab Bureau and was also a member of the Headquarters staff. He thus became immersed in the running of the Arab revolt and in intelligence work generally to the exclusion of many of his former activities. By and large the Sudan agency and intelligence department were ordinary government departments. Their budget was allocated by the Sudan government though the Egyptian war office contributed annually for intelligence work carried on in Egypt. The Sudan agent submitted an annual report on his activities. These reports were, however, never published owing to the confidential information which they contained.[5] The non-confidential parts were included in Wingate's annual memorandum.

The intelligence department in Khartoum was nominally under the Sudan agent and the director of intelligence, Cairo. In reality, however, its work was done by an assistant director in Khartoum under the direct supervision of Slatin. The department received monthly intelligence reports from the provincial governors and from its own agents. These were compiled into official intelligence reports and forwarded to the British war office. The department compiled the *Sudan Handbook Series* and its historical section prepared background material on Sudanese tribes, *ṣūfī ṭarīqas* and other matters of importance. The department was also responsible for the repatriation of tribes who had been dislocated during the Mahdia. In 1906 a special labour bureau was established within the intelligence department to cope with domestic slavery and with the growing demand of labour resulting from various development projects. The work of the department was carried out by regular staff, mainly composed of Syrians with a Roumanian and a Maltese to undertake special duties. The head agent was an old Sudanese officer and several prominent ex-Mahdists were included on its payroll. Part-time employees included the Shaykh of the Fallāta in Omdurman and many local dignitaries.[6]

The routine of intelligence work was vividly described by Butler shortly after he joined the department in 1911 :

> . . . *13th October 1911.* I've been in the Intelligence Dept. now about a month and have met quite an interesting lot of people. The Grand Mufti by name Sheikh al Tayyib Hashim . . . He is I understand quite loyal to the Government and of assistance to us. He is the brother of . . . Sheikh Abdel Gasim, Cadi of Wad Medani, a great friend of mine . . . Sayyid al Mekki al Morgani—Head of the Tijaniya Tarika . . . I don't think he could be trusted very far, or would be loyaler than suits his convenience or his purse . . . Omar Eff. Abdullahi, eldest son of the Khalifa, a pleasant young man, dressed in European clothes, intelligent face—He is now in the Fin. Sec's office . . . Son of Madi [Mahdi] by name Said Abd al Rahman . . . a dignified young Arab in Arab dress . . .

> I am told (Atiya)[7] that the people of the Sudan revere him and lots go to him at night to be healed . . . *16 October* full morning with Mudassa [Mudaththir] Ibrahim . . . ex tutor of Mahdi's sons—A great stand by and confidential adviser of Slatin's . . . *20 November.* Visited Omdurman and surprised by the poor living conditions of well to do people like the Mufti . . . *21 October.* A busy morning with Slatin . . . He outlined Govt. policy to me . . . *24 October.* Interviewed Ismail El Azhari, Kadi of Sennar.[8] A clever powerful man. Was sent away from El-Obeid because he took an important part in the morghanieh tarika dispute . . . *31 October.* As always had to go on rounds with various important chiefs and take them to the palace . . . *8 November.* Struve sent me down the amount of . . . slave captures up at Roseires and their disposal . . .[9]

This description affords a true understanding of the department's daily procedure. It acted as a kind of tourist bureau for provincial leaders visiting the capital. Daily visitors included its own informers in Omdurman as well as religious leaders from other provinces who had been banished from their region for various reasons. A tour of visits to the notables of Omdurman was part of its routine. The department's aim in these activities was to gauge public opinion in the country which, lacking representative bodies or a free press, had no way of expressing itself. The only Sudanese newspapers at the time were the *Sudan Times*, which was founded in 1903 by Fāris Nimr, the owner of *al-Muqaṭṭam* press in Cairo, and the *Sudan Herald* founded in 1912 by two Greeks. Both were under strong government influence and could not be regarded as a free expression of Sudanese public opinion.[10]

Wingate's relations with the Sudan agent and the intelligence department were closer than with any of the other departments. This can be partly explained by his personal inclinations as a one-time D.M.I. and by his belief that intelligence was his most comprehensive yardstick for measuring public opinion. Also the Sudan agent was Wingate's main link to the outside and apart from his official duties, supplied Wingate with confidential information regarding Egyptian politics and the inner workings of the British agency. Probably with this in mind Wingate selected the Sudan agents. Of the five agents during his tenure of office, three had served as his private secretaries prior to their appointment and one was Wingate's close friend during the Dongola campaign.[11] Apart from their specified duties Wingate consulted them on all major administrative problems and held their advice second only to Slatin's. He insisted that the Sudan agent should act only on his behalf and not as a free agent in his dealings with the authorities in Egypt. During Clayton's tenure of office in 1914–16, Wingate clearly denounced his undue independence and reprimanded him for trying to serve three masters at once namely, the army headquarters, the 'Arab bureau', and the Sudan government. He also disapproved of Clayton signing his own name to his numerous reports instead of using Wingate's, in which case '. . . more attention would have been paid to your appeals and views which after all emanate in the main from myself . . .'[12] As for the intelligence department in Khartoum Wingate relied on Slatin's view rather than on those of the British assistant director of intelligence. Only after Slatin's resignation in 1914 did the department achieve a more prominent position.

The 'three secretaries'.[13]

The financial, legal, and civil secretaries, were known as the 'three secretaries'. Unlike other directors of departments they were linked closely to the governor-general and acted as his advisers in their respective fields. All three of them had been on the central government board since 1908, and later became ex-officio members of the governor-general's council when it was constituted in 1910.[14] Their respective departments had a direct bearing on the welfare of the Sudanese people, while the civil secretary's office was also responsible for the well-being of all government officials.

The personalities of the three secretaries played an important role in moulding their departments and in formulating their relations with the governor-general and with the other government officials. Bernard Pasha, the financial secretary from 1900–23, was a Catholic of Maltese origin, and hence regarded as an outsider by Wingate and by most of the British officials in the Sudan, who attributed his shortcomings to his 'oriental' characteristics. Sir Edgar Bonham Carter, the legal secretary from 1899–1917, was the only civilian among the three secretaries. Of the senior officials his closest associate was Currie, the director of education, and together they became the spokesmen of the civil element within the Sudan Civil Service. In drafting the legal system of the Sudan, Bonham Carter enjoyed the assistance of Sterry, the chief judge, and co-operated fully with the grand *qāḍīs* who served under him. Of the four civil secretaries who held office during Wingate's governor-generalship, possibly only Phipps (1905–14) and Stack (1914–16) affected its character. Phipps was liked by most of his fellow officials but failed to gain much respect owing to the weakness of his character. Wingate regarded Phipps as his liaison officer with the provinces. Consequently, he acted as personnel officer but had little impact on policy making. It was left to Lee Stack to give greater prominence to the civil secretary's office. Stack, a man of pronounced views and strong character, was in a much better position to assert his personality. A former Sudan agent and Wingate's private secretary, he enjoyed the latter's confidence and was entrusted with wider responsibility than his predecessors.

The duties performed by the financial secretary were amongst the hardest and most unpopular undertaken by any Sudan government official.[15] As a consequence of being under the direct supervision of both the British financial adviser in Egypt and the governor-general of the Sudan, he was often called upon to reconcile views which were diametrically opposed. Harman, the first financial secretary of the Sudan, could not cope with this task and resigned in May 1900. He was followed by Colonel Bernard, who held that post until 1923. During that period the Sudan increased its revenue from £E 126,569 to £E 3,766,133. But, even more important, the country's revenue after 1913 exceeded its expenditure, thus achieving economic viability within fourteen years of the reconquest.[16] The duties and powers of the financial secretary were laid down in the 'Finance Circular No 1' in October 1899. He was to be responsible for all revenue and expenditure, whether in kind or in money. Every expenditure, even if sanctioned in the budget, had to be authorized by him. Appointments of officials, whether in central government departments or in provinces, had to be authorized by the financial secretary if their monthly salary exceeded £E 5. The controller of stores, who was in charge of all revenue in kind, and who supplied the requirements of all government departments and provinces, was under the direct control of the financial secretary. A special audit office was established in Cairo to which all provincial governors had to send their monthly accounts and vouchers.[17]

Soon after Wingate became governor-general he was warned about the excessive powers granted to the financial secretary.[18] Consequently, certain functions were transferred from the financial secretary to the governor-general. All appointments, except *ṣarrāfs*[19] and clerks, had to be sanctioned by the governor-general who also approved the salaries; the controller of stores had to keep the financial secretary informed, but was not to be under his control. Finally, applications by provincial governors for loans, had to be made directly to the governor-general.[20] Yet despite the curtailment of his functions the financial secretary's sphere of responsibility remained second to none, and was described by Cromer as '. . . not only the most important but also by far the most arduous in the Soudan . . .'[21] He continued to bear responsibility for the Sudan's budget and was thus in a position to object to any expenses or increases in salaries if he regarded them as unwarranted or incompatible with the country's finances. Furthermore, the financial secretary's views on finance had more weight in Egypt than those of any other Sudan government official including Wingate. Thus when the financial secretary opposed a majority decision of the governor-general's council, his views were in some cases accepted by the British consuls-general in preference to those of his colleagues.[22] This was well known to Wingate who resented it and wrote to Cecil : '. . . "Ikey" [Bernard] is at his old game of getting behind me to the Agency and I am naturally determined that his Dago methods shall not upset my relations with our present chief [Kitchener]—as he succeeded in doing with Lord Cromer . . .'[23]

Under these circumstances it was hardly surprising that Bernard had strained relations with nearly all the British officials. Though this state of affairs was partly due to Bernard's character, the majority of his difficulties were the direct result of his duties. It was because of this inherent tension between Bernard and his colleagues that Wingate sought to ease the situation by establishing the Central Economic Board in 1906, and the Central Government Board in 1908. Unfortunately this move did little to lessen the friction. When in 1914 Wingate decided to ask Kitchener to alter the regulations about financial control in the Sudan, he referred to Bernard's '*amour propre*' as one of the major considerations.

> . . . Hitherto, and in most financial questions as between Egypt and the Sudan, the anomalous position of the Financial Secretary . . . has always been a factor on which I have had to bestow an almost unnecessary amount of consideration . . .[24]

However, The World War intervened and the situation remained unchanged. Despite the general criticism, the overall impression of the financial department is one of efficiency and purpose. It remained throughout one of the most centralized departments in the Sudan and gave little scope to the initiative of individual governors or heads of departments.

The civil secretary's office underwent several changes during its first few years of existence. Until 1903 the Sudan agent was assistant civil secretary, and much of the work was done at his office in Cairo. In 1904 the controller's department became a section of the civil secretary's office and the department of prisons and police was also incorporated under an assistant director. The civil secretary was nominally in charge of the provinces and had to sift the governors' requests before submitting them to the other departments. His office controlled the movements of foreigners into the Sudan, and issued permits to trade in restricted provinces. It was also responsible for supplying *dhurra* (millet) to needy districts. Even requests for the erection of new pumps on the Nile, which required a permit from the Egyptian public works department, had to be sifted by the civil secretary. His main responsibility, however, was in the field of government personnel. Any demands for transfers made by the governors, heads of departments, and other individual officials, had of necessity to be directed to him. Following consultations with Wingate these proposals were then brought to the permanent appointments and promotions board. Yet, as in all spheres of administration, the final decision lay with Wingate.[25]

Police and prisons were under the assistant civil secretary from 1904. The Sudan police force, which had been part of the Egyptian army, assumed a civil character after the reconquest. In the first few years its staff was recruited from the Egyptian army. Yet from the very beginning the British officers had strong reservations concerning the suitability of Egyptians for police duties. They regarded the Egyptians as lazy and corrupt and claimed that the Sudanese mistrusted them.[26] Hence, governors were authorized to replace the Egyptians by locally enlisted men. In 1902 the police force consisted of 51 officers, 541 Egyptian, 647 Sudanese, 80 locally enlisted men, and 317 Arabs.[27] In 1905 it was decided to decentralize the police department and to place the police under the control of the provincial governors. The system of local enlistment was subsequently generally accepted so that by 1908 only 389 Egyptians remained in a police force totalling 2,979.[28] Apart from the regular police, there was also a force of locally enlisted *ghaffirs* in all provinces. They acted as watchmen in towns, and were used by village *'umdas* as messengers for weekly contacts with the *ma'mūr*.

In 1904 the department of prisons also ceased its independent existence and became part of the civil secretary's office. At the same time the prisons section was decentralized, leaving all criminals sentenced to less than two years' imprisonment in the charge of the province authorities. Hence only long-term convicts were sent to the central prison in Khartoum, and after 1911 also to Port Sudan, where they were usually employed in the prison workshop or by other departments. During the first years of the Condominium, excessive administration of corporal punishment caused concern to both Wingate and Cromer, but by 1904 there had been a considerable reduction.[29] Political prisoners including the Mahdist *amīrs* and their families, as well as those captured in various religious uprisings since the reconquest, were in a class by themselves. During the first few years they were imprisoned in Damietta, but in 1908 Wingate decided to transfer them to Wādī Ḥalfā, where they were kept in a special prison.[30]

Communications and agriculture

Communications and agriculture were the main administrative problems of the Sudan. There were three departments directly concerned with communications, namely the department of post and telegraph, the railways department, and the department of steamers.[31] By the beginning of the First World War the post reached the remotest parts of the country, by steamer, railway or camel, while the Sudan telegraph lines covered over 5000 miles. The railway, which had reached Khartoum shortly after the battle of Karari̅, extended eastwards to Port Sudan and to the south west via the Gezira to El Obeid. By 1916 nearly 1500 miles of railways were open to traffic. During the same period the steamer department could boast of two main routes. The first ran from Ḥalfā to Shellal, thus connecting the Egyptian railway system with that of the Sudan, while the second route ran from Karima to Dongola and brought the produce of Dongola to the Karima rail-head. A permanent steamer service also functioned between Khartoum and Juba to connect the capital with the southern provinces. Internal town transport was developed only in Omdurman and Khartoum, where a combined steamer and tramway service was inaugurated in 1905. It can easily be seen that in spite of the developments listed above, the communications-system for a country the size of the Sudan was woefully inadequate. The southern provinces could only be reached from the north during high Nile. The overwhelming majority of roads were dirt tracks which could not be used during the rainy season between April and October. As a result a great deal of the transport in the south was dependent on porters or animals and only slight beginnings were made in introducing mechanical vehicles.

Of all the departments in the Sudan, that of public works was the most highly and constantly criticized—a state of affairs which nearly brought about the dismissal of its director. Most of the criticism was levelled against the low standard of buildings erected by the department for provincial government officials. This criticism increased as time went on but failed to bring about any apparent improvement. In his report for 1906, Wingate tried to justify the department by saying that the low standard of buildings was due to budgetary reasons. In 1911 however, Wingate made an inspection of the Southern provinces following which he wrote that the government houses were: '. . . miserable huts which are tumbling down . . .'[32] The department was also attacked for devoting most of its energy and money to Khartoum, a criticism shared by most central departments. In 1908 the public works department was decentralized. District engineers were appointed in all the provinces, with instructions to submit their plans to the central department who would act as the supervisor and co-ordinator of the work. However the reorganization did not prove successful, and the whole system had to be reversed.[33] The failure of this department can be traced to a number of reasons. The budget was never sufficient, yet instead of limiting its projects, the department erected cheap buildings of poor quality. Communications also hampered its progress, as in many cases building materials had to be transported by camel. Lastly, most of the department's staff was either unqualified, or lacked the ability to adapt their knowledge to local conditions.[34]

From the economic point of view the most important asset of the Sudan was clearly agriculture. Yet in spite of this fact, the first step in agricultural administration had to wait until 1903, and even then development lagged well behind other spheres of administration until after the First World War.[35] Prior to 1910, there were two departments detailed to deal with agriculture. The department of woods and forests was established in 1903 with one director and a subordinate staff of six. However, owing to the shortage of manpower it was '. . . considered best . . . for each Mudir to be ex officio Director of Woods and Forests within his own Province . . .'[36] The department of agriculture and lands fared even worse. Restricted to two British officials and one clerk, it could hardly even cope with its clerical duties. There was not even a director for the department. Hence the head of the department of woods and forests was called upon to serve as acting director of agriculture and all matters relating to lands and development had to be dealt with by the civil secretary's office.

The absence of a proper departmental head was rectified in 1905 when it was decided to engage a professional director and to incorporate the functions of agriculture and lands into one department.[37] The new director who was a British estate agent, turned the department into '. . . a Central Estate office for Government properties . . .'[38] much to the detriment of agricultural development and agricultural education which continued to suffer from neglect. As a result the hoped-for improvements were negligible and in 1910, when the director of the department resigned, it was therefore decided to try yet another reorganization. The lands section, which had hitherto been the main stay of agricultural administration, now became part of the legal department, while agriculture and forests were united under the directorship of a former provincial governor. Detailed instructions regarding the functions of the new department were laid down by the governor-general's council. The main spheres of activity were to be agricultural development and education, while a special committee was to be set up to deal with future concessions.[39] The department, however, remained as weak as before, and was a constant cause of concern to Wingate and the central administration.

In 1915 the department of agriculture and forests suffered yet another upheaval. Following the resignation of its director, it was decided to split it once again. The agricultural section was affiliated to the civil secretary's office, while that of forests was put under the financial secretary.[40] Thus seventeen years after the reconquest, and with the Gezira development scheme nearing realization, the Sudan government was left without any department or personnel capable of undertaking this major project. This was clearly one of the great failures of the new administration. Luckily, the problem of land-settlement was dealt with by the legal department, while agricultural education and research were carried out by the department of education. The Central Research Farm at Khartoum North was managed by the education department, whose officials also undertook research into cotton growing in the Gezira. Hence two major aspects of agricultural development were being attended to, thus facilitating future development.

The department of education and its policy have been adequately described in numerous theses and articles.[41] It will therefore only be discussed in connection with the training of Sudanese personnel and with regard to the government's religious policy. Two works have also been written about the functions and policy of the medical department, which was part of the military administration until 1905.[42] Yet even after the establishment of a civil department, the health of the southern provinces was entrusted to the Egyptian army. The only hospital where adequate medical facilities existed was the central hospital in Khartoum. The other provinces were provided with small clinics which often had to exist without trained staff. The lack of communications with the outlying districts forced the government to use post offices as medicine stores and to train sanitary barbers for minor medical duties. Progress was hampered by financial considerations and by the tendency of the population to consult their traditional doctors.[43] The only other department whose policies and activities will be fully discussed is the department for the repression of slave trade, which was part of the Egyptian ministry of interior until 1910.

The provinces

The foundation of provincial administration was laid down during the reconquest. Under the Khalifa's rule Dongola, Berber, and other frontier regions were administered as military provinces and governed by military commanders. This system of government collapsed with the reconquest of Dongola in 1896 and of Berber in 1897. There was also little sense in reviving the pre-Mahdist Egyptian system of government. On the eve of the Mahdia the Egyptians planned to control the Sudan more closely. They divided the country into three independent *ḥukumdārīyāt*, each consisting of several provinces, under the direct control of Egypt. A special

Sudan minister was appointed in Cairo, who was responsible for the administration of the Sudan.[44] Having discarded this system, the British commanders of the Egyptian army regarded the Sudan as a *tabula rasa*, where the system of provincial administration could be determined by them. In April 1897, Kitchener presented to Cromer, a memorandum in which he stated his views on the future government of the country based on the following assumptions :

> . . . That the Sudanese absolutely despise the Egyptians . . . That there are forces in the Sudan that do not exist in Egypt . . . That the Sudanese . . . are not a difficult people to govern if the Government is one they respect . . . The present tendency is to govern Dongola Province exactly the same as any other province of Egypt, and this will naturally extend to other provinces when reconquered . . . I look upon this form of government as a grave danger to public security, and a very fertile cause of future discontent . . .

Kitchener suggested therefore, that '. . . the future administration of the Sudan should be that of a crown colony of Egypt; and resemble our form of colonial Govt. . . .'[45] Kitchener's intention was further clarified when he objected most strongly to a proposal to centralize the Sudan administration and put it under Egyptian government supervision.[46] According to Kitchener, this system was tried in Tokar following its conquest in 1891 :

> . . . The result was that Tokar was flooded with most unsuitable Egyptian employees; these were not well received by the people . . . Things went on for about a year in this way the discontent of the people growing, until the Governor informed me that it was openly said by the natives that they preferred Dervish rule . . .

Hence, Kitchener concluded, that the provinces should be administered by '. . . local administration suitable to the people, and that the chain of responsibility should be through competent officers having local experience . . .'[47] The system suggested by Kitchener was adopted with certain modifications in Dongola and Berber. The first governor of Dongola was General Hunter who divided the province into eleven districts. His directive to *ma'murs* was in many respects similar to Kitchener's later *Memorandum to Mudirs*.[48] Following the Italian evacuation of Kassala in December 1897, a third province was established. Thus with most of the Sudan still under the Khalifa's rule, there were already three provinces and two districts, Wādī Ḥalfā and Suakin, under Anglo-Egyptian military administration. This system was later extended to other provinces and prevailed throughout Kitchener's and Wingate's governor-generalship.

When Wingate became governor-general in December 1899, the Sudan was already divided into ten provinces. Another four provinces were established between 1899–1914, while the reconquest of Darfur in 1916, added the fifteenth province to the Anglo-Egyptian Sudan. Throughout these years there were constant changes in the internal boundaries of the provinces. Many of these changes were instituted in order to facilitate closer administrative control. In other cases boundaries were changed so as to unify tribes who had been split by an arbitrary border in the early years of the Condominium.[49] Each province was divided into a number of districts *(marākiz)*, which in turn were divided into sub-districts *(ma'mūriyāt)*. The number of districts and sub-districts depended largely on funds and on the availability of suitable officials.

The duties of governors, inspectors and *ma'mūrs* were laid down by Kitchener in 1899. They included responsibility for public security, the assessment and collection of taxes, the keeping and rendering of accounts, administration of justice and the registration of law. However, although these duties were rarely carried out during Kitchener's governor-generalship, they constituted the basis for future provincial administration.[50] The governors were also instructed to develop the agricultural and industrial resources of their provinces, and to supervise the functions of all other officials. They were warned not to purchase land in the Sudan, not to embark on trade, and not to have dealings with native women of their districts. An order published in 1902, forbade public servants of European origin, acquiring land in the Sudan except for their own residence, or to accept '. . . directly or indirectly any gift or any promise of gift from any native of the Sudan . . .' Thus when Stanton, governor of Khartoum since 1900, was offered presents by the people of his province, Wingate objected and suggested that '. . . a drinking fountain at the base of the Gordon Statue . . .' should be dedicated to him instead. This order did not apply to non-European officials who were allowed to receive gifts from relatives.[51]

The establishment of provincial headquarters was also laid down. Governors were warned that all appointments except *ṣarrāfs* and clerks at £E 5 per month, had to be authorized by the central government. The principal officials of each province were the British inspectors and the Egyptian *ma'mūrs*. The inspector was defined as:

> . . . the Mudir's staff officer in charge of the district to which he is appointed by the Mudir . . . He will not be a channel of communication between Mamurs and the Mudirieh—that is, Mamurs will forward direct to the Mudirieh all Reports and Returns called for . . .

The inspector's duties were to supervise the administration of the sub-districts within his district, and especially the operations of the police. His only executive task was in the administration of justice. The instructions sent by Kitchener to *ma'mūrs* were couched in rather more general terms. They were warned against taking bribes or molesting women, and instructed to be just but severe in repressing crimes. *Ma'mūrs* were given the power '. . . of sending offenders to prison for one day . . .' All serious crimes had to be referred to the nearest British officer. The first duty of the *ma'mūrs* was to prepare detailed reports about all the villages in their *ma'mūrīya*, so as to enable tax to be assessed correctly.

During the seventeen years of Wingate's governor-generalship the instructions laid down by Kitchener were generally followed. The governors' administrative duties were further extended when the department of police and prisons was decentralized in 1905. Following this decentralization governors were made responsible for the enlistment, training, discipline and pay of their police forces. Financially, the governors were dependent on the central administration. A certain relaxation of this dependency was afforded by the decentralization of the department of stores: every governor had his own budget for stores with which he could buy whatever he required. Yet in other spheres of finance, the governors remained as tightly controlled as before. Their financial independence was limited to '. . . all expenditure of £E 10—and under, for which provision exists in the Budget . . .'[52] In 1905, the financial secretary extended his control over the local provincial rates. These rates which had hitherto been spent by the governors without any supervision, were used for provincial services such as streets, sanitation, or *ghaffirs*. Furthermore, the amount of rates collected in each province depended largely on the initiative of the governor. From 1905 onwards governors were not allowed to impose local taxes without the authorization of the financial department. The rates as well as the expenditure were included in the annual budget, thus increasing the control of the central government. However, in the same way as before, the sums collected in any one province were spent on local services of that province. Out of £E 34,324 allocated to provincial services in 1905, £E 21,734 were spent in Khartoum, Khartoum North, and Omdurman. It was decided that certain provinces that could not raise the necessary sums locally, would be assisted by the central government. However, these sums were given as a loan on which 3% interest was charged.[53] Following complaints the governors were authorized in 1906 to spend the sums allocated to their provinces in the budget without further reference to the financial secretary.

Governors were less controlled in their other spheres of activity. The administration of justice, tribal affairs, assessment of taxes and land settlement were largely the responsibility of the provincial staff.[54] Here again the initiative of individual governors played an important role. Jackson, the governor of Dongola, completed the cadastral survey of his province in 1906, whereas other provinces had to wait for many years before the central government could undertake their survey. Similarly, in the field of irrigation, the invention of a special *sāqiya* by Jackson facilitated a more rapid agricultural development in his province.[55] Wingate whose relations with Jackson were never close, had to admit that Dongola was '. . . one of the most prominent features in the success of our Sudan Administration . . .[56]

The duties performed by inspectors largely corresponded to those laid down by Kitchener in his memorandum. Most of their time was taken up with the assessment of taxes and the administration of justice. In certain cases, where tribal organization was weak, the inspectors played an active role in the actual collection of taxes and in administering tribal law. Yet the shortage of officials compelled inspectors to diversify their activities and deal with cattle plagues, distribution of medicines and the compiling of provincial reports. Hussey, who was an inspector in Sennar in 1912, complained that most of his time was spent '. . . on matters of taxation, petitions from Sheikhs or from individuals . . . and lately to an increasing extent, answering queries from headquarters about matters which appeared to be of very little importance . . .'[57] Less information is available as regard to non-British officials. The staff of a *ma'mūrīya* included a *ma'mūr*, a *ṣarrāf*, one or more clerks, sanitary barbers and *ghaffirs*. The overall view of the non-British staff, as presented by their British superiors, is not very flattering. They complained about the unsuitability of the Egyptian *ma'mūrs* and constantly referred to their untrustworthiness, and to their getting involved in local politics. Hence, *ma'mūrs* were warned from clashing '. . . in any way with the exercise by Sheikhs of their proper responsibilities . . .'[58]

The major problem was the shortage of suitable officials. '. . . When a Merkaz has over seven hundred villages it is obvious a man must be either very stupid or very unlucky who pays his taxes . . .'[59] The provincial governors constantly complained about the shortage of staff, and insisted that the additional expenditure would be more than offset by an increase in revenue. This was proved in 1913, when an addition to the staff of the Upper Nile province produced an increase of £E 2,000 in the tribute paid by its tribes.[60] However, despite certain improvements, there was no major change throughout Wingate's governor-generalship. Thus the country's precarious finances dictated a course which decreased its potential revenue. The areas most seriously affected were the southern provinces and the Nuba Mountains. The vast territory of the south, combined with the lack of communications and the difficult climate conditions, made service in these areas less popular than in the north despite a special 'climate allowance', which was granted to all officials. As a result, the military character of the administration was more predominant in the south. The governor and most of the inspectors were British officers. Military administrative expeditions took the place of permanent government posts which could not be established due to lack of funds and a shortage of officials.

The military command of each province, apart from Khartoum, was vested in its governor. However, the military duties of the governors of the northern provinces were purely nominal, so that in 1911, Asser, then adjutant general of the Egyptian army, was able to suggest a separation of the military and administrative functions.[61] Clayton, who was at that time Wingate's private secretary, carried the argument further. He asserted that '. . . a governor has not the time, and every year has less of the knowledge, required to efficiently supervise the training, discipline and administration of the troops . . .' Hence he suggested that Wingate should '. . . divide the Sudan into a certain number of districts, irrespective of provinces, and give each district a Commandant and staff . . .'[62] All these suggestions were rejected by Wingate and the only provinces where military commandants were appointed were those whose governors were civilians. The supremacy of the governors' authority in all military and civil administrative matters concerning their provinces remained unchallenged throughout the Wingate era. Consequently, both military and civil administration suffered from a certain amount of neglect. In the northern provinces governors tended to neglect their military duties, whereas in the south the civil administration was often subjugated to military requirements. Wingate's reason for opposing the separation of military and civil administration is not hard to discover. As sirdar and governor-general he unified both aspects of the administration in his own person. He feared that the separation of the military functions would tend to undermine his own authority and to create an additional channel of military supervision over the Sudan.

The governor-general's council

During the first decade of his governor-generalship, Wingate set up numerous consultative bodies to advise him on administrative and economic problems. Among the more important committees were the Sudan government selection board, the central economic board, and the central government board. The duties of each of these bodies were defined by Wingate who also appointed the members. Moreover, it was left to Wingate's discretion to decide what to place on the committees' agenda. In these circumstances it could hardly be expected that they would play a significant role in policy making. Government decisions were generally reached in direct consultation by Wingate with certain members of his staff. Slatin and the Sudan agents were privately consulted about most problems, while the 'three secretaries' formed an inner circle of the central administration and aided Wingate in formulating his policy.[63]

The governor-general's council came into being in January 1910, but already in 1908 it was first suggested to Wingate by his civil secretary. Wingate had complained that many major administrative decisions were reached as a result of a brief discussion at the Cairo budget meeting between himself, the financial secretary and the head of the department or the provincial governor concerned. He therefore suggested giving the permanent selection board power to deal also with general administrative problems. Phipps, then civil secretary, made a more far-reaching suggestion and proposed the creation of a governor-general's council, which would deal with '. . . every odd, unusual, or unlegislated question . . .'[64] Over a year passed before the subject was taken any further. Wingate had, in the meantime, been sent on a special mission to Somaliland, and upon his return in June 1909, proceeded direct to England. It was from his home in Dunbar that he asked both Stack and Clayton for their views on constituting a governor-general's council in the Sudan.[65] Only in October 1909 was the first recorded move made by Gorst. In a private letter to Sir Edward Grey, he put forward the suggestion of '. . . instituting in the Soudan an executive legislative council on the lines of the Viceroy's Council in India . . .' and added that Wingate had already agreed to the suggestion. The 'Draft Ordinance for creating a council to assist the Governor General' was sent privately by Gorst to the foreign secretary on 7 October 1909.[66] The only substantial suggestion made by the foreign office was to include a 'native member' in the council: '. . . Wingate will perhaps be startled at the notion of a native member. I would not be, if I were in his shoes . . .'[67] Yet, in spite of Grey's recommendation, the suggestion of a native member was turned down by Wingate as reported by Gorst:

> . . . for the simple reason that there are no such people in the Soudan suitable to occupy a seat on the Council; nor are there likely to be for a long time to come. The Soudanese themselves are mere children, and the only Egyptians in the country are minor officials. Moreover, the inhabitants dislike the Egyptians, and much prefer the English . . .[68]

When Gorst, therefore, approached Grey officially a month later the only comment offered in the foreign office minutes was to the effect that the council would only give formal status to a position which already existed in practice.[69] This remark was certainly true with regard to the text of the ordinance itself. The council was to be constituted of four ex-officio members, namely the inspector-general, the financial, legal, and civil secretaries, and between two and four members appointed by the governor-general. It was authorized to promulgate laws, regulations and ordinances, and to decide the yearly budget. The governor-general could overrule the council's decisions or suspend their operation, in which case he had to state his reasons for doing so.[70] It was in a letter addressed to Wingate that Gorst laid down the nature of the relations between the governor-general and his council on the one hand, and the British consul-general on the other.[71]

One of the first tasks undertaken by the new council was to set down its own rules of procedure. These rules enabled the governor-general to refer to the council whatever he thought fit. Council could act, though only in an advisory capacity, on all matters concerning promotions, appointments, and defence, and was allowed to discuss these matters only if they were referred to it by the governor-general. Heads of departments and provincial governors could bring to council only business relating to their own departments or provinces, and the governors had first to obtain the sanction of the governor-general. The convening of council was left to the discretion of the governor-general who could also adjourn it whenever he saw fit.

The first meeting of the council was held at the governor-general's palace in Khartoum on 27 January 1910. According to the regulations, the discussions of the council were not recorded in the minutes. Only if a member dissented from the majority decision, was he required to give his reasons, which then became part of the minutes. During the first seven years the council held the following number of meetings: 1910 (25), 1911 (20), 1912 (14), 1913 (11), 1914 (12), 1915 (10), 1916 (4). Wingate presided over less than fifty per cent of the meetings and even then very rarely cast his vote. It was Slatin who used his extra casting vote as acting-president of the council at its second meeting, in February 1910. At its 9th meeting, the council decided that its members should take precedence over all other officials of the Sudan government.[72] The majority of the meetings dealt with problems of land ownership, personnel, agriculture, and trade, and a special series of meetings were devoted to the yearly budget. During its first year, the only serious disagreement occurred when the council had to deal with the salaries of its own members. Consequently Wingate and Gorst became the sole arbiters with regard to council members' promotions and pay. When, however, Gorst tried to interfere with the general terms of employment in the Sudan civil service, his suggestion was rejected by the council and Gorst had to withdraw.[73] During Kitchener's period as consul-general in Egypt, there were a number of clashes between him and the council, but all about minor matters, such as the payment of rent by government officials, or the increased charges on the government steamers. On one occasion Kitchener refused to approve the council's decision, and on several others ordinances passed by council had to be amended before Kitchener would sanction their publication.[74]

Judging by the record of the first seven years of its existence, the council's achievements were rather modest. It provided a permanent framework for the exchange of opinions among the various heads of departments, and thus enabled them to gain a broader outlook over government affairs. It did not, however, diminish Wingate's private consultations with his closer associates about most of the subjects which were later brought to the council. It is therefore hardly surprising that Wingate very rarely found his views overruled by the council's majority. The relations between the Sudan government and the British consuls-general in Cairo were hardly affected by the new council. It is true that a definite set of rules now existed, but misunderstandings occurred as before, and it is difficult to say that the consul-general's control over Sudan affairs increased in any way. As for the people of the Sudan, for whose benefit the government supposedly functioned, one can hardly see how the existence of a council, on which they had no representation and whose members were all British government officials, could make any difference to their well-being. Tribal and religious affairs were entrusted, as before, to the advice of Slatin, who, together with Clayton and Stack, formed the inner circle of the governor-general's advisers. Finally, judging by the diminishing number of the council's meetings and the narrow scope of its discussions it seems fair to assume that its functions declined rather than increased during that period.

CHAPTER V

Government Officials and the Training of Sudanese

THE administration of the Sudan emerged out of a military conquest. The British officers became administrators, and constituted the higher echelon of the country's central and provincial government until after the First World War. The necessity of including civilians in the administration was brought home to the Sudan government by the Boer War. Kitchener and many of the British officers left the Sudan to pursue their military careers, leaving in their wake large gaps in the administration. Hence a policy of recruitment was instituted in 1900, in the hope of enticing young British civilians to serve in the intermediate grades of the administration. The lower grades of the administration were filled by Egyptians and Lebanese, while the Sudanese were left to fill those posts which needed no qualifications. However, an educational policy was evolved whereby the administration hoped to replace the Egyptian officials by Sudanese.

The British military administrators

The advantages of British administrators were clearly defined by a British officer following a tour of inspection in the Sudan:

> . . . The special genius of our countrymen in general, and of our soldiers in particular, to act as bear leaders to barbarians . . . has never, and can never have, any better illustration than in the Soudan . . .[1]

The first list of appointees for the administration of the Anglo-Egyptian Sudan included eighteen British officers and one civilian. They were appointed as heads of departments and as provincial governors and inspectors. The only departments which had civilian directors and civilian staff from the outset were the departments of justice and education. The qualifications, which, according to Symes, enabled military commanders to become civilian administrators, were as follows:

> . . . They were quick to improvise and ready to tackle the most difficult situations with courage and common sense . . . They laid foundations of public tranquility and popular goodwill on which the structure of a civilized administration could be built securely . . .[2]

The impoverished Sudan was not in a position to afford highly specialized officials. It required men, able and willing to undertake any job whatsoever, even though the task was far removed from their basic qualifications. They had to open roads, make surveys, build their own stations, and lead military expeditions into the unpenetrated areas of their provinces. Duties of a more civilian character included land-settlement, the assessment of taxes, and the establishment of provincial administration working in harmony with the tribal and religious leaders within its boundaries. Even Cromer, who was one of the first to advocate the establishment of a Sudanese civil service, stated that '. . . these officers constitute the best possible agents for the administration of a country in the present condition of the Soudan . . .'[3] For Wingate there were additional advantages in appointing officers. As an officer and administrator he believed in the unity of civil and military duties. Moreover, as he was the sirdar of the Egyptian army, the choice of British officers for service in the Sudan was at his sole discretion and there was always a long waiting list to choose from. Once the officers had been appointed, Wingate could renew their contracts, or terminate them whenever he regarded it necessary.

However, it soon became clear that the officers' administration had many disadvantages. Most of the officers regarded their sojourn in the Sudan as a temporary phase. Those who wanted to pursue their military careers had to revert to the British army in order to get a substantive colonelcy. Others, who were willing to extend their contracts, had to go on half-pay and their work in the Sudan did not count as full service towards a pension. Wingate who wished to retain as many British officers as possible, repeatedly tried to alter their conditions of service. In May 1900 he sent his proposals to Cromer and suggested that the sirdar should be able to retain the services of British officers on full-pay, for periods ranging from two to ten years. He also argued that those officers who were retained beyond the period of ten years and were removed from the lists of their regiments should nevertheless remain eligible for promotion to brevet rank of colonel. Furthermore, according to Wingate, a gratuity of one month's pay for every complete year served in the Egyptian army, should be offered to officers serving beyond ten years.[4] The British war office only partially accepted these proposals. The limit of seven years' service at full-pay was retained, after which officers lost their claim for regimental promotion.[5] In 1902, Cromer appealed again to Lansdowne to alter the conditions. The war office agreed that officers would go on half-pay only after ten years' service, provided that Egypt would bear the extra cost.[6] Thus a compromise was reached, at Egypt's expense, which enabled Wingate to increase the number of British officers serving in the Sudan.

In 1914, the war office decided to limit the number of British officers serving in the Egyptian army to 184, unless their training and pension were also paid by Egypt. Kitchener, then consul-general, strongly objected to this proposal. He stated that the war office suggestions would compel Egypt to pay for the training and pensions of British officers serving in the Sudan administration '. . . and would inevitably lead to serious criticism . . .'[7] Yet despite Grey's support the war office refused to supply the required officers and suggested that Wingate should ask parliament for a grant in aid, instead of using '. . . indirect subsidies from Army funds . . .'[8] It is interesting to note that even as late as 1914 Wingate was still reluctant to solve the Sudan's administrative problems by employing civilians. He ordered Clayton to enlighten Kitchener about '. . . the danger of introducing large numbers of civilians (which is the only alternative if officers are refused) . . .'[9] The World War which broke out a few months later radically altered the situation. By 1916 the Egyptian army and the Sudan government were 86 British officers short of the required numbers, while the Sudan was faced with a problem similar to that created by the Boer War at the beginning of the century.

It is quite clear that the employment of officers undermined the continuity of central and provincial administration. Very few officers were willing to sacrifice their military careers in order to extend their service in the Sudan. Of the first thirteen military governors, only two served for more than five years. In the seventeen years of Wingate's governor-generalship there were forty-four military provincial governors. Of those, twenty-one served for 1–2 years; ten served for 3–5 years; and only thirteen served for longer periods.[10] While many of those officers lacked the qualifications of administrators, their abbreviated periods of service did little to enable them to get a proper training. Willis, then inspector in Kordofan, complained that '. . . they try too much to run the country as if it was a battalion—without the discipline of the ranks or the sufficiency of staff . . .'[11] Similar criticism was made by a correspondent of *The Times* who visited the Sudan in 1907. He claimed that in the Sudan '. . . no one other than a military officer is of any consequence . . .' This resulted in commerce and economic development being neglected, because the officers had little understanding of these subjects. '. . . Military despotism holds its sway, and civilian residents are kept in strict order. But there is no trade . . .'[12] It was the combination of the shortcomings of many military administrators and the difficulty of retaining them for longer periods of service which drove Cromer to propose the establishment of a Sudan civil service. In June 1900 he wrote to Salisbury: '. . . The only remedy is gradually to train up a number of young English civilians who will be prepared to stay in the country and acquire a thorough knowledge of the language . . .'[13]

The Sudan civil service

The first eight civilians, who were recruited in 1901, were appointed as assistant inspectors in the provinces. A suggestion made by Lansdowne, then foreign secretary, to recruit retired civil servants from India for service in the Sudan was rejected by Cromer: '. . . They are less likely than younger men to learn the language. Moreover, except as regards navigation, I have not found that Indian experience has been of much use here . . .' Cromer also reiterated his belief that the best way to establish a Sudan civil service was '. . . to bring in young civilians at the bottom who will gradually take the place of the military element . . .'[14] A system for recruiting young British university graduates was accordingly initiated in 1905. Between 1905 and 1916 fifty university graduates from Oxford, Cambridge, and Trinity College, Dublin were appointed to the Sudan civil service. Application forms were available at the universities and were forwarded by the universities' appointment boards to Cairo. It was then the duty of the Sudan agent to sift through the hundreds of application forms and letters of recommendation, and select a short list of candidates to invite to the meeting of the selection board, which met annually in London. The board was composed of British representatives of the Egyptian and Sudan governments. Wingate sat on the board in 1904 and 1905 as one of the Sudan's representatives, but following Cromer's suggestion he agreed that the Sudan should be represented by its senior civilian official and an additional military or civilian member of the civil service.[15] Wingate continued, however, to play an active role in the process of selection. He received hundreds of letters from friends asking him to recommend the appointment of their relatives. In most cases the requests were politely refused. However, in certain cases these solicitations seem to have had their effect. One of the candidates was accepted in the Sudan civil service following a letter which read: '. . . his father is the archdeacon of Exeter and all the boys are athletic, public school boys, and brought up under the best influence with strong religious belief . . .'[16] In yet another case Wingate wrote to Phipps, the civil secretary:

> . . . I enclose some correspondence I have had with Lady Tweeddale about her son Lord Edward Hay . . . I hope you and the other member of the Selection Board will use your influence to get him taken on as I think he is the type of man we want . . .[17]

The following letter to Cromer is even more illuminating, as it suggests that applicants were selected according to political considerations, although this was clearly forbidden according to regulations:[18]

> . . . Will you carry your mind back years ago to the time when you wrote me, at the request of Mr. Arthur Balfour, to take young Edward Pease into the Sudan Civil Service. It always struck me as a peculiar request as of course the Pease family were political opponents of the Cecils, but there had been some financial crisis in the family and you agreed that an exception should be made in giving young Pease a nomination . . .[19]

Despite these irregularities, the general entry route to a Sudan post was by application to the selection board, where nominees were judged according to their merits. The Sudan authorities refused to tie their hands by accepting civil servants according to the results of competitive examinations. The qualities required from nominees included academic and athletic achievements, robust health, and a general tendency towards outdoor activities. Reginald Davies, who joined the Sudan civil service in 1911, attributed his selection to his success in the 1910 boat-race. While Hussey decided to serve in the Sudan, '. . . as there was no special examination . . .'[20] Those selected as probationers had to undertake a one-year course of training, at their own expense, at Oxford or Cambridge. Studies included Arabic, law, and surveying, while a special course of anthropology was added to the curriculum in 1908. When they arrived in the Sudan they were appointed on probation as deputy inspectors, and remained in Khartoum for a further three months of instruction in Arabic, law and surveying. Most of them were then sent to the various provinces and initiated into the service proper. During their second year of service all British officials had to pass examinations in Arabic, and law, the results of which determined their promotion.

Most of the university graduates remained in the Sudan until they retired. Some became provincial governors, or heads of departments, others reverted to the Egyptian civil service, and a few were seconded to the British minister in Abyssinia for service on the Abyssinian side of the Sudan border. Of the 50 civilians appointed in the years 1901–16, 29 had become governors and 10 heads of departments by 1929.[21] Judging by achievements, the system of selection and the training provided in the Sudan civil service were both well suited to the administrative requirements of the country.

The civil service was composed of university graduates, yet British officers were continuously added to its ranks. Officers who wanted to join had to resign their commission in the British army before being appointed to permanent posts in the administration. As a rule, these officers had to complete ten years' service in the Egyptian army with at least five being spent in service of the Sudan government. However, these rules were not always followed and the appointment of officers to the civil service hindered the civilians' prospects of promotion. Bonham Carter stated the case for the civilians when he wrote: '. . . They see Military men being constantly brought over their heads . . . I am told by some of the civilians that they find themselves lower on the seniority list after three or four years' service than when they first joined . . .'[22] Wingate dismissed these arguments and wrote to Clayton: '. . . You will observe that Bonham Carter is on the war path on behalf of the improved conditions of civilians . . .'[23] However, the civilians' grievances were real ones and in 1914 Clayton proposed to establish the Sudan Political Service in order to avoid unnecessary friction. All officers undertaking administrative work were to belong to the new service, while civilians, as before, would belong to the Sudan civil service. Despite Wingate's agreement, the plan did not materialize. As a result of the outbreak of the World War, many of the officers who were to have formed the nucleus of the new service, were called up. The only result of Clayton's proposal was that the administrative branch of the Sudan civil service came to be known as the Sudan Political Service.[24] Clashes between military and civil administrators were not only the result of problems of seniority. Some of the officers—

> . . . were inclined to look on the Varsity recruit as a newly joined subaltern and expect the same attitude of mind as that of a young soldier . . . In consequence these particular officers were out to teach these young men where they got off . . .[25]

By and large, the military mistrusted the civilians as a class, an attitude which prevailed throughout Wingate's governor-generalship and was shared by many of the senior military officials.

Although there were no written regulations to exclude non-British Europeans from the Sudan civil service, the accepted policy was against accepting them. Thus when Wingate advertised for a director for the department of agriculture, Cromer wrote: '. . . I have erased the words "British Subjects", not that there is any intention of engaging others, but there is no necessity to say so in any official documents . . .'[26] One of the applicants for the post was a British subject who had served for many years in Cyprus. Wingate wrote: '. . . there is something Levantine about him and as you know that fact alone makes him undesirable . . .'[27] An applicant for the post of private secretary was turned down as he spoke '. . . English with a slightly foreign accent . . .'[28] If this was the attitude towards British subjects with a foreign background, it is hardly surprising that very few foreigners succeeded in penetrating the Sudan civil service. The few Germans and Austrians who held posts in the lower ranks of the Sudan administration were discharged and deported on the outbreak of the World War.

Egyptian and Syrian officials

The lower echelons of the Sudan administration were staffed by Egyptian, Lebanese and Sudanese officials, with a sprinkling of Greeks, Maltese and other nationalities added for good measure. During the Mahdia many Egyptians, and *muwalladīn*, who had served in the Turco-Egyptian government, continued to serve in the central administration. Following the reconquest, over 2,000 officials and ex-soldiers and officers of the Egypian army made their way to Egypt, hoping for compensation from the Egyptian government. '. . . They received only a pound or two and were soon starving on the streets . . .' Wingate who was then in charge of the Sudan office in Cairo, sent them back to Khartoum. He was later informed by Talbot, then head of intelligence, that their resettlement in the Sudan was impossible and that ' . . . a lot of the poor devils will die of starvation . . .' As a result of representations by Buṭrus Pasha Ghālī, the Egyptian foreign minister, the Commissioners of the Debt granted £E 65,000 to solve the problem.[29] Most of these old officials were unemployable, and the new administration was forced to recruit new officials for most of its services.

The principle adopted during the reconquest was that '. . . whenever sufficiently educated Sudanese have been found to place in official positions, they have invariably been given the preference and with good results . . .' However, there were only a few qualified Sudanese, hence a system was adopted '. . . of appointing [Egyptian] Mamurs and police officers who have been brought up in the military school under British supervision and who are directly responsible to their superior British officers . . .'[30] The British authorities attained several advantages by recruiting Egyptian army officers, rather than civilians. Officers could more easily be replaced by Sudanese, by re-transferring them to the army. Thus the Egyptians in the police force, who were drafted *en masse* from the Egyptian army, were replaced by Sudanese as early as 1903. The

Sudan railways which were built during the reconquest by the Egyptian army were put on a civilian basis by recruiting and training Sudanese to replace the Egyptians. Furthermore, the Egyptian army officers did not receive their pensions from the Sudan government and hence were cheaper to maintain. Lastly, the British authorities had adopted a policy of transferring the Egyptians from post to post so as to prevent them becoming involved in local politics or deriving material benefits from their official standing. Clearly it was easier to transfer military men, who were more disciplined and less burdened by family considerations, than civilians. Wingate reaffirmed the policy of transferring Egyptian *ma'mūrs* at short intervals when he wrote to Phipps: '. . . They [Egyptians] invariably become involved with the local people in an undesirable manner and their actions tend to throw discredit on the British Administration of the Sudan . . .'[31]

Certain departments, however, required qualified personnel and could not be supplied by the Egyptian army. Hence, most of the officials of the education and legal departments had, of necessity, to be recruited from Egyptian civilians. The British authorities soon realized that the better class of Egyptian officials could not be induced to serve in the Sudan unless offered considerable financial benefits. Currie complained that '. . . the Egyptian school master well paid as he is in Egypt . . . will not come to the Sudan for less than about 2½ times his pay—the good man I mean—Bonham [Carter the legal secretary] is in even greater difficulties than I am . . .'[32] Thus following the death of the Egyptian civilian inspector of Arabic in 1908, it was decided to fill the vacancy by employing an Egyptian army officer, after having failed to secure the services of a qualified teacher. The alternative course of offering higher salaries, in order to attract qualified Egyptians, was dismissed on financial grounds. Some of the Egyptians who served in the Sudan increased their income by accepting bribes. Others who did not resort to corruption soon realized that there was no future in the Sudan for them. The result was that many of the better Egyptian officials left the country as soon as they had earned sufficient funds to re-start their careers elsewhere.[33]

Financial considerations were not the major reason for the reluctance of the government to employ Egyptians. The British authorities questioned the loyalty of their Egyptian subordinates and resented their nationalistic sympathies. Following the Omdurman mutiny of 1900 the Sudan authorities decided to reduce the Egyptian army and to increase the number of British supervisors in the civil administration. Wingate was well aware that his policy was detrimental to the future of Egyptian administrators in the Sudan and wrote:

> . . . Our principle is not to allow these young officers to hold any of the higher Civil appointments, which are reserved exclusively for the young British Civilians. Therefore they have no hope of advancement in the Civil Service . . .[34]

This policy was consistently pursued throughout Wingate's governor-generalship, and was intensified during the World War as a result of Wingate's belief that a substantial number of Egyptian officials and officers '. . . sympathize with the Turks, or at any rate they do not sympathize with the new protectorate nor the appointment of the Sultan . . .'[35] The pronounced fear of Egyptian nationalism and of its effects on the people of the Sudan, brought about a plan for the reorganization of Gordon College which aimed at reducing the Egyptian teaching staff.[36] The reasons for the proposal were clearly stated by Wingate :

> . . . The Egyptian teaching element in the College has undoubtedly introduced a good deal of noxious propaganda of the Nationalistic type amongst the students . . . There are only two alternatives within the range of practical politics; either we must leave things as they stand and thereby risk increasing the new spirit which we are doing our utmost to eradicate, or we must anglicize the teaching . . . this will enable me to reduce a few of the purely Egyptian staff—a step of which the latter will not fail to realize the true significance; whereas parents will also understand our intentions and will appreciate our efforts to prevent the Egyptianization . . . of their children . . .[37]

In pursuing this policy the British authorities believed that they were serving the best interests of the Sudanese. The racial antagonism between the Egyptians and the Sudanese was regarded by the British as an indisputable fact; and became one of the basic considerations for the administration of the Sudan.

> . . . The fact is that the best class of Mohammedan Egyptians will not as a rule go to the Sudan, . . . Every dishonest or incompetent Egyptian official who is employed, tends to keep alive in the minds of the Sudanese the traditions of past Egyptian misgovernment, and to widen the breach which unquestionably separates the two races . . .[38]

With this in mind, the British authorities started looking for alternative officials to fill the gap until the Sudanese were ready to undertake these duties themselves. Their choice fell on two groups who were felt to have more in common with British interests than with Egyptian nationalism, namely the Copts and the Lebanese Christians. The Copts were first introduced into the Sudan by Muḥammad 'Alī in the 1820s, in order to manage the country's accounts. Many of them settled in the Sudan and served subsequent governments remaining in service throughout the Mahdia. The establishment of the Anglo-Egyptian administration brought many more Copts to the Sudan. They acted as head clerks, translators or *ṣarrāfs* in many of the provinces, and in several departments. Of the 281 Egyptians permanently employed in the post and telegraph department, more than half were Copts, and the proportion of Copts was even higher among the apprentices. There were also many Copts in the financial and civil secretaries' department, while Lebanese Christians predominated in the governor-general's office and in the intelligence and medical departments. The only departments where, for obvious reasons, the majority of employees were Egyptian Muslims, were the education department and the legal secretary's office.[39]

The importance of the Lebanese officials in the Sudan was clearly expressed by Wingate in 1908. Following the Young Turks revolution, he feared that Lebanese would find employment in the Lebanon and would cease to come to the Sudan, and wrote : '. . . so far they have been the backbone of our Sudan Clerical Staff . . .'[40] It is therefore surprising to read the following remarks which were made by Wingate in response to a letter he received from Cromer in 1903 : '. . . Your remarks on the Syrian and Coptic Bashkatibs are . . . entirely in accord with my own—I would much prefer Moslems . . .'[41] In the light of later developments, one can only assume that Wingate changed his views. Christians were well suited for the responsible positions they held, both on account of their qualifications and on account of their loyalty to Britain. They were vehemently opposed to the Ottoman Empire, and supported the anti-nationalist views in Egypt as expressed by *al-Muqaṭṭam*. Their anti-Ottoman sentiments were clearly stated when the Syrian community of Khartoum offered its services to Britain at the outbreak of the First World War and wrote to Wingate :

> . . . That until a just and upright government has been established in our country, we, the Syrians in the Sudan shall be considered no longer as Ottoman subjects but as a separate nationality owing allegiance only to Great Britain . . .[42]

In these circumstances it is hardly surprising that the Lebanese were regarded as second only to the British themselves in their loyalty to the British authorities in the Sudan.

The training of Sudanese personnel

The policy of gradual Sudanization of the administration was laid down even before the reconquest was completed. Cromer defined this policy more clearly when he visited Khartoum in 1903 :

> . . . It is, to say the least, very difficult to govern any country properly without some administrative assistance from its inhabitants. In the

Soudan the whole governing agency is practically foreign, for it must not be forgotten that the Egyptian is quite as much a foreigner as an Englishman . . . I do not doubt, therefore, that Sir Reginald Wingate . . . will do all in his power to create a class of Soudanese who will before long be capable of filling some of the subordinate posts under the Government. High education is, of course, for the time being quite out of the question, but if we limit our ambition to reading, writing, and arithmetic we ought to be able to produce some satisfactory results . . .[43]

With this in view, the Sudanese authorities set about the establishment of an educational system geared to provide Sudanese officials for the lower grades of the administration. They also decided to appoint as many Sudanese as possible to posts where education was not regarded as essential. '. . . To satisfy religious feeling in each Mudiria, two Ulemas, one Imam, and one Muazzin were appointed . . .' Efforts were made to reopen as many *kuttābs* as possible by offering government subsidies to the teachers.[44] In the area of central government, the Sudanese filled the subordinate posts in the police and prisons department. The steamers department recruited ex-slaves in Omdurman to man its wood stations and dockyards, while '. . . the sailors and the reises were all berberines . . .'[45] The Sudan medical department recruited Sudanese barbers *(ḥallāq)* to augment its services. By 1908 one hundred paid sanitary barbers were employed by the department throughout the Sudan. Their service included the registration of births and deaths, vaccination, and minor operations. Sudanese women were trained to become nurses but were reported to be 'indolent, incapable of learning and quite unfit to be left in charge . . .' Ta'āīsha played a predominant role in the Sudan railways, while the Hadendowa became skilled bridge builders. Even the intelligence department had several Sudanese on its pay-roll.[46] In the provinces Sudanese were appointed as shaykhs and *nāẓirs*, but only the lowest-paid clerks in the provincial headquarters were of Sudanese origin.

Education was therefore clearly required, and the director of the education department defined its aims in his first annual report. These included the creation of an artisans' class; the diffusion of an elementary education to enable the masses to understand the elements of government; and the training of an indigenous administrative class.[47] In order to achieve these aims, different types of educational institutions were required. Instructional workshops were established in Kassala, Omdurman, and at the Gordon College, where pupils were instructed in metalwork, woodwork, stone-cutting, and in ginning of cotton. By 1908, the fifty-four boys who had graduated from the workshops had found employment in their respective trades. However, the better class Sudanese refused to send their children to these workshops. The governor of Khartoum expressed his concern when he wrote: '. . . I lately tried to get some apprentices for the Gordon College Workshops but failed. All want to become Effendis . . . Are not the seeds of a second Indian experience [being] sown . . .'[48] Several departments established their own workshops. Sudanese were trained as telegraphists in a special school at Khartoum. The steamers and boats department had over sixty trainees at its Khartoum workshop, while the railways trained their required artisans at Atbara. In 1908, the first Sudanese youths were sent to India to be trained as forest rangers.

In order to disseminate the rudiments of education among the mass of the population, the government relied on the existing *kuttābs*. A few model *kuttābs* were established in the northern provinces, with teachers trained and paid by the government. Their syllabus included the traditional teaching of the Qur'ān, to which the rudiments of writing, reading, arithmetic, and geography, were added. The third aim set down by Currie was the training of an administrative class. To achieve this aim, six primary schools were established at Ḥalfā, Suakin, Berber, Omdurman, Khartoum, and Wad Madanī. By 1903 there were 600 boys studying at these schools, all receiving an English education. The graduates of these schools were directed by the government, to take up employment in whatever department most required their services. In 1905 all the school graduates were sent to the survey department to undertake the cadastral survey of Berber province. '. . . The saving effected . . . by the provision of these native trained boys may be estimated at from £E 3,000 to £E 4,000 per annum in wages . . .' By the end of 1906, over seventy graduates had been absorbed in the central administration and in the provinces.[49] There were, however, two pressing needs which could not be met by these schools, namely the supply of teachers and of *qāḍīs*. Consequently, a training course for young shaykhs was established in Omdurman in 1902. Its pupils were from selected Arab families, and went through a three years' course of training to become teachers in the government's *kuttābs*. In 1903 a *qāḍīs'* training course was set up at Gordon College. The *qāḍīs'* and teachers' courses were combined in the first three years of their studies, and two additional years were added for specialization in the respective fields. Up to 1908 Arabic was the medium of education. The government's reasons for not introducing an English education were '. . . to prevent these young Sheikhs from being so Europeanized . . . that they may not become permanently out of touch with their subsequent environment and duties . . .' However, the standards achieved were so low that the administration decided to send future candidates to the primary schools for their initial education. The forty teachers and *qāḍīs* who graduated up to the end of 1908, were all absorbed in the government service '. . . Each of them represents a saving of something like £E 100 a year in salary, as compared with the rate of pay of an Egyptian with corresponding qualifications . . .'[50] The immediate result was the dismissal of as many Egyptian *qāḍīs* as possible. When Bonham Carter wanted to appoint Egyptian *qāḍīs* in 1907 and in 1916, he had to overcome Wingate's reluctance before the appointments were approved.[51] The *qāḍīs'* training college also enabled the government to reduce the number of Sudanese students who were sent to al-Azhar, as it was feared that they would be imbued with Egyptian nationalist or pan-Islamic ideas.

In the years until the First World War, the educational policy continued to be dictated by administrative needs. The demand for introducing secondary education was therefore postponed by Currie who argued:

> . . . in a country like this, if a man responsible for educational development does not submit every phase of his policy to the test of what the economic needs of the country are . . . he will merely walk in the old educational rut . . .[52]

Hence, prior to the establishment of the secondary schools, he surveyed the needs of the various government departments and concluded that a technical trend was more urgently required. Two courses were, therefore started in order to supply the needs of the departments of survey, irrigation, and public works, a two-year course for surveyors and a four-year course for subordinate engineers. Owing to financial difficulties in 1909–10, the final year of the engineers' course had to be cancelled. Nevertheless, none of the graduates had difficulty in finding employment in government service.

The three southern provinces were not included in these educational schemes. The initiative taken by southern governors in establishing schools in their provinces was rebuked by Currie, who feared that the schools would help in spreading Islam. The only educational facilities provided by the government for the inhabitants of the south were those required by the military administration. In 1903 the first thirty boys from the southern provinces were admitted to a three years' course at Gordon College. '. . . By this plan it is hoped that the efficiency and status of the future black officer may be considerably raised . . .' The scheme was further developed a year later by the decision to establish a permanent military school at Khartoum. Thirty Sudanese graduates from the government's primary schools were admitted yearly into the cadets school for a three-year course. Following their graduation they were drafted as officers into the army, thus replacing Egyptian officers.[53] A special effort was made in the southern provinces to substitute Sudanese for the Egyptian Muslim army-clerks. When difficulties were experienced in finding suitable cadets, Wingate wrote, '. . . this looks as if Currie was confining his attention to Egyptians and half-breeds, of course we have to provide education for this class, but not at the expense of the Sudanese who are to be our real mainstay in the future . . .'[54] By 1911, Asser reported that the army was '. . . on a fair way to the extinction of the Egyptian from such stations . . .' He added, however, that:

> . . . the Sudanese Katibs of the Equatorial Companies, have . . . too much of the Effendi about them . . . Education seems to deprive the Oriental of any standing qualities he may have possessed and replaces them by an effeminacy which seeks for soft jobs . . .[55]

The aims set down by Currie, on his assuming the directorship of Education in 1900, were partly achieved. By 1914 many graduates of the government primary schools and of the higher educational courses at Gordon College were employed in the lower ranks of the government and army administration. Even the sons of the three *khalīfas* and of many prominent Mahdist *amīrs* were absorbed in the government service.[56] Shortly before retiring from his post, Currie proposed to make further changes by appointing Sudanese to higher administrative positions, even if efficiency suffered as a result.[57] This suggestion however, was not implemented. Only a preliminary step was undertaken in 1915, when the first Sudanese were appointed as sub-*ma'mūrs*. The full implementation of Currie's proposal had to wait until 1924.[58]

Certain sections of the population viewed the introduction of government-sponsored education into the Anglo-Egyptian Sudan with great suspicion. They believed that government schools would give a Christian education and that school graduates would be forced to become soldiers or officers. These suspicions prevailed in some of the provinces and were particularly strong among the nomad tribes of Kordofan and the Red Sea, with the result that progress was retarded.[59] In the towns and larger villages progress was generally more rapid. Yet the fact that a high percentage of the pupils were Egyptians or *muwalladīn* caused deep concern to the administration, whose major aim was to educate a *bona fide* Sudanese clerical class. In 1903 the total number of pupils at the four government schools was 577, out of whom only 180 were Sudanese; 179 *muwalladīn*; 128 Egyptians and the remainder from numerous other nationalities.[60] Apart from Khartoum and Omdurman, where the general attitude towards education was favourable, the Blue Nile and Sennar provinces were the strongest supporters of education. It was in these two provinces that a 'voluntary' education tax was first imposed, following a suggestion made by certain sections of the inhabitants. The Blue Nile province was also the pioneer of girls' education in the Sudan. This sphere was previously dominated by missionaries, as the government had decided not to get involved in it. In 1907, the first girls' school was opened in Rufā'a by Shaykh Bābikr Badrī and following its inspection by Currie it received a regular government subsidy.[61] The rapid growth of education, however, had its hazards. There were many parents who regarded education as a guarantee of a government post for their children. Hence the government, which was directly responsible for this attitude, was obliged to warn the parents that there was no certainty that their offspring would obtain government employment.[62]

The conditions of service of Sudanese officials differed from those offered to Egyptians, Lebanese, or Europeans. According to the Sudan Pension Ordinance, all Sudanese officials belonged to 'Class A', and had to serve a minimum period of twenty-five years before retiring. Furthermore, Sudanese earned their pension at a lower rate than that offered to other officials. In 1914, the pension ordinance was amended, so as to prevent Egyptians earning less than £E 16 per month becoming eligible for pension under the more favourable conditions. The reason was probably that by then there were sufficient Sudanese to fill these lower paid posts. In general, Sudanese were offered lower salaries than those paid to Egyptians or Syrians of equal qualifications. The reason for this was that the British administrators believed that an official serving in his own country should not qualify for the extra remuneration offered to foreigners. Even on the Sudan railways, the lower-paid Sudanese had to travel second or third class while on duty whereas other officials were entitled to first class tickets. In common with all other government officials, the Sudanese were prohibited from engaging in trade. Sudanese, whom the government wanted to reward for their services, received robes of honour or religious robes, which were bestowed by the governor-general, in preference to the Egyptian decorations, which were controlled by the Khedive.[63]

The relations between British and non-British officials[64]

The British community in Khartoum was on the whole a rather exclusive society. The British officers had their own club, and preferred the company of their fellow-countrymen to that of the Sudanese or Egyptian officials. There were, however, certain occasions when the British officers felt obliged to mix with the Muslim officials. Such an occasion was *mawlid al-Nabī*, and a description of the festivities by Balfour, one of the British officers, indicated the gulf that existed between the two peoples:

. . . I went to the weirdest show last Wednesday the Mohammedan feast of Mouled el-Nabby . . . we were led to a table completely covered with dishes, on each of which was some form of cake or sweet more impossibly unwholesome than the next . . . In another crowd all held hands and jumped up and down making a noise like a dog barking in unison. This goes on until they get too giddy to stand or are sick . . .[65]

Another British official related how he offered the food given to him by a *fakī*[66] to his dog Mūsā, while his pony was honoured with the name Muftī.[67] This nomenclature could hardly have been conducive to more cordial relations between the British officials and the inhabitants of the Sudan.

In the provinces, relations were closer, especially in the outlying districts, where weeks would pass before the British inspector enjoyed the company of one of his compatriots. Yet the little evidence there is tends to show that the British inspectors did not regard their fellow officials very highly. The following passages from Willis's diary, written when he was inspector at the Nahūd district in Kordofan, illustrate his attitude to, and treatment of his subordinates.

. . . *20 Mar. 1909* . . . Had to beat el-Bashir for lying and playing the fool . . . Ali Gula is a fearful liar . . . *16 Jan. 1912* . . . Abu Zaid Hagar who is supposed to be Omda of these hills does not know even where they are . . . *31 January 1911* . . . The show at Port Sudan (the King's visit) seems to have been no end of a fantasia—all the Nazirs got putty medals and will all be too big for their boots . . . *31 August 1912* . . . Nazir ['Alī Julla] is up to every game—slavery, guns, female ivory, gunpowder—and has been collecting from all his folk to cover his expenses to Port Sudan which he says were £500 and were as a matter of fact nil . . .[68]

The absence of social relations between the British officials and the Egyptians and Sudanese is hardly surprising. They belonged to different civilizations and were of a different mentality and creed. Moreover, the British were taught to mistrust the Egyptians, and regarded the Sudanese as incompetent. Since many of the British believed that any sign of friendship or cordiality towards their co-officials would be interpreted as a sign of weakness, it is no wonder that they tended to place their relations with the inhabitants and non-British officials on an extremely autocratic and paternalistic footing. Atiyah, a Lebanese Oxford graduate, who arrived in the Sudan in the 1920's, commented on the arrogance of the British teachers at Gordon College. He described the social barrier which existed between the races, even on an academic level, which was in complete contrast to the cordial relations he had experienced with his fellow undergraduates in England.[69] Relations seem to have been somewhat better during Wingate's governor-generalship. Bābikr Badrī, the founder of the first girls' school in the Sudan described the help he had received from the British officials and from the director of education. His relations with them were limited to matters of common concern. Moreover, it appears that the British treated Badrī with more respect and understanding than a fellow teacher from Egypt who in front of the class described the people of the Sudan as a race of slaves.[70] The difference between Badrī and Atiyah lies in the fact that they were of different creeds, mentality and generations. Atiyah, a Christian Lebanese, who received an English education since early childhood and later studied at Oxford, was a young man when he arrived in the Sudan. His education and outlook were similar to those of his British superiors and he naturally expected to be treated as an equal. Badrī, a Muslim who received a traditional education in a *khalwa*, was already over forty when he started his career as a teacher. His limited education and his previous experience under the Khalifa's rule, enabled him to accept the paternalistic attitude of his superiors without resentment. Moreover, Atiyah arrived in the Sudan after the assassination of Sir Lee Stack in 1924, which had brought about a further estrangement between the British officials and their subordinates. On the basis of this very limited evidence, one may only assume that the relations between the British officials and their Sudanese subordinates were better than those of the Egyptians. The British officials succeeded in establishing a direct link with the people of the Sudan, which was largely based on their sense of duty and on their just treatment of the inhabitants. Summing up the achievements of sixteen years of British rule in the Sudan, Symes wrote the following about the British administrators :

> . . . The British official is recognized as the *deus ex machina* of a regenerated Sudan. He is not omnipotent . . . but he is just, he can organize and supervise, he has a passion to probe to the facts of a matter and, above all, in intention he is kindly and well disposed. His mistakes are, as often as not, attributed to his subordinate non-British officials; and his virtues have undoubtedly built the fabric of the new Sudan . . .[71]

Wingate had a definite political aim when he instructed Symes to write this memorandum, namely to sever the links between Egypt and the Sudan. Yet whatever view one may take of this policy, Wingate's claim about the supreme position of the British administrators as compared with their fellow Egyptians, was fully corroborated by future events.

CHAPTER VI

Religious Policy, Islam and Christianity

THE religious policy to be pursued by the Sudan government was first enunciated by Lord Cromer in 1899, in his speech at Omdurman.[1] It was further elaborated by Kitchener in his memorandum to the provincial governors :

> . . . Be careful to see that religious feelings are not in any way interfered with, and that, the Mohammedan religion is respected. At the same time, Fikis teaching different Tariks [sic] . . . should not be allowed to resume their former trade. In old days, these Fikis, who lived on the superstitious ignorance of the people, were one of the curses of the Soudan, and were responsible in a great measure for the rebellion . . . Mosques in the principal towns will be rebuilt; but private mosques, takias, zawiyas, Sheikhs' tombs, & c., cannot be allowed to be re-established, as they generally formed centres of unorthodox fanaticism . . .[2]

Cromer had also warned Salisbury against allowing Christian missionary activities in the Muslim provinces of the Sudan, which he feared would be interpreted by the inhabitants as the first result of the British conquest.[3] In advocating this policy Cromer enjoyed the full support of the Anglican Bishop of Jerusalem, who regarded it as wise '. . . to restrain the undisciplined invasion of the Soudan by missionary agents . . . until the Government of the country is fully and firmly settled . . .'[4] This policy which implied the preservation of the *status quo* in the Muslim north whilst encouraging the gradual Christianization of the pagan tribes, was the first step in what in later years became known as Southern Policy.

Islamic policy in the northern provinces[5]

The principle underlying the Sudan government's policy towards Islam was to encourage orthodox Islam while striving to lessen the impact of Sufism.[6] The government aimed at establishing a Sudanese Muslim leadership which would find itself aligned to the interests of the established administration. It regarded Sufism as a movement based on superstition which could endanger the new regime by encouraging Mahdist uprisings. In order to promote its policy, the government issued a proclamation in 1901, which was widely circulated throughout the Sudan. In it the government undertook to do everything in its power to encourage what it regarded as the true Islamic religion, by building mosques, encouraging *waqfs*, and by appointing *'ulamā'* to teach the *Sharī'a*, and act as *qāḍīs* in the various provinces. However, those who were not within the sphere of orthodox Islam were warned against interfering in religious affairs. The proclamation was defined by Cromer as:

> . . . an attempt on the part of the Sirdar to strengthen the orthodox body of Moslems which it had been his policy to form and support as against the numerous heretical Moslem sects of which the Sudan had ever been a hot-bed . . .[7]

Another step in the same direction was the appointment of the 'Board of Ulema' in June 1901. All government decisions on matters regarding Islam were henceforth to require the sanction of the board. Yet once again Wingate's main worry was Sufism. '. . . Tarikas . . . have been rather on the increase but I hope with the aid of the Council [of Ulema], to quietly but firmly deal with them . . .'[8] In practice all religious questions were within Slatin's sphere of responsibility. The 'Board of Ulema' consisted of some of his closest friends whom he often consulted. By collaborating with the Board the government's decisions acquired an Islamic sanction. Reporting on certain of the Board's members, many years later, Willis wrote that they '. . . continue to play the "Vicars of Bray". They have not very much influence, but then I imagine they were not meant to have . . .'[9]

There were several additional ways in which the government sought to support orthodox Islam. The authorities aided the establishment and maintenance of mosques, and assisted Muslims who went on pilgrimage to Mecca. The government also supported the teaching of the Qur'ān in government-approved and subsidized *kuttābs*, whose teachers studied under orthodox Muslims. Lastly, the administration of justice in all spheres related to the personal status of Muslims was entrusted to the Muslim *Sharī'a* Courts. The erection of new mosques started immediately after the reconquest. In certain provinces most of the new mosques were privately built and financed by a method of subscription.[10] Others were officially recognized and received financial assistance from the government. By 1904 there were 413 mosques in the Sudan distributed over the northern provinces. Of these 189 were defined as 'Public Mosques' and 224 as 'Private Mosques'. Some of the public mosques were not only subsidized by the government but also built by the department of public works. Yet, by and large, the discrepancy in the number of mosques in the various provinces suggests that the initiative of the inhabitants and their financial resources played an important role.[11] Provinces like Kordofan and Kassala had very few mosques. When the governor of Kassala requested government assistance in order to build a mosque in the province's capital, the government offered a subsidy of £E 20 on condition that the inhabitants raised an equal sum. By 1905 there was still no mosque in Kassala, while in El Obeid the only mosque consisted of an open square with a straw shelter in the middle.[12]

The part played by *awqāf* in the building and maintenance of mosques seems to have been insignificant. *Waqf* was not a traditional institution in the Sudan and seems to have been unknown in Sudanese land-tenure before the Turco-Egyptian conquest.[13] There were, however, a few exceptions. The central mosque of Khartoum, which was inaugurated in 1904, was largely financed by Egyptian *waqfs*. The same applied to the mosques of Ḥalfā and Tokar. Despite these exceptions most of the mosques were built and maintained by the local inhabitants aided by the government. The government also assisted in providing and paying for the personnel required by the mosques and the *kuttābs*. Yet, owing to the precarious government finances this was more a token of government support than substantial assistance. The government could afford to be more generous in granting religious robes to the country's religious leaders. These were conferred by Wingate during the *'īd al-fiṭr* or *al-'īd al-kabīr*, both of which were observed as official holidays. The class of *'ulamā'*, which came into existence as a result of these measures, depended on the government for its economic well-being as well as for its political powers, and became the most prominent supporter of the new regime.

An additional measure undertaken by the Sudan government to encourage orthodox Islam was the assistance it granted for the pilgrimages to the holy places of Islam. Wingate knew that the Mahdi's interdiction of the pilgrimage, had caused considerable resentment. Hence, by encouraging the pilgrimage, the government hoped to gain local support and to strengthen the orthodox Muslim elements. In 1900 the British agency in Cairo prepared a special report on the conditions of the pilgrimage to Mecca. The report suggested that the Sudan government should be empowered to open a quarantine at Suakin, in order to overcome the international regulations by which all pilgrims had to travel to Tor, some seven hundred miles from Suakin, to the internationally controlled quarantine. The report concluded : '. . . It is most undesirable that any obstacles should be placed in the way of the freedom of the Sudan pilgrimage . . .'[14] However, the Sudan authorities were unable to overcome the regulations imposed by the international conference of the quarantine board at Venice. The result was that pilgrims avoided the quarantine and landed at Massawa or along the coast. In 1907 the Sudan government succeeded at last in opening its own quarantine at Suakin. Hence, despite continued interference by the international quarantine board, the Sudan government was able to appoint its own officer and to provide its own arrangements for the pilgrims. Special pilgrims' villages were built at Suakin where pilgrims were accommodated according to tribal origin and where they lived under their own shaykhs until they resumed their journey.[15] Throughout these years the government assisted the indigent pilgrims by paying their quarantine fees and their upkeep in the Suakin villages. In the years 1911–13, the annual subsidy granted by the government amounted to over £E 3,000, while the pilgrims themselves contributed only about £E 400–600 per annum.[16] Even during the World War the pilgrimage was only stopped for a few months and was resumed in July 1915. Special precautions were, however, taken to stop enemy agents or propaganda from infiltrating into the Sudan.[17]

The reasons for the government's favourable attitude towards the pilgrimage are not hard to discover. Wingate was interested in gaining the support of orthodox Islam. By hampering the pilgrimage he knew that he would alienate those elements within the Muslim community whom he was anxious to cultivate. Secondly, owing to the sparse population of the Sudan and its meagre labour force, the Sudan government was keen on attracting immigrants from West Africa, who were popularly called Fallāta and Takārīr. Many of these settled in the Sudan either before or after their pilgrimage. Despite their slave-dealing and religious fanaticism, these western immigrants made an important contribution to the country's economy.[18]

Despite the government's official rejection of Sufism, it could not disregard its impact on the Muslim inhabitants of the Sudan. Furthermore, the Khatmīya order, which was widespread in the eastern and northern Sudan, was in a separate category. During the Turco-Egyptian period the Khatmīya was favoured by the authorities. Its leader, during the early stages of the Mahdia, was Muḥammad 'Uthmān al-Mīrghanī II, who denounced the Mahdi and consequently escaped to Egypt where he continued to receive government assistance. Following his death in 1886 he was succeeded by his son, 'Alī al-Mīrghanī, as shaykh of the Khatmīya. The loyalty of the Khatmīya and its leaders to the anti-Mahdist cause was soon to be rewarded. Sayyid 'Alī al-Mīrghanī was awarded the C.M.G. in 1900, thus becoming the first and only notable of the Sudan to receive a British decoration until the First World War. Furthermore, the central mosque of the Khatmīya which was destroyed during the Mahdia was rebuilt by the government in the Khatmīya quarter of Kassala despite the official policy not to assist *ṣūfī zāwiyas.*[19] Only the refusal of the British authorities to recognize him officially as the paramount shaykh of his *ṭarīqa*, caused Sayyid 'Alī al-Mīrghanī some bitterness. Yet despite constant appeals the government could hardly appoint an official shaykh to a *ṣūfī ṭarīqa* which, although respected, never acquired official recognition. In 1912, however, Wingate wrote a letter to Sayyid 'Alī, which granted him semi-official recognition as head of his family :

> . . . The Morghani family lives in various places and are therefore under the local authority of the district in which they are living; but I have no doubt that all of them, like the Government, look upon you as their own head and chief . . .[20]

The Khatmīya leadership continued to be divided between Sayyid 'Alī and his brother Aḥmad al-Mīrghanī and was a cause of endless friction. The latter settled at the *ṭarīqa*'s headquarters in Kassala, where he enjoyed a dominant position. Both brothers continued on the government's payroll, and when Cecil in 1916 suggested that their subsidy should be stopped, Wingate objected strongly, stating that they were '. . . amongst the few who are genuinely and entirely on our side . . .'[21] Wingate had good reasons for being grateful to the Mīrghanīs for they consistently supported his policy of reducing Egyptian influence in the Sudan. Moreover, fearing the competition of other *ṣūfī ṭarīqas*, notably the Majdhūbīya, they were only too glad to inform against them.[22]

The attitude of the government to the other *ṭarīqas* can be defined as one of suspicious tolerance. Sufism, its teachings and rituals, were regarded as dangerous fanaticism by most of the British officials who had only a limited knowledge of its true significance. Describing his impressions of the members of one of the *ṭarīqas*, a government inspector wrote : '. . . It is when one sees such men that one realizes the difficulty of any truce with Islam . . .'[23] Another inspector recorded his impressions of a *ṣūfī* celebration of *Mawlid al-Nabī;*

> . . . on all their faces is a sort of "far away" rapt expression, not a pleasant dreamy peaceful look, but a look that makes one picture them waving blood stained swords, as they hack their way through the forces of "unbelievers" to the cry of "Allah Akbar" . . . their barbaric discords adding to the weirdness of the scene, and the pious ecstasy of the religious maniacs . . .[24]

One of the principles guiding the government's attitude towards *ṣūfī* orders was not to interfere in their internal affairs. However, the important role played by the *ṣūfīs* in local politics brought about an increasing interference by government officials in the appointment of *ṣūfī* shaykhs. This happened in El Obeid in 1911, when Ismāʿīl al-Makkī died. Savile, then governor of Kordofan, appointed Shaykh Ibrāhīm al-Mīrghanī as shaykh of the Ismāʿīlīya order as he was sure of the latter's co-operation with the government.[25] Although officially the Sudan government did not change its policy towards *ṣūfī* orders, the reality of the Sudan forced it to modify its policy over the years. This was most apparent in the case of *ṣūfī zāwiyas* which were being rebuilt throughout the northern provinces. Even the attitude towards *ṣūfī* shaykhs was gradually modified and with the outbreak of the World War, they were recognized by the government as an essential part of Sudanese Muslim leadership.

Religious uprisings and religious-political prisoners

Wingate was firmly convinced that considerable sections of Sudanese Muslims were still Mahdists at heart. '. . . The fact that Mohammed Ahmed was an impostor has by no means driven out of their heads that the "expected Mahdi" will eventually come . . .'[26] Hence the government was always on the alert. Hardly a year passed without some religious uprising, or certain *fakīs* being arrested and deported. In 1900 'Alī 'Abd al-Karīm was arrested with twenty of his followers. '. . . At a meeting of the principle religious dignitaries . . . the sect was denounced as heterodox and dangerous . . .' and its members were deported to Ḥalfā.[27] In July 1901, the Sudan authorities were alarmed about '. . . Dervish like terikas . . .' in the Gezira. Consequently, Shaykh 'Abd al-Maḥmūd Wad Nūr al-Dā'im and several other religious leaders were arrested, only to be released a few weeks later when the alarm proved a false one.[28] In August 1901 the 'Board of Ulema' was instructed to investigate the alleged anti-government preachings of a former Mahdist, Shaykh Mahdāwī 'Abd al-Raḥmān, who had recently returned from banishment in the south.[29] In 1903, a *fakī* from Bornu, Muḥammad al-Amīn, was reported to have declared himself as the mahdi. The civil secretary suggested that '. . . a little killing in the neighbourhood . . . will have a good effect . . .' Wingate, who was on holiday in England, approved of sending a punitive expedition but urged that '. . . Mahon . . . [should] do all he can to establish Govt. authority without unnecessary bloodshed . . .'[30] Muḥammad al-Amīn was arrested with his followers on 12 September and was hanged in public at El Obeid. In justifying this extreme sentence Wingate put forward the following arguments which were repeated in similar cases in the coming years:

> . . . The movement which he [Muḥammad al-Amīn] had instigated was considerably more widespread and subversive of Government

authority than had been anticipated . . . Had he been left at large for even a very short time longer, he would have succeeded in alienating a considerable number of tribes; and in view of the comparatively small number of troops . . . it is not improbable that he would soon have acquired an influence in the country which would have jeopardized Government authority . . . Colonel Nason's decision to carry out the extreme penalty of the law without delay shows how fully that officer realized the importance of dealing decisively in a matter which would have only become more difficult had the question of execution been postponed . . . Colonel Nason's prompt action will, in my opinion, act as a powerful deterrent to further disturbances . . .[31]

Slatin, who fully approved of the death sentence, maintained that the reports about the so called mahdi were very exaggerated.

In 1904 Muḥammad Adam declared himself as *nabī* 'īsā at Singa, in Sennar province. The Egyptian *ma'mūr* who set out to arrest the pretender was killed and '. . . in the melee which ensued Mohammed Adam and his followers lost their lives . . .' Thus read the official report which, however, failed to mention that two of the *nabī* 'īsā's followers, who were captured alive, were executed against the express wishes of the acting consul-general in Egypt but with Wingate's full approval.[32] 1905 was a year without religious disturbances. Wingate remarked optimistically that '. . . this is an indication that slowly but surely the effects of the mighty upheaval, for which the Mahdi and the Khalifa were mainly responsible, are gradually dying out . . .'[33] A major incident which occurred in 1906 in the Nuba Mountains and which was first thought to have been instigated by religious or racial motives was discovered to have been prompted by the government's measures against slave raiding. However, early in 1907, two *nabī* 'īsās who declared themselves in al-Qaḍārif and Wad-Madanī, were promptly banished to Ḥalfā and Khartoum.[34]

The major religious uprisings during Wingate's governor-generalship occurred in April 1908. A young British inspector and an Egyptian *ma'mūr* were murdered by 'Abd al-Qādir Muḥammad Imām Wad Ḥabūba and his followers in the Masalamīya district of the Blue Nile province. In the battle which ensued ten of the government troops and thirty-six rebels were killed. In the course of the resulting interrogation Wad Ḥabūba declared :

. . . My desire is that the Sudan should be governed by Moslems according to the Mohammedan laws and the Mahdi doctrines and precepts . . . I know the people of the Sudan better than the government does; I have no hesitation in saying that their friendliness and flattery is nothing but hypocrisy and lies, I am ready to swear that the people prefer Mahdism to the present Government . . .[35]

Wad Ḥabūba and twelve of his followers were sentenced to death.

However, only the leader was executed as the British foreign office intervened and instructed Wingate to commute the sentences.[36] Practically all of the Sudan's British officials were united in condemning the British government's decision. Currie wrote: '. . . Once again England falls back on the blood stained policy of attempting to conciliate its enemies by giving away its friends . . .'[37] Their main objection was that by commuting the sentences, the government gave in to Egyptian nationalist pressures, which labelled the Wad Ḥabūba incident as 'Another Dinshawai in the Sudan'.[38] The 'Board of Ulema' fully backed this view and stated that the Wad Ḥabūba rebellion was a direct result of the government not carrying out '. . . their (the Ulema) decision, given at the time of the Milleniumists' trials, [1901] that all teachers of Mahdism should at once be put to death . . .'[39] The *'ulamā'* and other notables of the Blue Nile province sent a telegram to the government professing their loyalty. '. . . May God punish the evil doers for their deeds. We promise before God and you that we will inform the Governor at once of the first signs of such uprisings . . .'[40] Wingate in his proclamation to the '. . . Ulema, Fikis, Omdehs, Sheikhs, Notables, and people of the Sudan . . .', warned that the government '. . . will feel compelled to modify its present policy of gentleness and indulgence . . . and you will then learn the might of the Government and its powers to enforce its orders . . .'[41] In his private correspondence, Wingate reiterated his belief that had Wad Ḥabūba succeeded in gaining a victory over the government troops,

> . . . he would have been a prophet endowed with all sorts of miraculous gifts and we should have most of the Gezira at his heels. There is no doubt there is plenty of latent Mahdism and until the generation born and brought up in that faith has died out we shall be subject to these outbreaks . . .[42]

Wingate and Bonham Carter vehemently denied the rumours that the Wad Ḥabūba rebellion was in any way connected with problems of land settlement, and reaffirmed their contention that it was of a purely religious nature. In a secret memorandum Wingate enumerated the new dangers threatening the Sudan, and demanded an immediate increase in the military force in the country or an adequate system of internal communications.[43] Reports of a new *nabī* 'Īsā filtered from Kordofan, and rumour had it that 12,000 pilgrims were invading the country from the west. The intelligence department was ordered to keep a careful watch over suspected religious notables.[44]

It is clear that the Wad Ḥabūba incident was treated as a far more serious threat to the security of the Sudan than previous incidents of a similar nature. An analysis of Wingate's report suggests that he misinterpreted the facts. Wad Ḥabūba and his supporters first murdered Scott-Moncrieff and Muḥammad Sharīf. They later surprised the government troops by attacking them on the night of 2 May and inflicting on them heavy casualties. Yet on 4 May, without any further military action, Wad Ḥabūba was captured by local villagers and brought in to the governor of the Blue Nile. As a result, the whole movement collapsed and most of those implicated in the rebellion were captured.[45] The rebellion was broken, therefore, not as a result of a military victory by government troops, but by the lack of support afforded to the rebels by the local inhabitants. This clearly implied that the people of the Blue Nile were afraid to be implicated in an anti-government movement and were more interested in pursuing their personal welfare and cultivating their land than in any renewed religious uprising. The explanation of the extremely serious view taken by Wingate and the British officers of the Wad Ḥabūba rebellion should be sought in a different direction. It was the first Muslim uprising since the reconquest in which a British official was murdered and a great number of losses were incurred by the government in the ensuing battle.[46] Secondly, since 1904 there had been no Muslim rebellion and Wingate had therefore hoped that Mahdism was a thing of the past. Lastly, Wingate realized that without adequate communications the chances of attaining real security were slight. Hence he decided to exploit the opportunities afforded by the Wad Ḥabūba rising in order to press the British government for a substantial loan.

There were no major religious rebellions in the following years, but *nabī* ʿīsās continued to appear periodically while a close watch was kept on many *ṣūfī* shaykhs. In 1909 suspicion fell on Sayyid ʿAbd al-Mutaʿāl, leader of the Idrīsīya in Dongola, whose nephew had declared himself mahdi in Yemen. In the same year two of Wad Ḥabūba's followers were captured and executed.[47] Religious unrest continued in 1910, only to be explained away by the appearance of Halley's comet. Phipps, who was acting governor-general at the time, arrested several Taʿāisha near Singa and reported that '. . . the bag of 267 spears and 7 Fikis seems very mixed . . .'[48] At the same time a new *nabī* ʿīsā appeared at Shanābla in the White Nile province. The policemen who were ordered to arrest the *fakī* and his son were '. . . compelled to fire at them, with the result that the son was shot dead and the fiki mortally wounded . . .'[49] In August 1910, a *fakī* and his three sons were arrested in Berber on charges of religious fanaticism culminating in the murder of an *ʿumda* and a policeman. All three were sentenced to death.[50]

Towards the end of 1910, the government became aware, for the first time, of the dangers of the immigrants from West Africa. These immigrants, known as Fallāta or Takārīr, were Muslim pilgrims, many of whom passed through the Sudan on their route to the Ḥijāz. They settled in the Sudan in great numbers and established their own colonies. After the battle of Burmi, in 1903, some 25,000 Fulānī refugees fled to the Sudan from the British administrators in Nigeria. They were welcomed by the Sudan government on account of their thrift and industry and were allowed to settle on the Blue Nile under their leaders Mai Wurno and Aḥmadu of Misan. In the years after 1910 these immigrants were responsible for many religious uprisings.[51] In November 1910 Najm al-Dīn proclaimed himself *mahdi* at Shaykh Ṭalḥa on the Blue Nile. In consequence, tension ensued between the Takārīr and the local Mahdists. Najm al-Dīn himself succeeded in escaping, but was shot dead in 1914 in Kassala province.[52] In 1914, one of the Fallāta gathered some followers and killed the British officer who tried to arrest him. The following year, Aḥmad ʻUmar, a Fallātī from Sokoto who had settled in Omdurman, proclaimed himself *nabī* ʻīsā, and retreated with his followers to Jabal Qadīr. He sent messengers to all the Fallāta villages to join him, but met with little success. He was finally caught with thirty-one of his followers near Jabal Qadīr. By 1916, the Fallāta's reputation for religious unrest was so deep rooted, that the government stationed a special garrison in Sennar during the Darfur campaign.[53] Only two other religious uprisings need be mentioned. Both occurred in 1912 and were caused by Muslim pilgrims. In April 1912, a Tunisian *fakī* proclaimed himself mahdi near Jabal Qadīr and was duly shot dead with seven of his followers. In June of the same year a Tripolitan *fakī* was deported from the Sudan for preaching pan-Islamic propaganda.[54]

The rather extensive list of religious uprisings during the first seventeen years of the Condominium is noteworthy for the following reasons. It proved that resentment of foreign rule prevailed throughout that period. However the comparative ease with which these upheavals were overcome, despite inadequate communications and military forces, proved that they failed to gain popular support. This was probably due to the fact that most of the Muslims of the old generation were still under the impact of the Khalifa's crushing defeat and were not inclined to risk their welfare, or indeed their lives, by participating in a religious rebellion. Yet their belief in Mahdism was by no means a thing of the past. This was clearly proved after the World War when Sayyid ʻAbd al-Raḥmān al-Mahdī, emerged as a respectable political leader and succeeded in gaining support for his neo-Mahdist movement.

The government's attitude towards the Mahdist prisoners and

their families was a direct result of its general religious policy, and therefore warrants a brief survey. The principal Mahdist *amīrs* were imprisoned in Damietta until 1908. Prisoners caught in later religious uprisings were kept in the Ḥalfā prison. Many of the less important *amīrs*, as well as those who changed sides before the battle of Karari, were not imprisoned, and some of them even held government posts. When Muḥammad 'Uthmān Abū Qarja returned from captivity in Darfur in 1907 he was also allowed to settle on his lands in the White Nile province.

In 1908 the government decided to move the imprisoned Mahdist *amīrs* from Damietta to Wādī Ḥalfā and Port Sudan, thus placing them out of the reach of the Egyptian nationalist press, while at the same time removing them from the eyes of inquisitive British Liberal M.P.s who persistently worried about the health and well-being of these prisoners. Wingate, who feared that the Egyptian nationalist press would start a campaign against this move, suggested that the transfer should be carried out secretly. Slatin objected and claimed that there was nothing to fear as the prisoners had previously asked to be transferred to a less damp climate.[55] The Mahdist *amīrs* were therefore moved openly and although several liberal M.P.s continued to question their well-being, the government was not unduly worried. These Parliamentary questions received similar answers year by year, namely that by releasing these *amīrs* the peace of the Sudan would be threatened and the lives of the *amīrs* would be endangered by a hostile population. In 1909, Slatin agreed that all Mahdist *amīrs*, except 'Uthmān Diqna, should be released from their chains. In 1912 the government allowed twelve of the *amīrs* to reside in specified towns in the Sudan. By then the alleged danger to their lives had apparently disappeared.[56] 'Uthmān Diqna, who was reported to be '. . . quite crazy and lives just like an animal . . .', continued to reside in the Wādī Ḥalfā prison.[57]

While the government viewed the prospects of rehabilitating the older generation of *amīrs* with certain misgivings, it tried its best to educate their offspring as useful citizens. After the reconquest, several of the *amīrs'* children were sent to Egypt in order to receive a proper education. By 1908 Wingate regretted having sent them to Egypt, as they absorbed Egyptian nationalist ideas, and decided to transfer them to the Sudan. Many of them were later absorbed in government departments and in provincial administration where they proved quite satisfactory.[58] The only instance where one of the young generation of *amīrs* was reported to have been involved in a religious, anti-government movement, occurred in 1915. Ḥasan Sharīf, son of the Khalīfa Muḥammad Sharīf, took part in a conspiracy in Omdurman, and was duly banished to Mongalla province. Thus the Anglo-Egyptian administration was following Mahdist and Turco-Egyptian precedents, in banishing criminals to the south. Owen, then governor of Mongalla, remarked, '. . . I tell him [Ḥasan Sharīf] he is lucky to come and see this part of the Sudan for nothing, when tourists pay hundreds of pounds . . . I fear he doesn't see the joke . . .'[59]

Government policy during the First World War

In 1906, when there was a danger that a war might break out between Britain and Turkey, as a result of the Taba Incident, Wingate wrote, '. . . If religion is made the pretext for coming to blows we must be prepared for trouble on the part of the inhabitants in spite of their hatred for the Turks . . .'[60] At the outbreak of the World War the Sudan government was therefore gravely concerned about the loyalty of its Muslim inhabitants. It published a proclamation warning the inhabitants that according to the Condominium agreement the country was still under martial law. Internal censorship was imposed throughout the Sudan, and all enemy aliens except missionaries were deported. Special arrangements were made to '. . . prevent Turco-German Jehad propaganda from the west . . .' from being smuggled into the Sudan.[61] A scheme for military tribal levies was prepared by the adjutant-general and included those tribes regarded as trustworthy. Special precautions were taken with some of the *ṣūfī* shaykhs and the arrest of several extremists '. . . had a sobering effect on hotheaded youths . . .'[62]

The major steps undertaken by the Sudan government were of a rather more conciliatory nature. Upon his return to the Sudan, Wingate delivered a speech to the *'ulamā'* at Khartoum. In it he tried to convince them that the war was not between Muslims and Christians, but against the misguided rulers of Turkey who had aligned themselves to Germany in order to fight Britain '. . . the one power who, by her actions and the sentiments of her people, has ever been a true and sympathetic friend to the Moslems and to Islam . . .'[63] Thousands of copies of this speech were distributed throughout the Sudan. A speech on similar lines was delivered by Wingate to the Egyptian officers, some of whom were of Turkish origin. More important, however, was the personal approach. Wingate travelled to many provinces where he met the principal tribal and religious leaders and was assured of their loyalty. This was accompanied by a government inspired press campaign, followed up by a tour of all the provinces by their respective governors during which protestations of loyalty were collected from the dignitaries.[64] One of the more practical measures undertaken by the government was not mentioned in the official dispatches, and had little to do with its religious policy. The years 1912–14 were bad drought years in the Sudan. The government, therefore, imported large quantities of *dhurra* from India. When the War broke out it was able to distribute cheap *dhurra* to the poverty stricken provinces which together with the supply of pumps for irrigation had a considerable effect on the cultivators' sense of loyalty. The result was that apart from a few insignificant incidents the Sudan remained quiet.[65]

The only uprising of any importance was that of Fiki 'Alī in 1915. Fiki 'Alī was one of the most powerful and loyal Nuba *makks*. However, rumours spread by a Nubāwī who had returned to the Nuba Mountains from imprisonment in Khartoum convinced him that the British were on the verge of defeat and were about to be replaced by a Muslim government.[66] Fiki 'Alī was captured and sentenced to death, but succeeded in escaping *en route* to El Obeid. An arrangement made by the British inspector enabled the *makk* to give himself up on the condition that his sentence would be commuted. Those implicated in the uprising included a few men of the Nuba Territorials, as well as Muḥammad Faqīr the *nāẓir* of the Misīrīya.[67]

With the coming of the World War, the government also modified its attitude towards the *ṣūfī ṭarīqas* and sought the support of many of the religious leaders who had hitherto been treated with suspicion. Al-Sharīf Yūsuf al-Hindī, who in 1909 was publicly charged and condemned by the 'Board of Ulema' for interfering in tribal affairs, became *persona grata* and was recommended for a C.M.G.[68] The shaykhs of the Idrīsīya, who had previously been under government surveillance, were acting on behalf of the intelligence department in its communication with the Sanūsī. Jackson, the governor of Dongola, was asked by Wingate '. . . to keep them in good humour . . . it would be a good thing to show some special mark of consideration for the family . . .'[69] Sayyid 'Abd al-Raḥmān al-Mahdī, who for years had been regarded with suspicion by the authorities, emerged as one of the staunchest government supporters. When a religious Mahdist uprising occurred at Jabal Qadīr in 1915, Wingate was able to report: '. . . I am glad we knocked out the Gedir Fiki—(private) the man who informed about him was Abderrahman the late Mahdi's son—rather satisfactory . . .'[70] Sayyid 'Abd al-Raḥmān, and five hundred other religious and tribal leaders signed the *Sudan Book of Loyalty*, pledging their full support for Great Britain and her allies during the war.[71]

The loyalty of the Sudanese Muslims during the First World War was regarded by the British authorities as absolute proof of the rightness of the government's policy and, moreover, as a personal triumph for Wingate. Cromer, speaking in the House of Lords, said:

> . . . The state of affairs in the Sudan, was one of the greatest indirect compliments that had ever been paid to the wisdom and beneficence of English administration . . . The main credit for the success achieved was unquestionably due to Sir Reginald Wingate and the officers under his command . . .[72]

Symes, then Wingate's private secretary, stated the Sudan government's view when he wrote that the loyalty of the Sudan will continue '*. . . so long as the population knows that their religious interests are being preserved intact and that the present Government is permanent . . .*'[73] Wingate claimed that Britain's support of an Arab Khalifate, in 1915, had considerable effects on Muslim opinion in the Sudan. However, there is no reason to assume that the loyalty of the Sudanese depended on British Middle Eastern policy either in 1915 or when Britain supported the Arab revolt in the following years.[74] The general impression one gets by reading the correspondence between the British officials and Wingate is that the mass of the Sudanese were loyal to their own interests, and showed little concern for the war or its outcome. The government probably gained more loyalty by looking after the material welfare of the inhabitants than by its attitude to Islam. As for the religious leaders, the government gained their support by modifying its previous policy. The non-orthodox Muslim leaders who were previously viewed with suspicion became a part of the government's establishment. The climax of this support came in 1919 when 'Abd al-Raḥmān al-Mahdī, Yūsuf al-Hindī, and Ismā'īl al-Azharī were included by Stack in the Sudanese delegation to Britain. All three of them had been previously suspected by the same government whose cause they were now called upon to serve.[75] The inherent suspicion of Egypt and Turkey, which was shared by many of the Sudanese leaders of the older generation, and the conviction that British rule was better, stronger, and more permanent than that of its predecessors, were probably the major factors which rallied the Sudanese leaders to the British cause.

Christianity in the Muslim provinces and the role of Bishop Gwynne[76]

In their relations towards missionaries and Christianity the British authorities found themselves in an awkward position. Most of the higher and intermediate officials, whether British, Syrian, or Egyptian Copts, were of the Christian faith. However, the government firmly believed that any attempts to proselytize the Muslims were not only bound to fail but would create an atmosphere of Muslim fanaticism. Hence, the government tried to draw a line between the observance of its own Christian beliefs and the activities of missionaries. The latter were regarded as a necessary evil and their proselytizing was limited as much as possible to the southern, non-Muslim provinces.

The Anglo-Egyptian Sudan had been nominally included in the Anglican diocese of Jerusalem since 1899. However, Bishop Blyth of Jerusalem was warned not to '. . . exercise active episcopal functions in that country . . .' and only in 1903 was the rule relaxed, and Gwynne appointed as the first archdeacon of the Sudan.[77] Already then it was considered as desirable to develop a separate Anglican bishopric in the Sudan, and funds were raised in order to make this possible. By 1908, £19,000 had been collected for the new bishopric, and Gwynne was appointed as the suffragan bishop of the Sudan. A proposal by Gorst to establish a united bishopric of Egypt and the Sudan was rejected by Wingate on political grounds with the able support of Bishop Blyth.[78] In 1912, the Sudan became a separate and independent bishopric and Gwynne was appointed as its first bishop and dean of the newly consecrated Khartoum Cathedral. Thus, from the very beginning, the development of the Anglican church was intimately connected with Gwynne who was also a prominent member of the CMS.[79]

Gwynne and Harpur of the CMS arrived in the Sudan in December 1899, following an agreement between Cromer, Kitchener, and the CMS headquarters, that the society would establish its first missionary station at Fashoda.[80] The CMS, however, did not adhere to this agreement and instructed its missionaries to remain in Omdurman. Kitchener, then governor-general, on being informed by Gwynne of the CMS decision, was very '. . . surprised to hear that our Committee had instructed us to remain in Omdurman . . .' However, Kitchener did not object to the CMS missionaries remaining in the north and '. . . showing friendliness to the Copts . . .'[81] When Wingate became governor-general a few weeks later he was informed that Gwynne and Harpur had '. . . found a few tame Christians to whom they administer all that is necessary . . .'[82] In March 1900, a Coptic bishop arrived in Omdurman and the two CMS missionaries had to seek new venues for their missionary zeal. Once again the CMS insisted that the missionaries stay in Khartoum and as a result of these circumstances Gwynne became chaplain of the British detachment in Khartoum.[83] Cromer quite rightly suspected Gwynne's motives for wanting to obtain this appointment. He wrote to Salisbury and Lansdowne that Gwynne would now have an excuse to further his missionary ambitions among the Muslims.[84] This was also the motive which prompted the CMS to agree that one of its missionaries should undertake the duties of chaplain which were clearly outside the missionary sphere.[85] Wingate's decision to appoint Gwynne as chaplain was probably the result of a number of reasons. The British detachment in Khartoum required an Anglican priest but was too small in numbers to warrant the appointment of an army chaplain. Gwynne had in the meantime gained the confidence of several British officers who strongly recommended his appointment. Lastly, Wingate may already then have toyed with the idea that by offering Gwynne an official appointment he would become part of the Anglican establishment and forsake his missionary ambitions.

Gwynne himself was in no doubt as to where his loyalty lay. When in 1901 he was asked by Cromer to help in raising funds for an Anglican church in Khartoum, he complied knowing that his services to future CMS activities would be enhanced by his accepting the offer. Similar motives induced the CMS to accept Gwynne's appointment as archdeacon of the Sudan in 1905, despite Wingate's insisting that in order to secure the appointment Gwynne had to resign from the CMS. Wingate argued that a missionary could not be head of the church in a country where proselytizing was forbidden. However, he promised that the severance of Gwynne's relations with the CMS would be only nominal. The CMS concluded that Gwynne should resign his membership as he would '. . . be able to do more for the Society and at less expense than if he had remained a member . . . at the same time he is to be in a much more prominent and recognized position . . .'[86] When, a few months later, the CMS decided to establish its first missionary station in the south, Gwynne, the archdeacon of the Sudan, was appointed as 'Head of the Gordon Memorial Mission'.[87]

Although Gwynne was hardly in a position to undertake active missionary work, he tried his utmost to help his fellow missionaries, and to further missionary enterprise. In some cases this led to Wingate rebuking him for neglecting his duties as head of the Anglican community.[88] It was not, however, until 1912 that Wingate became really worried about Gwynne's intentions. He opposed Gwynne's appointment as an independent bishop of the Sudan, fearing that he might be tempted to assert his independence from the government. The appointment was, therefore, postponed until Wingate was certain of his own authority over church affairs.[89] In 1914 Gwynne tried once more to alter the relations between church and state in the Sudan. He proposed the establishment of a Church Council in which voting would be by proxy and in which Gwynne himself would be empowered with the veto.

Wingate's main worry was the support given to Gwynne by a number of prominent officials:

> . . . I need hardly say that I view with grave apprehension any independent power being given to the Clerical party . . . which will require to be very carefully curbed if we are to keep missionary and other propaganda matters within safe limits . . .[90]

Once again it was Bishop Blyth who came to Wingate's aid in limiting Gwynne's independence to purely clerical matters. Satisfied with this achievement Wingate noted: '. . . It only emphasized the wisdom of our decision years ago, that the head of the Anglican Church in the Sudan should on no account have any direct attachment to any missionary body . . .'[91] However, all the evidence tends to show that it would have greatly simplified matters had the bishop of the Sudan lacked proselytizing ambitions. For Gwynne, despite his resignation from the CMS remained at heart a missionary.

Wingate himself was by all accounts a religious man, although he believed that any interference by missionaries in the Muslim north was bound to result in trouble. He was, therefore, quite prepared to play an active part in any Christian activity which had no missionary content. Bishop Blyth, who visited the Sudan in 1906, was very impressed by the sincere religious atmosphere among the government officials, '. . . The fact that they are not ashamed of their own religion impresses the natives who respect them for that . . .'[92] On the other hand, Bishop Gwynne wrote, '. . . I maintain that the Moslems despise us for neglecting the observance of our faith . . .'[93] The truth was that the British officials of the Sudan, whose Christian belief was centred around the moral content of their religion, had no desire to impose their beliefs upon others. Hence Blyth, as an Anglican Bishop, expressed his satisfaction, while Gwynne regarded any religion without missionary connotations as bordering on heresy.

Khartoum Cathedral was built through the efforts of Wingate and his fellow officers who claimed that it would '. . . more than anything else, prove to the Oriental mind the permanent nature of our occupation . . .'[94] The foundation stone was laid in 1904, and Wingate appealed to the British people to raise the necessary funds. Gwynne, as bishop, had to take an active part in the fund raising and was pitied by his fellow missionaries who regarded the building of a Cathedral as '. . . perfectly mad . . . when money is urgently needed for real necessities . . .'[95] By 1912, the Cathedral was completed and the Bishop of London was invited to attend the consecration ceremony. To Wingate's dismay the Bishop attacked Islam in a sermon he delivered to CMS missionaries in the Albert Hall shortly before his intended visit to the Sudan. Wingate wrote to Gwynne: '. . . the Bishop of London puts himself on a level with the fanatical Sheikh Ali Youssef of "El-Moayyad" . . .'[96] Kitchener proposed cancelling the Bishop's visit. However, the consecration took place on 26 January 1912, and no further incidents occurred. Wingate was firmly convinced that the consecration ceremony and the Bishop's visit '. . . was to be made a peg on which to develop a strong anti-Govt. policy as regards religious matters, more especially missions, education &c . . .' Hence, he decided to revise and stiffen all regulations regarding missionary activities. A previous decision to have Sunday as a day of rest for British officials was cancelled as a result of the Bishop's London sermon. Officially, therefore, Friday remained the day of rest for all government officials except in the southern provinces and Port Sudan. The observance of Sunday by Christians was encouraged by Wingate whenever possible. Church of England services were held in all towns where the number of British officials was sufficient to justify it. The special link between the government and the Church of England was clearly demonstrated by the fact that services were held in the government houses and in the governor-general's palace until the churches were erected.[97] Other Christian denominations had their respective churches in Khartoum. A free grant of land was given to the Greek Orthodox community in 1901 to build a church. Similar grants were made to the Copts and to the Church of England. The Austrian Catholic missionaries built a Cathedral and opened schools in Khartoum and Omdurman. The Greek communities in Khartoum and Port Sudan formed societies which undertook religious and educational functions as well as offering assistance to their poorer compatriots. The large Coptic community also established its own school in Khartoum. However, constant troubles between the Coptic Bishop and his flock hampered the development of more comprehensive communal services. The only other religious community to be founded in the Sudan was the Jewish community, whose synagogue and communal services were inaugurated by the grand rabbi of Alexandria in 1908.

Missionary activities in the northern provinces

The government's policy of forbidding missionary freedom of preaching north of the 10th parallel was set down by Cromer and maintained with slight modifications throughout Wingate's governor-generalship. The missionary societies were allowed to establish medical stations and to open schools in the Muslim provinces, and there were three missionary societies which functioned in the Sudan during the early period. The Verona fathers, usually referred to as the Austrian missionaries, had worked in the Sudan since 1848.[98] During the Mahdia their stations were closed and some of the missionaries were imprisoned. The Verona fathers were the first to arrive in the reconquered Sudan and undertook to comply with the government's policy of non-proselytization. Hence, although they opened schools and medical stations in the north they concentrated their efforts in the southern, non-Muslim provinces.[99] The American Presbyterians arrived in the Sudan in 1899 and established their first station on the river Sobat in 1901.[100]

The CMS's connection with the Sudan began after Gordon's death in 1885, when, at a meeting in London, £3,000 were allocated to a Gordon Memorial Mission in the Sudan. Following the reconquest the society repeatedly requested permission to open missionary stations in the northern Sudan. Despite the government's refusal the CMS ordered its members to stay in Khartoum and undertake what work they could find. The society built its headquarters in Khartoum on land leased from the government. Yet, although this land was granted for building the society's depot for its future activities in the south, the CMS bided its time and waited for its chance to undertake missionary activities among the Muslims. In July 1900, the CMS managing committee decided: '. . . That the Committee do not see their way to near prospect of manning two Missions in the Eastern Soudan . . . They decidedly prefer to aim at opening and maintaining a Mission at Khartoum . . .'[101] The CMS, in fact, was less justified in keeping its missionaries in Khartoum than any other missionary societies. The Presbyterian and Austrian missions had many adherents among the Christian population and were, therefore, allowed to start schools and medical stations in the north. The CMS did '. . . not have a single native adherent and no children of adherents to educate . . .' Hence they were not permitted to undertake educational and medical work.[102] Following an interview with Cromer in 1902, Gwynne wrote, '. . . I had an interview with the great Lord C. last week. He knows nothing of education still less of the work of Christian missions and yet his opinion on both is final here . . .'[103] Only in 1903, following Cromer's visit to the Sudan, were the restrictions on missionary education relaxed. The CMS was allowed to open a school in Khartoum provided that Muslim children were enabled to withdraw from Christian religious education. A government order forbidding missionaries to preach privately to Muslims was also relaxed. The CMS was allowed to preach to its domestic servants or at its mission, provided it did not hold public meetings.[104] But the government's continued pressure on the CMS to establish a mission in the south went unheeded. Instead the CMS proposed to prepare :

> . . . a carefully worded memorial to the Sirdar referring to his admirable civil government of the Sudan and embodying the many urgent reasons . . . for Christian Mission work amongst its Mohammedan population . . . The memorial should be signed by a very large number of influential people, including as many members of the Royal family as it is possible to induce to do so . . .[105]

The CMS founded a girls' school at Khartoum in 1903, shortly after receiving Cromer's permission. The society, however, had no intention of complying with Cromer's request that every Muslim parent should give his written consent to his child receiving religious education. Hence, Gwynne expressed his satisfaction when Wingate failed to press this point and instead relied on Gwynne's goodwill. The result was that the CMS concentrated its efforts on getting Muslim girls to attend its schools. As for their participating in religious education, '. . . a few parents have occasionally said that they do not wish their children to do so, but they generally attend in the end . . .'[106]

An article in *al-Mu'ayyad* in December 1906 convinced the Sudan authorities and Cromer that stricter measures had to be applied to the missionary schools. This article accused those responsible for the CMS girls' school of breaking their promise to Muslim parents whose daughters attended the Christian religious education despite the undertaking that they would be exempt.[107] There is no doubt that the accusations were justified, and that the Sudan authorities were aware of the true situation. Gwynne did not deny the charge. He stated, however, that the article represented an opinion of a minority of Egyptians whose sole motive was to arouse anti-British feelings. He therefore suggested inviting the Egyptian Muslims to open a school for their own girls, as the government had no funds to open one.[108] A special government committee which investigated the situation in the missionary schools proposed the imposition of government inspection on all missionaly schools. Stricter conditions were laid down for conducting the schools, and a special clause stipulated that no child would be allowed to attend religious education without the written consent of its parents.[109] In January 1907, Phipps, then civil secretary, undertook an inspection of all missionary schools. His report revealed that all the Muslims at the Catholic schools were exempt from religious instruction. However, there were eleven Muslim boys at the Presbyterian school, and 59 Muslim girls at the CMS girls' school, who were subject to religious instruction.[110] Cromer, realizing that the major problem was the CMS girls' school, proposed opening a government school instead. Wingate was reluctant to accede to Cromer's request. He argued that if the government was to open a girls' school the CMS would agitate in the British press and would also object to government inspection of their schools.[111] Thus the government decided not to persist with this project and the CMS opened additional girls' schools at Omdurman and Atbara.

By 1912 there were seventeen missionary schools, educating nearly 1,000 pupils, in the Muslim provinces, whereas in the south, which should have been the missionaries' mainstay, there were only four schools, all run by the Austrian Catholics.[112] In the same year Wingate introduced even stricter control over missionary education as a counter-measure to Gwynne's increased authority following the consecration of the Khartoum Cathedral. Missionary schools were to be inspected regularly by the governor-general's representatives. Their syllabus and teaching staff had to be approved by the authorities and, as previously, any child had to bring the written approval of his parents if he wanted to participate in religious education.[113]

The relations between the government and the other missionary societies were less strained than with the CMS. Giffen, of the Presbyterian mission, who arrived in the Sudan in 1899, related that relations between government officials and missionaries were very friendly. However, many of these officials regarded missionary activities as superfluous or even harmful. '. . . "The religion the people already have", it was said, "is good enough for them; it is all they need, and all they can comprehend" . . .'[114] The British officers found the Catholic mission most to their liking. The Austrian missionaries complied with government orders, undertook the work in the southern sphere which was allotted to them and concentrated on industrial education which the government was anxious to develop. The reasons for this more worldly attitude were probably that the Catholics, as foreigners, were less likely to interfere in administrative problems, or indeed to expect aid from the government. Moreover during the Turco-Egyptian period, the Verona fathers had made no attempt to proselytize Muslims and had concentrated in the pagan south so that the new restrictions did not interfere with their work. As for relations between the missionaries and the Muslim population, there is no evidence to show that they were strained, apart from occasional anti-missionary articles in the Egyptian press. Most of the missionaries had a very low opinion of Islam, which they expressed quite openly. Even Gwynne, who spent many years among the Muslims and was on friendly terms with many of them, persisted in these views and regarded Islam as a major factor in the country's backwardness.[115]

Islam in the southern provinces

The process of Islamization of the southern provinces made considerable progress during the Turco-Egyptian period as a result of trading penetration. During the Mahdia Islam in the south suffered a set-back owing to the brutality of Mahdist raids and its fanaticism. Thus the Anglo-Egyptian Sudan, by virtue of the Islamic character of its army and the lower ranks of its officials and as a result of the more permanent nature of its administration, became an agent for spreading Islam in these provinces. During the early years of the Condominium there was no consistent government action to halt the spreading of Islam in the south. The posts which were occupied by the Egyptian army attracted the northern *jallāba*[116] and became centres for spreading Islam. Wingate was aware :

> . . . that for one Christian officer or official who goes into the Southern districts there are hundreds of Moslems each one of whom is, by the very nature of his religion, an embryonic missionary; moreover, the Moslem religion appeals to the blacks very much more than the Christian religion can . . .[117]

However, apart from throwing the south open to missionaries, there was little he could do. The government, fearing the effects of Muslim education, decided not to extend its educational facilities to the south. When, in 1904, the governor of Baḥr al-Ghazāl started a school for the children of the provincial staff, he was ordered by Currie, the director of education, to close it. Currie argued that by employing a Muslim teacher '. . . the net result of his teaching must tend towards Mohammedanism . . .'[118] Wingate, who supported Currie, suggested the employment of a Lebanese teacher and stated his views about the government's religious policy in clear terms :

> . . . I am not at all keen to propagate Mohammedanism in countries in which that religion is not the religion of the inhabitants. As a Govt. I do not intend interfering with religious beliefs and prefer to leave all that in the hands of the Missionaries . . . Then again the language question comes in; the language of the Bahr-el-Ghazal is not really Arabic, and therefore if any foreign language is taught, it ought to be English . . .[119]

Towards the end of 1904 it became clear that Islam was making progress in the Baḥr al-Ghazāl. In consequence the governor decided to stop even the teaching of reading, writing and arithmetic. A proposal made in 1906 to re-open the school for the children of government employees was again rejected by Currie who suggested that any eligible children should be educated in Khartoum. These purely negative measures, designed to discourage Muslim education, soon proved a complete failure. Islam made rapid progress in the Baḥr al-Ghazāl as well as in the Nuba mountains and in the Mongalla province.[120] Stack, then Sudan agent in Cairo, commented:

> . . . It is sad to think that when by our administrative and civilizing efforts we are able to induce the heathen tribes of the Sudan to live at peace with their hereditary foes, the Arabs, the former incline at once to Mohammedanism . . .[121]

Following a tour of the southern provinces in 1911, Bishop Gwynne proposed '. . . to clear out the Egyptian Mamours and replace the Sudanese troops by police raised and employed locally and the encouragement of good British trading companies . . .' Furthermore, he accused some of the British officers of aiding the progress of Islam by building mosques in the southern provinces. Wingate, whilst admitting the fault of some of his officers, reiterated his belief that only the missionaries could provide the antidote to Muslim propaganda.[122] The years after 1910 witnessed an increased attempt by the government to repulse the progress of Islam. The *jallāba* were restricted by government orders and needed a special permit to trade in the south.

In March 1911 Wingate took an important step in instituting what later came to be known as the 'Southern Policy'. Following a tour of inspection of the southern provinces he stated that the system which prevailed in the Sudanese battalions, whereby all recruits became Muslims, had helped in spreading Islam. He therefore suggested replacing the Egyptian army in the south, by locally recruited units under the command of British officers. Wingate pledged Gorst to complete secrecy and asked him to '. . . avoid any reference to the religious aspect . . .'[123] Thus the Equatorial Battalion came into being. The official reasons for recruiting the new battalions were stated to be financial and territorial. The Equatorials were cheaper than regular army units, and their services were required in occupying the Lado Enclave. By 1914 there were five Equatorial companies, and the number of Egyptian army units was accordingly decreased.[124] However, Wingate's intention of excluding Muslim officers and officials, could not be realized as there were not enough British officers and educated southerners.[125] The only area in which the government succeeded in excluding Muslim influence from the territorial battalions were the new districts of Gondokoro and Nimule which were ceded to the Sudan following the border settlement with Uganda. In the other southern provinces the government persisted in trying to eliminate the Muslim element as '. . . quite apart from the religious question *per se*, it would of course be politically undesirable for the Equatorials . . . to become Moslems . . .' This process of elimination was slightly retarded owing to the World War and to a mutiny of the Equatorials at Yambio in 1915.[126]

In April 1912, a few months after the first Equatorial battalion was raised, Wingate suggested a similar plan for the Nuba Mountains. Recruiting started in March 1913 and a year later the first company of the Nuba Territorials assembled at Kadugli. Most of the company consisted of ex-slaves from Jabal Miri, while the *makks* of the other mountains dissuaded their men from joining fearing that this would result in a loss of authority. The rising of Fikī 'Alī, *Makk* of Jabal Miri in 1915, afforded ample proof of the company's loyalty, as only two of his former slaves joined in the revolt. Wingate wrote optimistically that he hoped the Nuba Territorials would soon 'acquire such a reputation as not to merit the term "abid" . . .'[127]

Missionary societies in the south

The southern provinces were opened to missionary activities shortly after the reconquest. It was not, however, until 1900–1901 that the first missionaries proceeded to the south to survey their future areas of activity. Following a suggestion made by the representatives of the CMS and the Presbyterians, the Sudan government divided the areas south of parallel 10° into three spheres. The Austrian mission was allocated the left bank of the White Nile; the American Presbyterians were allowed to operate in the Sobat and Zarāf valleys; whilst the CMS received permission to work in the Baḥr al-Jabal and in the area between the American and Austrian societies.[128]

The Lado Enclave, which reverted to the Sudan in 1910, was claimed by both the Austrian mission and the CMS. As a result of the CMS's poor record, Wingate decided to allot the area to the Austrian mission. However, he compensated the CMS by granting them part of the Azande district in the Baḥr al-Ghazāl.

In 1913 the government followed a new departure by allowing missionary activities north of latitude 10°. Following an appeal by Gwynne, Wingate allowed the Sudan United Mission to open a station at Melut, north of Kodok. Gwynne, who had accompanied the new missionaries to Melut, wrote, '. . . I came here a fortnight ago to start a new mission and try and thwart Islam in its threatened hold on the pagans . . .'[129] Wingate also enabled the Austrian mission to re-open its station at Dilling in the Nuba Mountains, which had been closed on the Mahdi's order in 1883. In both cases the areas were regarded by Wingate as non-Muslim, and missionaries were introduced in order to check the advance of Islam.[130] A year later the Austrian missionaries declared that '. . . Gebel Dilling had become rather too Mohammedan for them. . .', and in 1916 the station was closed for the duration of the World War.[131] The division into spheres did not apply in these new areas, or in the frontier districts which were ceded to the Sudan from Uganda in 1913. But in other parts of the southern Sudan the division into spheres continued to be applied.

The government set down a number of regulations to which all missionary societies had to adhere. Missions were instructed to '. . . place themselves unreservedely [sic] under control of its local head in the country . . .' They were further ordered to '. . . act only with the approval and permission of the Governor General of the Sudan . . .' Missionaries were forbidden to trade, except for bartering for their immediate necessities. They were ordered not '. . . to act as intermediaries between natives and the Government . . .' Although these regulations were formalized only in 1912, they developed in the preceding years primarily as a result of practical requirements.[132] In 1905 the Austrian missionaries were granted government payment for their educational work in the Baḥr al-Ghazāl. The following year Gwynne suggested that all missionaries should be granted a special reduction on the Sudan railways and steamers. He argued that '. . . Missionaries are doing more than any other Englishman to develop their part of the Soudan . . .' The government accepted his suggestion and a reduction of 50% was granted to all missionaries travelling in the Sudan.[133] The order forbidding missionaries to trade was based on Wingate's belief that '. . . the Boxer movement in China was to a large extent caused by Missionaries becoming extensive traders . . .'[134] In 1912 Wingate realized that missionaries could not exist in the outlying districts without being permitted to barter. Hence, he ordered trade regulations to be relaxed and decided to exempt the Austrian missionary stations from paying certain taxes.[135] These regulations indicated that while striving to keep a clear distinction between missionary and government activities, the Sudan authorities attempted to assist the missionaries wherever they could.

The government's attitude to the different societies stemmed from their usefulness to the government rather than their creed. The British officials were, in the main, adherents of the Church of England. However, once it became clear that the Roman Catholics provided the only effective missionary services in the Sudan, the government showed its gratitude by granting them preference. Constant efforts to induce the CMS to occupy its sphere in the south failed to produce results. In 1904 Wingate warned Gwynne that unless the CMS made a start he would have to apportion the districts of Gondokoro and Wadelai to the Austrians. In 1905, the CMS at last decided to establish its first station in the Mongalla province and issued the following proclamation :

> . . . the course of history by which the British rule is established as a rule of peace in the Nile Basin; the remarkable Call to the Society from the ruling authorities in that land to send a mission there . . . all combine to make the Committee feel that the hand of God is manifest in the ordering of this new venture of faith . . .[136]

The CMS decided to link the work in the Southern Sudan with their activities in Uganda, and instructed Dr Cook, one of its missionaries in Uganda, to stay in Mongalla for six months. It was probably as a result of the vehement views held by Cook that the new missionaries viewed the government officials with suspicions bordering on hostility.[137] Hadow, the secretary of the new mission, failed to reach an understanding with the governor of Mongalla. Before long he despaired of the prospects of proselytization and suggested leaving only two missionaries in Mongalla and transferring the rest to other countries.[138] Despite Gwynne's protests the CMS decided to accept Hadow's proposals and withdrew most of its missionaries. In 1908, the CMS was compelled to abandon its station for a short period, and asked Gwynne to arrange for the government to supervise the mission's property. By this time Gwynne was thoroughly disillusioned with the CMS. He wrote to Wingate : '. . . I shall tell them when I get home that I either have a voice in the management of the mission or I wash my hands of the whole business . . .'[139] Constant appeals by Wingate, Gwynne, and the two CMS missionaries who had returned to Mongalla, failed to induce the CMS headquarters to extend their missionary activities. It was only in 1913, that the CMS decided to open a new station at Yambio aided by Australian missionaries.

In those circumstances it was hardly surprising that the Sudan government refused to extend the sphere granted to the CMS and preferred the work of the Austrian mission. This view was clearly expressed by Wingate in 1912, when he tried to convince the CMS to forego their rights in the Azande district :

> . . . I have no hesitation in saying that I should infinitely prefer to see the Roman Catholic Mission allowed to extend their stations into the Riketa and Yambio districts . . . The CMS . . . have neither the means nor the organization to be anything like as useful to the Government as the Roman Catholics are . . .[140]

Wingate's reliance on the Austrian Mission was clearly demonstrated during the World War. Most of the Catholic missionaries were technically enemy aliens, and as such should have been interned or deported. Wingate, however, declined to treat them as other aliens, as Cromer had suggested, and instead decided to place them under government observation by concentrating them in certain stations. In a report on missionary activities, prepared by Willis after the War, there was nothing but praise for the Austrian mission. As for the CMS, he proposed that '. . . the best thing to do with this Mission is to get it to go away . . . The CMS is too slow and bullies too much . . .'[141]

Missionary education in the south

Until 1926 education in the southern provinces was based exclusively on missionary initiative. The government refrained from opening schools, even in cases where there was a genuine demand for education, on the grounds of lack of finance and fear of Islam. Every encouragement and inducement was offered to the missionary societies to open elementary and technical schools. Consequently, the Austrian mission opened four schools in the Baḥr al-Ghazāl and two in the Upper Nile province. The CMS opened its first school in Malek in 1906 and a second one at Bor in 1915. The American Presbyterians opened a school at Doleib Hill in the Sobat valley in 1902. However, only the Austrian missionary schools were regarded as proper schools and their teachers were paid by the education department. The governor of Baḥr al-Ghazāl, defined the government's aims as follows:

> . . . The Government does not want to make more Moslems, it wishes to technically instruct the natives, through the medium of their own language teaching them a certain amount of English . . . religious education can be given to those whose parents desire it in the Missionary schools . . .[142]

Thus, the government's priorities were clearly defined. The principal aim was to stop the process of Islamization while the proselytizing efforts of the missionaries were treated as being only of secondary importance. The government was not altogether successful in pursuing this policy. The missionaries complained, justifiably, about the government's inconsistency and insisted that it was impossible to induce the southerners to learn English, as long as Arabic remained the official government language. Wingate admitted the soundness of these arguments and suggested introducing English as the semi-official language in the Baḥr al-Ghazāl:

> . . . if the new system is started very quietly and tentatively—without any fuss and without putting the dots on the i's too prominently—the desideratum may become a *fait accompli* almost before anyone has

realized that a change has taken place. It is very much easier to deal with an accomplished fact should opposition be eventually raised . . .

At the same time Wingate proposed introducing Sunday as a weekly holiday in the remote districts of the Baḥr al-Ghazāl and Mongalla provinces. He wrote that although he realized that the introduction of English and of the Christian Sunday might cause Muslim resentment,

. . . we must remember that the bulk of the inhabitants of both . . . Provinces are not Moslems at all, that the whole of Uganda has accepted Christianity almost without a murmur, and that furthermore English is a very much easier language to learn that Arabic . . .[143]

By April 1911, Sunday had been introduced as a day of rest in the Lado Enclave and in the following years English became the accepted means of communication in the south. In the early years of the Condominium this policy could hardly have been implemented. The threat of the Belgians in the Lado Enclave and the punitive expeditions against turbulent tribes required the presence of Egyptian and northern Sudanese Battalions in the south. Hence, Arabic and Islam were enabled to penetrate the southern provinces. The turning point occurred in 1910. The transfer of the Lado Enclave and the organization of the Equatorial battalions allowed the British authorities to pursue an active anti-Islamic policy. Aided by exclusive missionary education, the government took its first decisive step by introducing English as the semi-official language of the south. This laid the foundation of a separate political and administrative development in the southern Sudan. In adopting this policy the government believed that it was acting in the best interest of the inhabitants of the Sudan. The unhappy relations between the northern *jallāba* and the southern tribes during the Turco-Egyption period, and the raids of the *anṣār* in the south during the Mahdia, were regarded as ample proof that separation was essential. An additional argument justifying this Policy was forwarded by the first British inspector of the Lado Enclave, who argued that a complete separation of the south was required for the economic development of that area :

. . . Little can be done for the Negro provinces whilst they are starved so as to turn over all available funds to the Arab provinces, and whilst they are subject to laws or regulations made for the benefit of the latter . . . So the Negro provinces should be put in a class by themselves, under a vice-governor . . . and allowed to work out their own salvation . . .[144]

During Wingate's governor-generalship there was very little criticism of the policy he adopted in the southern provinces. Even had such criticism existed, the lack of a free press in the Sudan did not enable the inhabitants to express their views. The Egyptian nationalist press was pre-occupied with Egyptian problems. When it ventured into Sudanese politics it was more concerned with criticizing British supremacy, with denouncing the treatment of Muslims in the north, and the activities of the missionaries in the Muslim provinces. However, the government's Southern Policy was already challenged in 1907 by a British Liberal M.P. He demanded that the promotion of missionary activities in the south be stopped and that the separatist policy be abandoned.[145]

CHAPTER VII

The Administration of Justice

THE Condominium Agreement was not in itself a constitution. It gave formal recognition to the prevailing situation following the reconquest. At the same time its preamble stated the necessity of providing laws for the country, and set down the procedure by which they were to be enacted. It excluded the enforcement of Egyptian laws or decrees in the Sudan and barred the jurisdiction of the Egyptian mixed tribunals from the country. The Agreement stated that Europeans would not enjoy any special privileges, thereby excluding the extension of the Capitulations to the Sudan. It further laid down the procedure for the enactment of laws. Complete powers were granted to the governor-general to promulgate laws and regulations, and change them whenever necessary. Finally, it imposed martial law over the Sudan, thereby extending even further the powers of the governor-general.[1]

The legal system

The first law to be enacted by the Anglo-Egyptian authorities dealt with land ownership in the Sudan. Following that, the Sudan Penal Code and the Code of Criminal procedure were drafted by Brunyate, the legal adviser of the Egyptian government. No Civil Code was enacted, instead the *Civil Justice Ordinance* was promulgated in 1900, having been drafted by Bonham Carter, the newly appointed legal secretary. The Sudan was thus provided with legal codes, largely based on those of India, but following the Egyptian procedure with regard to the hearing of cases. The Sudan Penal Code followed the Indian Penal Code of 1837, and the *Civil Justice Ordinance* was based on the Indian Civil Procedure Code as adapted in Burma. Questions concerning the personal status of Muslims were to be decided according to the *Sharīʿa.* Customary law was to be applied whenever possible, '. . . courts were instructed to decide cases, in default of local legislation, in accordance with "justice, equity, and good conscience" . . .' Cases of conflict of jurisdiction, between the civil and Mohammedan Courts were to be decided by a special council.[2]

The codes and ordinances were at first only extended to the provinces of Khartoum, Dongola, Berber, Sennar, Kassala, and Wādī Ḥalfā. In the Baḥr al-Ghazāl and the Upper Nile provinces, justice was administered according to tribal law, and martial law was resorted to whenever necessary. In Kordofan, the vast areas and scarcity of government officials, made the enactment of the new laws impossible. Only in 1906 were the Sudan Penal Code, the Code of Criminal Procedure and the *Civil Justice Ordinance*, enforced in all the northern Provinces. The governors of the Upper Nile, Baḥr al-Ghazāl, and Mongalla were authorized to decide in what cases to take proceedings according to the above codes.[3]

In 1910 Wingate stated his views about the Sudan legal system as follows: '. . . In the Sudan we have endeavoured to graft the experience gained in India on the system we found existing in the Sudan and so far I have every reason to believe we have evolved something which is acceptable to the natives . . .'[4] Thus three legal systems developed side by side. The first was based on the legal codes and administered by government officials. The *Sharī'a* law was administered by Mohammedan law courts and supervised by the grand *qāḍī* and by the British legal secretary. The customary or tribal law was administered by tribal chiefs under the supervision of government officials. An additional way of obtaining justice was by petitions. The people of the Sudan were encouraged to petition their nearest government official, but could also appeal to the inspector-general, the legal secretary or the governor-general. Officials and judges were instructed '. . . to see personally every petitioner however unreasonable or obviously misdirected his petition may be, and to hear what he has to say . . .'[5]

The central judicial staff consisted of the legal secretary, three judges, and the advocate general, all of whom were British. In 1904 civil courts were established at Khartoum and Suakin. Other centres such as Berber, Dongola, and Ḥalfā were visited by the civil judges three times a year. In 1908 the Sudan courts of justice were inaugurated in Khartoum and it was decided to institute a high court and a court of appeal. Justice was, however, mainly administered by non-qualified officials acting as magistrates. All governors and some inspectors were magistrates of the first class. Inspectors and other British officials, as well as a few non-British employees, were magistrates of the second class. Egyptian *ma'mūrs* and other non-British officials were magistrates of the third class. Up to 1905 only officers could be appointed as magistrates. In 1905 *The Magisterial and Police Powers Ordinance* enabled the governor-general to appoint also civilians and inspectors of the slavery repression department who were previously excluded.[6]

Every province, including Khartoum, had a governor's court consisting of three magistrates. It was presided over by the governor or his nominee, acting as a magistrate of the first class. These courts were authorized to pass any sentence within the law. The minor district courts also constituted three magistrates and were qualified to pass sentences not exceeding seven years imprisonment, or a fine not exceeding £E 50. Magistrates' courts of the second and third class could only hear cases summarily and pass sentences not exceeding two months' imprisonment, or a fine not exceeding £E 5.[7] In 1908, a special court was established in Khartoum, to hear all cases connected with land ownership. At the same time five British officials were appointed as land settlement officials in the provinces of Berber, Blue Nile, White Nile, Ḥalfā, and Dongola. It became clear that the appointment of provincial judges would have over-extended the budget, so that special, non-qualified, judicial inspectors were appointed, whose duty it was to hear all the cases in the provinces, by travelling to the various district headquarters.[8]

By and large, the agreed practice was to try criminal cases, wherever they occurred, by provincial staff, leaving the generally more complicated civil suits to legally-trained officials. The logic behind this practice was that punishment for a criminal offence varied according to ideas, habits, and the degree of civilization, '. . . The same crime committed by a Sudanese black, a Jaalin Arab, or a Kababish nomad would probably not be fairly met by the same punishment . . .'[9] Inspectors of the nomad Arabs were told that '. . . camel stealing and raiding even if murder results, are, as once were cattle lifting on the Scottish border, but manly exercises . . .'[10] The fact that punishment was in the hands of the local administrator, also tended to boost the latter's authority in his district. Governors were allowed a wide lattitude in interpreting the Sudan Penal Code as a tribal society could ill afford to lose the benefits of blood money as a result of imprisonment or execution. According to the Penal Code, capital punishment or life imprisonment had to be imposed for murder. However, '. . . what usually happened . . . was a petition to the Governor General to remit the death penalty . . . The Governor General would then refer the matter to the provincial Governor to try and make a settlement between the two sides . . .' Following the payment of blood money, the death sentence would be substituted for a '. . . moderate term of imprisonment, so that the people might recognize that the Government has its right too . . .'[11] Another principle was that '. . . claims, other than those connected with land, arising out of events taking place during the Mahdia should be refused . . .'[12] As years passed, new legislation was introduced, creating new offences. Some ordinances applied to non-Muslims only, while others were limited to one or two provinces.

New ordinances were published in the *Sudan Gazette*, and explained in the annual reports of the legal department.

By virtue of the Condominium Agreement, Wingate exercised complete authority over new legislation. Despite his control, which might have caused friction, his relations with the senior staff of the legal department were on the whole good. Yet, he expected them to co-operate fully with other branches of government administration and had little patience with legal technicalities. Hence, when Sterry, the chief judge, decided a case contrary to what Wingate regarded as being in the best interests of the country he complained that it was '. . . quite useless . . . to argue with these legal people on matters of expediency, policy, etc., etc.—they no more understand it than the man on the moon . . .' What the Sudan required were law officials '. . . who were capable of looking at a situation from the point of view in which those actually responsible for the administration have to consider them . . .'[13] Needless to say, Wingate's view prevailed, and cases were decided according to the principle that legal considerations had to be waived whenever administrative policy so required.

The administration of justice in the provinces

The administration of justice in the provinces was, by and large, entrusted to the provincial inspectors and was described by one of them in the following words:

> . . . in a primitive society no distinction is generally made between administrative and judicial functions. They are both part of the single function of the chief or ruler . . . in some respects the District Commissioner in a primitive society is in the same position . . .[14]

This, and the scarcity of legally trained officials, forced many an inexperienced junior inspector to settle cases ranging from trespassing and cattle thieving to adultery and murder. Their duties comprised, '. . . those of Judge, Magistrate, Mayor, Registrar . . . and almost every kind of civil work . . .'[15] The legal training given to these young inspectors was nominal. Following their appointment, they spent the first few months in Khartoum, where they were trained in the various government departments and were made familiar with the Sudan's legal system. Only in 1908, when the first judicial inspectors were appointed, was a more comprehensive legal training required. One of the first legal inspectors in Berber province described his duties as follows:

> . . . My job was to sit in the Civil Court in El Damer and hear the civil cases and also to keep the register of lands up to date which had

taken us four years to compile. I also visited Atbara Berber and Shendi once every month to hear civil cases . . . Also when the Governor so directed I sat as one of the members of a Mudir's court (three magistrates) to try some serious crime . . .[16]

In Kordofan the judicial inspector's job was not so straightforward. He spent most of his time roaming around the districts allotted to him. His duties varied from one district to another, and depended largely upon the competence of the shaykhs, *nāẓirs*, or other tribal chiefs. He was called upon to settle divorce cases concerning Dinkas which ought to have been decided by the tribal chiefs, according to customary law. In the absence of *qāḍīs* and *Sharīʿa* courts he sometimes had to settle cases concerning the personal status of Muslims. Generally, the tasks of the judicial inspectors in Kordofan seem to have been very much those of ordinary inspectors. They assessed the tribute, appointed shaykhs, and were generally in charge of administration. Their short legal training enabled them to criticize the judicial proceedings of their untrained colleagues. Yet, as long as a greater number of qualified staff could not be afforded, nothing could be done to overcome these deficiencies.

A typical mishap occurred in Talodi, in the Nuba Mountains in 1906. Two tribal chiefs, who had led an attack against the local government post were court-martialled and hanged without reference to Khartoum or Cairo. The sole reason for this hasty justice was that there were '. . no effective means of safeguarding the prisoners . . .' The court consisted of one British and two Egyptian officers who, having heard twelve witnesses for the prosecution and two for the defence, sentenced the accused to be hanged.[17] Bonham Carter criticized this action severely, and demanded that the commanding officer at Talodi be reprimanded. He stated '. . . that it is dangerous if officers think that the summoning and confirming of court martial can be justified merely on the ground of local convenience . . .'[18] Slatin reacted in much the same manner and Cromer concluded '. . . that apart from hasty procedure, and the wholly undefendable reasons given for hanging the Sheikhs, it is even questionable whether they deserved hanging at all . . .'[19] This however, did not stop Cromer from justifying the proceedings in his correspondence with the foreign office.[20] With the extension of the railways and telegraph to Kordofan, hasty executions were avoided in later years. Yet the judges were as amateurish as before, and when in 1915, another rebel was tried in the Nuba Mountains a local inspector was appointed to act as president of the *mudīr's* court.[21]

The administration of Islamic law

In 1882, Colonel Stewart reported :

> . . . There is in each province a Mehkeme or Sheriyat Court with a Cadi on a monthly salary varying from 100 to 1250 piastres. This official cannot inquire into criminal cases, but in civil suits, should both parties agree, he can be appealed to. His chief business is, however, connected with inheritances, marriages, divorce, & c. . . .[22]

The part played by the *Sharīʿa* courts during the Turco-Egyptian period, was subordinate to that of the provincial courts and the central court at Khartoum. During the Mahdia, the secular courts ceased to exist. The Mahdi, and afterwards the Khalifa, asserted a personal paramountcy in all matters of law. Justice was based on the Qur'ān, the *Sunna,* and the edicts and decisions of the Mahdi. Next to the Mahdi was the *qāḍī al-Islām* who provided the channel of communication between the Mahdi and the provincial *qāḍīs.* Most of these *qāḍīs* were laymen, as the *qāḍīs* who were trained in Egypt were generally not trusted by the Mahdi. Throughout the Mahdia the judiciary was dependent upon the administration. In the provinces the governors were dominant, and no *qāḍī* could be appointed without their approval. While in the centre the will of the Khalifa was predominant and the judiciary became a subservient tool.[23]

This had been the situation when, after the reconquest, the Anglo-Egyptian authorities decided to re-establish the Muslim judiciary, much on the lines that existed prior to the Mahdia. *The Sudan Mohammedan Law Courts Ordinance* was promulgated in 1902. It provided for the establishment of a high court consisting of the grand *qāḍī*, the *muftī*, and one or more other members. The *mudīrīya*, *muḥāfaẓa*, and *ma'mūrīya* courts were to consist of one *qāḍī* each. The Mohammedan Law Courts were competent to deal with any question regarding marriage, divorce, inheritance, guardianship, *awqāf*, and all problems concerning the personal status of Muslims. They were also competent to decide upon any question other than those mentioned, provided that all parties, whether Muslims or not, made a formal demand to be bound by the ruling of the Islamic law. Conflicts of jurisdiction between the civil and *Sharīʿa* courts were to be decided by a council consisting of the legal secretary, the grand *qāḍī*, and the judicial comissioner.[24] Until 1916 no judicial commissioner was appointed. Hence the third member of the council was appointed by the governor-general and was invariably of the senior British officials of the legal department.

In 1915 the Sudan became one of the first Muslim countries, following the *Ḥanafī* school, to introduce a reform of the divorce law. *The Mohammedan Law Courts Organization and Procedure Regulations* enabled the grand *qāḍī* of the Sudan to order a departure from *Ḥanafī* jurisdiction whenever he thought necessary.[25] As a result, the reform of family law in the Sudan, much on the lines advocated by Qāsim Amīn and Muḥammad 'Abduh, anticipated that of Egypt. The Sudan Judicial Circular, No. 17, provided for judicial divorce for a wife whose husband failed to support her. It enabled a wife whose husband was presumed dead, to remarry, and granted judicial divorce to wives deserted for more than one year. It also granted divorce to wives whose matrimonial discord was such that only divorce provided a solution. Thus the family law, which represents the very heart of the *Sharīʿa*, was reformed at last. The importance of this reform lay in the fact that it departed from *Ḥanafī* jurisdiction. Thus the principle of reforming Muslim law, according to any one of the four *madhāhib* was introduced into the Sudan, and was to effect future modifications of Islamic law.[26]

The Mohammedan Law Courts Organization Regulations of 1905, were of a purely administrative nature. They enabled the grand *qāḍī* to hear and decide any case whether previously heard by a Mohammedan court or not. They also fixed the fees of the Mohammedan courts and ordered that all suits should be heard in the district where the defendants resided.[27] *The Procedure Regulations for Mohammedan Courts*, published in 1906, stated that any judgement passed by a Mohammedan court should be executed by the government officials or police officers, whenever required.[28] In 1912, the *Maazun Regulations* were published.[29] *Ma'dhūns* were to be appointed on recommendations by shaykhs, *'umdas* or notables and had to register all marriages and divorces within their district.

A special inquiry about the *waqfs* of the Sudan, which was ordered in 1901, showed that the few *waqfs* that existed were not properly registered in the *Sharīʿa* courts and that their produce was being misappropriated.[30] The management of these *awqāf* was entrusted to the Sudan Mohammedan Law Courts, as Wingate had decided to stop any interference in Sudanese *awqāf* by the 'Egyptian Wakfs Administration'.[31] Apparently this was not fully implemented. The *awqāf* of Kordofan were managed by the provincial headquarters at El Obeid, who built the central market on *waqf* property and used its rent for building a mosque. Even in Khartoum the *awqāf* were transferred to the supervision of the grand *qāḍī* only in 1911. The annual income of these *awqāf* was £E 250 and was used for the maintenance and construction of mosques.[32]

All the legislation and regulations connected with the Mohammedan courts were issued by the grand *qāḍī* subject to their approval by the governor-general. The grand *qāḍī* also submitted annual reports, the summaries of which were included in the reports of the legal department. Most of these reports dealt with the administration of Islamic law in the provinces and with problems of personnel. Commenting on the low standard of the *qāḍīs*, Bonham Carter noted that '. . . the salaries paid to them are wretched and would be disgraceful if regarded as a normal salary for a legal official . . .' He added, however, that '. . . their decisions . . . though probably wrong in form and possibly in law are based on a knowledge of the people and are usually regarded by them as just . . .'[33] In 1904, the grand *qāḍī* introduced a new scale of fees for the *Sharīʿa* courts, as the previous scale had been too high for a poor country like the Sudan.[34] In the following year he suggested that the registration of transactions relating to land should be left entirely in the hands of the *Sharīʿa* Courts. The grand *qāḍī* stated that these courts had lost more than half of their original jurisdiction and were confined to matters arising out of family relations. He felt that this diminishing range of jurisdiction undermined the authority of Islamic law, which he regarded as superior to all others. Needless to say the grand *qāḍī's* attempt to increase his control was resented by the Sudan authorities.[35]

The grand *qāḍīs* and the inspectors of the *Sharīʿa* courts, during Wingate's governor-generalship, were Egyptians. The only Sudanese holding a central position in the judicial hierarchy was Shaykh al-Ṭayyib Aḥmad Hāshim, *muftī* of the Sudan.[36] The first grand *qāḍī* of the Sudan was Muḥammad Shākir, who resigned in 1904, having been appointed head of the *ʿulamāʾ* of Alexandria. He was followed by Muḥammad Hārūn, late inspector of the Mohammedan law courts. He belonged to the conservative trend in Islam, and stated that '. . . Mohammedan law is founded on equity . . . *and does not require at any time any alteration or amendment* . . .' Cromer, who held very definite views on Islamic reform and was a great admirer of Muḥammad 'Abduh, stated that:

> . . . it is natural that a conservative Mohammedan should hold these opinions . . . but of course . . . they are sheer nonsense. Mohammedan law requires a great deal of alteration or amendment . . . I am inclined to think that a Kadi who holds the views set forth in the report I have just been reading is not altogether the man you want . . .[37]

Whether as a result of Cromer's pressure or not, Muḥammad Ḥārūn resigned in 1908, and was replaced by Muḥammad Muṣṭafā al-Marāghī who held the post of grand *qāḍī* until 1919. Al-Marāghī, an Azharite and a disciple of 'Abduh, had previously served as *qāḍī* of Dongola and Khartoum, and was on the Egyptian *waqf* administration. His reforming zeal was brought to bear on the Islamic laws and earned him the respect of all the British judges.[38]

All of the provincial *qāḍīs* during the formative period were also Egyptians. Yet, by 1912, twelve of the district *qāḍīs* and twenty-two assistant *qāḍīs* were graduates of the *qāḍīs'* course at Gordon College. The number of provincial and district *Sharīʿa* courts increased from twenty-eight in 1903 to forty-five in 1912. Of these, eleven were provincial courts, and the others, district and sub-district courts. In 1908, the grand *qāḍī* decided not to increase the number of courts, despite ever-growing pressure of work, as he regarded the raising of *qāḍīs'* wages as more essential. The department's budget did not provide for the inspection of the provincial *Sharīʿa* courts, and their *qāḍīs* had to cope as best they could. The result was that many districts remained without courts and were visited by a *qāḍī* only once or twice a year. Hence, many cases, which should have been settled by *Sharīʿa* courts, were referred to the British inspectors.[39]

Administratively, the *qāḍīs* were under the supervision of the British governors and inspectors. It was through the governors that the *qāḍīs* applied for leave, while the inspectors forwarded their confidential reports on *qāḍīs* to the legal secretary without reference to the grand *qāḍī*. Governors also were not allowed to communicate with either the grand *qāḍī* or the inspector of the Mohammedan courts and had to refer always to the legal secretary.[40] The appointment of *qāḍīs* for the central administration and the provinces was entrusted to Slatin and Bonham Carter. Muḥammad ʿAbduh, who visited the Sudan in 1904–5, advised its authorities on the suitability of Egyptian *qāḍīs*. It was on his recommendation that Muṣṭafā Sulṭān and Muḥammad Muṣṭafā al-Marāghī were appointed to serve in the Sudan.[41] The avowed aim of the Sudan authorities was to train Sudanese *qāḍīs* in sufficient numbers, in order to forego the services of the Egyptians, who were regarded as unreliable and expensive. From 1908 onwards this aim was nearly achieved. All junior posts were filled by Sudanese *qāḍīs* and only a few senior positions continued to be held by Egyptians.

The government's policy of entrusting all matters concerning the personal status of Muslims to the *Sharīʿa* courts was both necessary and wise. It enabled the government to avoid unnecessary friction with the Muslim inhabitants and helped establish an orthodox Muslim leadership whose interests were bound up with those of their British rulers. The scope of jurisdiction which was granted to the *Sharīʿa* courts was basically similar to that of other provinces of the Ottoman Empire during the same period. Under the Turco-Egyptian authorities, the establishment of a system of civil justice had already undermined the *Sharīʿa* courts. During the Mahdia this process was reversed and Islamic law, as interpreted by the Mahdi and the Khalifa, became predominant. The introduction of codes and the establishment of a department of justice, to apply them, enabled the Anglo-Egyptian authorities to limit the *Sharī'a* courts' area of jurisdiction once again. Efforts to extend their authority over matters such as land ownership, were resisted by the authorities. But the paramountcy of Islamic law was upheld in all matters concerning the personal status of Muslims.

Tribal and customary law

The civil law courts had only partial jurisdiction over the southern provinces and over the nomadic tribes of the north. The *Sharī'a* courts were also not extended to the non-Muslim southern provinces. The jurisdiction of these vast areas was to be left to tribal and customary law and was to be administered by shaykhs and chiefs recognized by the government. Their decisions were liable to review by a British magistrate, and no sentence of capital punishment could be passed by them. Among the nomadic tribes of the north, justice was administered by the *nāẓir* according to the accepted tribal laws, and only a few cases came under the codes. '. . . But the increasing acquiescence in the interpretation by the British officials of tribal and communal law and custom . . .' was regarded as a hopeful sign of the times.[42] The government's assumption was that customary law could be interpreted and overruled by British officials, and that tribal chiefs could become part of the administrative hierarchy without losing their influence over their people. Governors could imprison or remove tribal chiefs for excesses, thereby undermining the latter's authority. Moreover, the very existence of government posts where most cases could be settled, enabled the tribesmen to flout the authority of their chiefs regardless of the intentions of the local government officials. Finally, the gradual pacification of the southern provinces also tended to make the need for strong tribal leaders less apparent.

Matthews,[43] the governor of the Upper Nile province declared himself as a staunch supporter of customary law which he regarded as '. . . worthy of deep consideration, and after purgation of Dervish contamination, of general adoption . . .'[44] In 1908, he wrote:

> . . . as long as we decide cases according to equity and common sense, and avoid legal technicalities, we shall hold the confidence of these tribes . . . Provided neither cruelty nor extortion is practised we should be careful to avoid the danger of robbing chiefs of their power . . .[45]

Yet by deposing the *makk* of the Shilluks for '. . . Misappropriation and unjust treatment of his tribe . . .', Matthews undermined the authority of his successor. The newly appointed *makk* was not expected to rule his tribe according to his own standards '. . . Major

Matthews is endeavouring by every means in his power to inculcate in this somewhat uncivilized potentate the elements of justice and honesty . . .'[46] In the Baḥr al-Ghazāl the powers of the tribal leaders were '. . . limited to one month's imprisonment, all cases for which such punishment is considered inadequate being dealt with by the nearest Inspector . . .' In deciding these cases inspectors did not necessarily comply with the Sudan codes: '. . . and cases are tried by courts not legally empowered to deal with such cases . . . what is principally needed is for the punishment to be just and prompt . . .'[47]

It is hardly surprising that the powers of tribal chiefs diminished constantly to the dismay of the British inspectors. Following a tour of the Dengkur district in 1905, the inspector complained that most of his time was taken up by deciding cases '. . . which never get settled until an inspector goes round, instead of being decided right off by the Sheikh or elders . . .'[48] Similarly, another inspector complained that the Dinka shaykhs had no control over their men and he was called upon to settle all their cases. Paradoxically, only those tribal leaders who owed their allegiance to the government were accepted by the provincial authorities, yet the fact that they were bound to the government undermined their authority within their tribes. When Yambio, chief of the Azande, was killed in battle, the British inspector decided to appoint Oku, who '. . . openly stated that his following was so small that he could not maintain his position if the troops were withdrawn . . .'[49] The natural successors to the chieftainship were turned down for fear of their excessive powers. It is small wonder that by 1908, the powers of the Azande chiefs had declined to such an extent that the British inspector had to settle '. . . a large number of cases nearly all being questions of ownership of women . . .', and clearly falling within the jurisdiction of customary law.[50] The chiefs refused to hold court, for they did not know the government's rules and were afraid of exceeding their powers. Hence, the administrators were forced to conduct tribal affairs by dealing directly with the tribes. By 1911, the Sultan of the Azande had lost most of his power, and was openly disobeyed by his sons and people. It is therefore hardly surprising that the administration of justice in the Baḥr al-Ghazāl was summed up as follows: '. . . An increasing preference for the decision of an inspector is noticeable throughout the province, and in the Eastern district, especially, every petty case is submitted to him for adjustment . . .'[51]

The deterioration of customary law in the Nuba Mountains followed a similar pattern. During the first few years administrators hardly ventured into the mountains, and only the Arab tribes who inhabited the valleys came to settle their cases in the scattered government stations. The *Makk* of Taqalī stopped his people from bringing their cases to the government as he feared '. . . that he will lose his authority and power over his subjects . . .'[52] The administration of customary law remained in the hands of the Nuba *makks* who were assisted by the *kujurs* (priests) and by the councils of elders. Among some of the tribes the *kujurs'* position was paramount. They vehemently resisted any government encroachment upon their authority. However, by 1913, military expeditions had subjugated many of the Nubas and had broken the powers of both *makks* and *kujurs*. Consequently, the administration of justice passed into the hands of the inspectors.[53] Only those tribes, remote enough from a government post to be left in peace could administer their own customary law. The Nuer of the Upper Nile were rarely visited by government inspectors. Moreover, the area they roamed was so vast that many of them never saw an English inspector until 1922. The supreme authority continued to rest with the witch doctors, who were regarded '. . . as much a curse in the Southern Sudan as the illiterate fiki is in the North . . .'[54]

In some provinces customary law had deteriorated yet the introduction of civil codes was regarded as premature. The governor, therefore, devised his own scale of punishments much to the embarrassment of the central government. Wingate commented on the high percentage of corporal punishment in Mongalla when he wrote to its governor :

> . . . I see that the infliction of this form of punishment in your provinces [sic] is not only greatly in excess of the other provinces quoted, but has also, in several cases, been illegally administered—notably in the case of the flogging of a woman in the Bor district which, although possibly not repugnant to native custom and conditions, is wholly contrary to British administrative methods and principles . . .[55]

Another pitfall of the administration of tribal law by government officials was their tendency to codify these laws. A compendium of all Dinka laws was prepared by a British inspector, and tribal law was administered by government officials aiming '. . . to govern the inhabitants of the Southern Sudan entirely by their own "tribal codes" . . .' In the years 1903–6 more than 1,600 cases were decided by government officials according to Dinka laws. However, decisions were sometimes contrary to tribal law owing to the superficial knowledge of the officials concerned.[56] The obvious dangers of codifying these laws were soon pointed out to the Sudan government :

> . . . Such a code can scarcely escape destroying or at least damaging the capacity of traditional laws and customs to mould themselves to new circumstances; and it runs the risk of perpetuating misunderstand-

ings which are sometimes inevitable when people of higher civilization attempt to grasp the principles underlying the legislation of tribes with whom they are imperfectly acquainted . . ."[57]

Despite this warning Sudan government officials continued to administer tribal justice according to their own interpretation, thus undermining tribal leadership and obstructing the natural course of development of tribal laws and customs.

CHAPTER VIII

Tribal Policy

THE population of the Sudan at the time of the reconquest was largely a tribal one. Despite the dislocation of tribes during the Mahdia and the weakening of their economic and social structure, the tribes continued to perform a major function in society. Hence the British authorities in the Sudan realized that the reconstruction of the country depended first and foremost on the pacification of the tribes, their resettlement and their loyalty to the new regime. To achieve these aims with a minimum of administration and expense, the authorities used different measures in the northern and southern provinces. The northern Sudan, with its Muslim and largely Arabic speaking population, was the more easily accessible to the new administrators. Moreover, most of the government's officials were either Egyptians or Lebanese, who had a common language with, and in many cases the same religion as, the indigenous inhabitants. Consequently, after an initial period of pacification, the government could establish direct administrative control over most of this area with little recourse to military expeditions.

The southern provinces were in a different category. The negroid tribes of the Sudan occupied the area roughly south of latitude 10°, with the Baḥr al-'Arab forming a natural frontier between them and the Muslim north. Inhabited by a multiplicity of tribes without a common language, culture, or religion, the vast areas of the south had defied the continuous efforts of the Turco-Egyptians and the Mahdist state to establish a semblance of organized government in that region. Ravaged by successive waves of invaders, the tribal society of the south was not only dislocated but in many cases on the verge of a complete breakdown. Hence the Anglo-Egyptian forces, who began to penetrate the south two years after the reconquest, had to rely on military stations and armed expeditions to a far greater extent than in the northern provinces. The process of gradual pacification was not completed even by the end of Wingate's governor-generalship and continued well into the 1920s.

Pacification and resettlement

Collaboration between several of the northern tribes and the Anglo-Egyptian forces started in 1896–7, during the Dongola campaign. Seeking relief from the Ta'āishī autocracy, some of the riverain tribes, especially the Ja'alīyīn, raised tribal levies who participated in the final stages of the advance on Khartoum.[1] The intelligence department under Wingate and Slatin did not rely merely on chance. Letters offering *amān* (clemency) to tribes and individuals were sent by the intelligence department to all the provinces and to the Mahdist *amīrs* who were not of Baqqāra origin. Although some of these letters found their way to the Khalifa 'Abdallāhi, the intelligence department was well rewarded and received numerous requests for *amān*.[2]

The principles of tribal administration had been defined by Kitchener in his *Memorandum to Mudirs*. Governors, inspectors and *ma'mūrs* were instructed to '. . . acquire the confidence of the people, to develop their resources, and to raise them to a higher level . . .' They were further advised to seek the co-operation of '. . . the better class of native, through whom we may hope gradually to influence the whole population . . .'[3] The first step was the establishment of government posts throughout the Sudan, the number of which was limited only by the state of the country's finances and the availability of personnel. They were entrusted with the establishment of law and order, and also assisted in the resettlement of the tribes in order to increase the area of cultivation. In the southern Sudan progress was less rapid. Fashoda was the only district over which the government extended its authority during 1899. The prospects of establishing a proper administration in these areas must have seemed rather gloomy. Maxwell then governor of Khartoum, wrote : '. . . the country is only fit for Hippos, mosquitoes and Nuers to live in . . .'[4] The government had neither the power nor the means to establish its authority in the south. Salisbury's suggestion that they should occupy Baḥr al-Ghazāl from Uganda was turned down by Cromer on political grounds.[5] Instead, in 1900, Wingate sent agents to several southern tribal leaders inviting them to Khartoum '. . . where matters could be explained to them, and flags issued to them to hoist in their territories. Four representatives arrived in Khartoum on the 14th April 1900 . . . representing eleven chiefs of the Bahr-El-Ghazal . . .' The government's anxiety to establish a semblance of authority in the remote south nearly led to a fiasco. Several British and Egyptian flags were hoisted on the French side of the border.[6]

In the winter of 1900, the first government expedition was dispatched to the Baḥr al-Ghazāl and several posts were set up. But a patrol which was sent to the province in November 1901 met with resistance and resulted in considerable loss of life, including that of a British inspector. The punitive expedition which followed this murder was ruthless in its methods, and set a pattern for future relations between administrators and inhabitants.[7] Many of the southern tribes viewed any form of government with the utmost suspicion and withdrew into the interior whenever they sighted a government patrol. By 1905 there were nine military posts in the Baḥr al-Ghazāl and a total force of some 1300 men and 64 officers. The military character of the province was clearly visible, and it was only after the Equatorial battalions replaced the Egyptian army in 1912–13 that the administration assumed a more civilian character. When Bishop Gwynne visited the Zande district in 1911 in order to establish a CMS station, he was given an Azande interpretation of British rule in the southern Sudan :

> . . . You put the Egyptians in the front when you conquered the dervishes and you put the ex-dervishes in front rank when you conquered us and now one or two British rule many hundreds all over the Sudan . . .[8]

The situation in the Upper Nile province, which until 1906 included Mongalla, was much the same. The southernmost post was established at Mongalla in 1901. However, government control did not extend beyond the immediate vicinity of the posts. Of the major tribes of the province only the Shilluks were brought under effective control. The Dinka kept aloof from the government, while the Nuer maintained an openly hostile attitude and resented government interference in their tribal affairs. The most turbulent tribes, however, were the Beir and Anuak who inhabited the area between the Baḥr al-Zarāf and the Abyssinian border. In 1912 the government launched a punitive expedition against these tribes and decided to establish its administration on purely military lines.

The pattern of government penetration into the Nuba Mountains followed a similar line. The few government posts were not able to control the intertribal fights between the various mountains, let alone the constant raids between the Nubas and their Arab neighbours. Wingate, who knew that some of these feuds had been going on for many generations, wrote to Cromer, '. . . I have categorically refused to allow Government to be drawn into inter-tribal quarrels . . .'[9] However, the underlying reason appears to have been that the government feared an intertribal coalition which might revolt against its authority. An intelligence report on Kordofan stated : '. . . there is little chance of a combination between the tribes without the introduction of some powerful object of common interest such as religion . . .'[10] Moreover, the Nuba Mountains were part of Kordofan province until 1914. Yet, instead of improving the communications between them and El Obeid, the provincial capital, Asser, the adjutant-general, ordered the improvement of the road from Talodi in the Nuba Mountains to Tonga on the Baḥr al-Ghazāl.

> . . . You then have a force which is not dependent on the railway or on the North of Kordofan, and in case of the Arabs threatening the railway or Obeid, you can with the Southern and independent force turn the tables on them by threatening their houses and lines of communication . . .[11]

While the government generally refrained from interfering in intertribal feuds, it did insist that its own authority should be respected. In the Nuba Mountains, as in other southern provinces, this was partly achieved by punitive expeditions. When Wingate paid his first visit to the Nuba Mountains in 1912 he wrote, '. . . This is the first time in which this country has been at rest or that it has had any chance of developing its resources . . .' Two years later Wingate again reported that the peace and prosperity of the Nubas had reached a new peak. However, successive punitive expeditions during the years 1908–1914 and the revolt of Fiki 'Alī in 1915, tend to suggest that Wingate's optimism was premature.[12]

In order to pacify the tribes the government tried to limit the large quantities of arms and ammunition which had been abandoned by the defeated Egyptian and Mahdist armies and had subsequently come into possession of the tribes. An ordinance for regulating the carrying of firearms was among the first laws to be promulgated by the Anglo-Egyptian authorities. However, the government continued to hand out firearms to shaykhs and others as a reward for their services to the government.[13] Further legislation limiting the import and use of arms and ammunition was enacted in the following years. Yet, despite the increased fines and imprisonment, the legislation seemed to have had little effect.[14] Arms smuggling continued, especially on the Abyssinian and the western borders. In the southern provinces the *jallāba* were implicated in the illegal arms trade, in spite of the restrictions the government imposed on their movements. But by far the largest concentration of illegal firearms was in the Nuba Mountains. Many Nubas had served in the Khalifa's *jihādīya*[15] and had retained their arms following his defeat. In 1908 it was estimated that there were 20,000 Remington rifles in the Nuba Mountains alone.[16] The increased number of government posts and the greater security they brought enabled the authorities in Kordofan to undertake the disarmament of the tribes, and by 1911 the number of illegal weapons had decreased.

Legislation concerning the import and sale of alcoholic liquor was first introduced in 1899. To begin with it had little effect on the tribal population as it did not apply to *merissa* (millet beer), or palm wine, the most popular drinks. Provincial governors were ordered to ensure that no liquor was sold to the inhabitants. Cromer, however, continued to be concerned about the excessive consumption of alcoholic drinks in the Sudan. This was largely the result of pressure by the foreign office which in turn was caused by the lobbying of the Anti-Slavery-Societies.[17] In consequence, *The Native Liquors Ordinance, 1903* was promulgated. It forbade the manufacture and sale of all liquors, including *merissa,* without licence. It further stipulated that '. . . any person having over 30 litres of Merissa shall be deemed to have some for sale unless he proved otherwise . . .'[18] In the following months this ordinance was enforced in most of the northern provinces as well as in Fashoda and the Baḥr al-Ghazāl.

Wingate, however, was continuously pestered by the English press and by questions in the House of Commons concerning the excessive consumption of liquor in the Sudan. Although these allegations were denied by Wingate, it appears that many crimes were caused by drunkenness among the tribes. Consequently, a new ordinance for the prevention of drunkenness was promulgated in 1907. It gave to any police officer or *ma'mūr* the right to arrest drunkards without a warrant and to impose on them a specified fine or imprisonment. Further legislation was introduced in 1908 which forbade the selling of '. . . any alcoholic liquors to any native of the Sudan . . .'[19] During all these years Wingate maintained that no alcoholic liquors were sold to Sudanese and that the many cases of drunkenness reported were the result of excessive consumption of *merissa.* In 1912 Wingate had to admit that large quantities of imported liquor were in fact sold to the Anuak and the Nuer. He therefore issued an order '. . . to totally prohibit the transport of liquor, except for the reasonable consumption of Europeans . . .'[20] The more practical method of imposing heavier import duties on liquors was suggested by the director of customs, and was adopted by the governor-general's council in 1914.

While arms and liquor were the two main spheres in which legislation was thought to have a direct bearing on the pacification of the country, several other ordinances also had a direct effect on tribal administration. *The Wild Animals Preservation Ordinance* of 1900 sought to regulate the hunting habits of the Sudanese and to impose taxes on Europeans hunting for pleasure. Legislation to protect the country's forests was passed in the following year, and the *Contraband Goods Ordinance* was promulgated in 1902. Finally, a special ordinance '. . . for preventing the import sale and use of Hashish . . .' was enacted in 1907.[21]

Following the initial period of pacification the resettlement of the tribes, which had been dislocated during the Mahdia, became a dominant feature of tribal policy. In 1900 the government called on the Baqqāra tribes in the Gezira to return to Kordofan, and in the following months nearly 30,000 made their way to the west.[22] Many Dinka and Shilluk refugees were also assisted in making their way back to the south. Resettlement continued over a number of years, organized and assisted by the intelligence department. The government's aim in encouraging this mass migration was threefold: to decrease the population of Omdurman; to encourage cultivation; and to restore the tribal map of the Sudan to what it had been before the Mahdia. The population of Omdurman, which continued to be the largest town in the Sudan, decreased from approximately 150,000 in 1892 to about 40,000 in 1900.[23] Although the decrease can be partially attributed to the death-toll resulting from the reconquest, internal emigration also accounted for this sharp decline in population.

In order to encourage cultivation the government made available agricultural loans to assist landowners to erect *sāqiyas* and to purchase cattle. Returning tribes were also provided with cheap *dhurra* for the first few months and with good seeds to start cultivation. On resuming cultivation the newcomers were exempted from paying taxes during the first year. Another measure undertaken to encourage resettlement was the colonization of released Sudanese soldiers who were settled in military-agricultural settlements on the Blue and White Niles. This scheme was started in 1900, and by 1913 all these colonies were reported to be flourishing and no longer required government assistance. A further measure was the encouragement of immigrants from the bordering countries, and by 1912 there were over 16,000 Fallāta who had settled permanently in the Sudan. As a result of these measures, cultivation increased rapidly, and in 1908 it was realized that without additional irrigation facilities there was no further scope for expansion. Furthermore, efforts to improve agricultural techniques were frustrated by the apathy and total indifference of many tribes.[24]

Tribal leadership

After the reconquest the Anglo-Egyptian authorities sought the co-operation of the shaykhs in order to impose the new administration upon the tribes, and to hasten their return to agriculture. Government officials were therefore instructed to remember that:

> . . . not only are Sheikhs 'Public Servants' but they perform work of the greatest importance and responsibility . . . [it] is the general aim

> of the Government to associate them as a class with the work of the administration . . .[25]

However, the government made it quite clear that it would determine the functions of the shaykhs and that government officials would have the authority to overrule their decisions. Thus from the outset the government regarded the shaykhs as its tribal agents who could be appointed, overruled, and dismissed just as any government official.

A government order of 1902 appertaining to the procedure of appointing new shaykhs stated :

> . . . Mudirs and Administrators should . . . send their recommendations in this respect, with full details as to hereditary title, influence & c. of the particular Sheikh to the Assistant Director of Intelligence Khartoum, for the approval of H.E. the Governor General . . . probationary Commissions will be made out . . .[26]

This procedure was followed throughout Wingate's governor-generalship. Shaykhs were judged according to government standards of ability and their readiness to comply with orders. Full details about the appointed shaykhs and their qualifications were published in the annual reports of the provinces; and, in the case of important shaykhs, in the *Sudan Gazette*. Some of these shaykhs failed to pass their period of probation, while others were dismissed for a great variety of reasons ranging from incompetence and lack of authority to malpractices and autocratic behaviour. In certain cases the provincial governors decided that the number of shaykhs was out of proportion with the population and hence had to be reduced. The governors argued that by having fewer shaykhs those who remained would tend to work harder and increase their efficiency.[27] Thus tribal leadership became fully dependent upon government administration.

> . . . The policy adopted has been to raise the status of the Sheikh as far as possible in the eyes of his people by trying to impress on them (and on him) that he is the representative in his own village of the Government . . .[28]

Tribal leaders who tried to assert their independent authority were not trusted by the government even if their loyalty was beyond doubt, as it was conceivable that their power, not derived from the government, might be directed against it. In certain cases the *nāẓir* of the tribe was officially approached before one of his shaykhs was dismissed. However, there is no evidence to suggest that the *nāẓir's* view could have swayed the government's decision. Consultations with the elders of the tribe were also undertaken when new shaykhs had to be appointed. Yet, once again, the final decision rested with the government official:

> . . . Muglad, 12 November 1911 . . . Had a strenuous moment with ten gentle Arabs, who as usual wanted to have their own way whatever happened . . . However got them into line and swore in several new sheikhs . . . Idris el-Sakin was the only man his people stuck to . . .[29]

The posts of *ʿumdas* and *nāẓirs* were introduced into the Sudan during the Turco-Egyptian period. In 1863, Mūsa Pasha Ḥamdī divided certain districts into *aqsām* and appointed indigenous *nāẓirs* as their administrators. The term *ʿumda* was substituted for that of *shaykh al-balad* in nineteenth-century Egypt and was used in the villages of the northern riverain Sudan. Following the reconquest both terms were re-introduced into the Sudan by the new administrators. It seems that *nāẓirs* were appointed only for nomad tribes such as the Kabābīsh, Hadendowa, or Misīrīya, and that they were in a superior position to all the other tribal shaykhs. *ʿUmdas* were re-introduced in the riverain north but their exact functions seem to have hardly differed from that of other shaykhs. The government's policy was to undermine the authority of both *nāẓirs* and *ʿumdas* and to strengthen the heads of the subordinate tribal units. *ʿUmdas* were introduced in the Baqqāra tribes of Kordofan in 1911 in order to decrease the influence of their *nāẓirs* and to make the tribes dependent on direct government authority. The result was that while the *nāẓirs* lost much of their influence, the *ʿumdas*, who had no hereditary powers, were not strong enough to assume control.[30] The same policy prevailed in the Nuba Mountains and in the southern provinces:

> . . . Meks of the pliant Merkaz hanger-on type were appointed who were not only personally unsuitable and unacceptable to the people, but who were often impossible of acceptance to the people as not being of correct royal lineage . . . The equivalent of the Arab type of Omda scurrilously known as Kelb el Hakuma [sic] was by no means uncommon . . .[31]

Among the southern tribes the deposing of the *Makk* of the Shilluks was probably the most noteworthy example. In 1899 Jackson, who had been in Fashoda, appointed Koor as *makk* of the Shilluks. By 1903, however, he was found to '. . . have been guilty of misappropriation and unjust treatment of his subjects . . . and was in consequence deposed and banished from the country . . .'[32] The new *makk*, who was duly appointed, had to accept '. . . the "XI conditions" of Mekship . . .' which were laid down by the British governor in order '. . . to show the power of Government . . .'[33] Consequently, the powers of the new *makk* were so diminished that the governor himself complained of the *makk's* lack of authority. The inevitable result of this policy was the further deterioration of tribal leadership. There were certain exceptions to this policy, notably amongst the camel owning tribes of Kordofan. 'Alī Wad al-Tōm, the *nāẓir* of the Kabābīsh throughout this period, enjoyed a large measure of autonomy in administering his tribe. This was probably the result of a number of factors. Firstly, the Kabābīsh remained a truly nomadic tribe which by virtue of its greater mobility could maintain a larger measure of independence. Secondly, the Kabābīsh, many of whom had been staunch opponents of the Khalifa, had to be rewarded by the British authorities; and lastly, 'Alī Wad al-Tōm was by all accounts an extremely capable leader who knew how to remain in the government's good books without losing his independence. Yet the Kabābīsh were by all accounts an exception, and the weakening of central tribal leadership which was extended to most of the other tribes was a logical conclusion of the government's policy of undermining tribal coalitions.[34]

Many of the *nāẓirs* were dismissed during this period for a great variety of reasons. 'Abdallāh Jādallāh, the *nāẓir* of the Kawāhla in Kordofan, was dismissed in 1909. For years he had collected tribute from his tribe and used part of it for the *mahr* (bridal money) he was required to pay for marrying the Mahdi's daughter. The new *nāẓir* was elected by a council of elders, and gained the confidence of his tribe as well as that of the government.[35] Muḥammad al-Faqīr, *nāẓir* of the Misīrīya, who had for years been suspected for malpractices and slave trading, was dismissed in 1915 for being implicated in Fiki 'Alī's revolt. The new *nāẓir*, Muhammad Dafa' Allāh, was appointed following a meeting with the shaykhs and *'umdas* of the tribe.[36] Yet, however justified these dismissals were, they could not fail to undermine the stability of tribal leadership which had already suffered during the Mahdia.

With the decreasing powers of shaykhs and *nāẓirs* one could hardly expect that the duties performed by them would be of major significance. The area of jurisdiction of the numerous shaykhs was determined by the government according to its own consideration. '. . . Owing to administrative exigencies, the Beja tribes were at first partitioned between three provinces: Berber, Red Sea, and Kassala. Tribal unity . . . naturally suffered . . .'[37] Along the borders the situation was even worse, as the artificially drawn borders cut across many tribes. The duties entrusted to the shaykhs included: the digging of wells; the building of roads and rest houses; the guarding of communications; and various tasks of an administrative nature such as reporting deaths. The major functions, however, were to assist the government in the administration of justice and in the collection of taxes. In both these spheres the shaykhs held a subordinate position. The assessment of taxes was performed by the provincial inspectors and governors with the active participation of Slatin, while the shaykhs could only appeal against the government's decisions. It was then their duty to divide the agreed tax or tribute among the various sections of the tribe and to be responsible for its collection. The diaries of several government inspectors indicate that even this duty was often performed by the officials rather than by the shaykhs. Savile, whilst inspector in northern Kassala, described his methods of collecting tribute. His *entourage* included an officer and twenty-five soldiers. On arrival at a well, where the cattle had to be brought for watering, he erected a *zarība*, (cattle pen), and when the tribes arrived with their cattle he—

> . . . took a portion of each herd of cattle and drove them into the zariba and kept them as hostages for the tribute; taking care to take about three times the value of tribute in live stock . . .

Following this procedure the tribes had little alternative but to redeem their flock by paying the tribute demanded from them. '. . . The tribute was chiefly in gold nose rings and beads, all absolutely filthy. The people almost all assured me that they had no money . . .' When one of the tribesmen tried to cheat Savile out of 5d., he duly confiscated his sheep and gave it to his soldiers as extra rations.[38]

The rewards which the government offered the tribal leaders were inadequate throughout the period. Initially, the government granted the shaykhs minor tax exemptions. Thus a shaykh was not liable for land tax on one feddan if he cultivated 100 feddans, or more. When the *Taxation of Animals Ordinance* was amended in 1903, the legal adviser wrote that its main object—

> . . . was to enable the Governor-General to exempt Omdas and Sheikhs, a class who do much work for the Government without pay, and have frequently to move about, from the payment of tax in respect to one riding animal . . .[39]

In addition, shaykhs who provided detailed lists of the owners of animals within their tribes were granted a remission of 5% on the taxes they collected. In 1903 the government ordered that all shaykhs should receive an equal and fixed percentage of all taxes collected by them '. . . provided the Mudir is satisfied that the Omdas and Sheikhs have performed their regular duties in a satisfactory manner . . .'[40] The government's failure to compensate the *'umdas* and shaykhs for their labours was quite apparent. Certain governors demanded that the remuneration granted to the shaykhs of nomad tribes should be fixed at 20% of the tribute they collected. Even Wingate, who was well aware of the government's financial difficulties, had to agree with his provincial governors that the remuneration of shaykhs was insufficient. *Nāẓirs*, who during the Turco-Egyptian period had been exempted from taxation, and in addition derived numerous benefits from their tribesmen, lost their privileged position under the new regime and received instead a low monthly salary.[41] Hence, they continued to levy internal tribal taxes which were not recognized by the government. Thus *ṭulba* and *fiṭr* were paid by the shaykhs of smaller tribal units to the *nāẓir*, while *ḍayʿa* was levied on clients from other tribes.[42] The government, though fully aware of the situation, failed to rectify it owing to financial considerations. Instead it rewarded its shaykhs by granting them 'Robes of Honour' which could be withdrawn by the governor-general at his discretion. In consequence the authorities hoped to make the tribal leaders part of the administrative establishment without incurring heavy expenses.

The government clearly failed to establish the authority of tribal leaders which was one of its declared aims. The disruption of tribal cohesion and the loss of leadership during the Mahdia made the achievement of this aim extremely difficult. The general impression obtained from reading the provincial reports, as well as the private correspondence and diaries of British officials, is one of confusion. The government constantly claimed to be interested in furthering the independence of tribal leaders, whereas the inspectors and governors undertook an ever increasing share of their responsibilities. Indeed the position of shaykhs had become so degraded that in certain cases slaves were elected by their fellow tribesmen to fill that post. This was based on sound common sense. The shaykh's major duty was to assist in tax collecting and hence he was bound to get into trouble with the government. '. . . A person whom no one cared two straws about was the obvious man to be offered as candidate—or as a sacrifice! Hence a slave was chosen . . .'[43]

> . . . The ambiguous position of the Sudan chiefs had resulted from the assumption that they could be used as part of the administrative hierarchy and still maintain their traditional relationship with their people . . . The attempt in the early days to utilize them as part of the Government's machinery while withdrawing some of their powers had resulted in a chaotic situation . . .[44]

Punitive expeditions

Armed expeditions were a permanent feature of tribal administration throughout Wingate's governor-generalship. They were aimed primarily at subduing turbulent tribes and protecting their tax-paying neighbours. In the frontier areas they had the additional task of fighting against the slave trade and arms runners. The government could not afford to establish military posts in the remote districts of the southern provinces. Hence armed administrative patrols were undertaken by the government in order to demonstrate its power to the tribal population who otherwise would not have known of the government's existence.

During the early years of the Condominium the government was concerned with establishing posts and with opening a way through the *sadd* to the Baḥr al-Ghazāl. Once a semblance of government was established, tribal resistance started, and was soon punished by military expeditions. A minor affray with the Dinka near Rumbek towards the end of 1901, was followed by a more serious conflict with the Agar Dinka, culminating with the murder of Scott-Barbour, a British inspector. Wingate, who at the time was inspecting the While Nile province, ordered the British officer commanding the punitive expedition '. . . to deal without mercy with all those he captures who were present at S.B's [Scott-Barbour] murder . . .'[45] Consequently, '. . . the villages of Sheikhs and headmen implicated were burnt and their cattle and grain confiscated and the men themselves shot when taken, and beyond all doubt found guilty . . .'[46] But, a few months later, the Agar Dinka struck again. They attacked the tribes who had been friendly to the government, burnt their villages and stole their cattle. A new punitive expedition was therefore launched and several more tribesmen were shot. The British officer in charge of the expedition reported optimistically that the Agar Dinka had now become truly friendly to the government.

A similar procedure was followed in the first government expedition against the Nuer in the Fashoda district, in April 1902. The British officer in charge of Fashoda sent a message to Denkur, one of the tribal leaders of the Nuer, that he should come to offer his submission to the new government. When no reply was received, a punitive expedition was undertaken :

> . . . about 250 head of cattle were captured, 400–500 sheep and goats, and about 50 tusks of ivory, which should more than pay all expenses incurred. Estimated value of loot £600 . . . Many of Denkur's villages were burnt . . . he himself must have lost all prestige . . .[47]

Three months later the Nuer retaliated by attacking their neighbours, the Dinka, who had assisted the government. The governor of Fashoda who summed up the results of this expedition wrote :

> . . . The Government has undoubtedly lost rather than gained ground, owing to the unfortunate results obtained by the expedition of Denkur

in April last when the inhabitants fled before the government troops and returned to find their village burnt and cattle vanished . . .[48]

Thus the pattern of southern administration was set and was intensified during the following years. In the years 1903–5 the government sent three punitive expeditions to subjugate the Azande of the Baḥr al-Ghazāl province. In 1905 the mission was finally accomplished. Yambio, the Sultan of the Azande, was killed in battle and the tribe, which had previously been harassed by the army of the Congo Free State, submitted without much resistance. The inevitable result was that the Azande chiefs lost control of their tribe which, in consequence, had to be administered by government officials.[49]

Not all the senior British officials agreed with this policy. Matthews, the governor of the Upper Nile province from 1902–8, advocated peaceful penetration and insisted that '. . . the act of going through the country without molestation of the natives, cannot but appeal to the savage mind . . .'[50] Following the first punitive expedition against the Azande, Matthews insisted that the tactless behaviour of its British commander was largely responsible for the subsequent hostility of the tribe.[51] He also strongly opposed a punitive expedition against the Nuer in 1905, as he insisted that the '. . . hostility of the Nuers to the presence of a British official has been deliberately fabricated by the Dinkas . . .'. Matthews concluded that no armed intervention was necessary in an inter-tribal conflict.[52] He persisted in his views, until he left his province in 1908, and stated in his final report :

> . . . Government is a necessity, of course, if we are to occupy their country, but in some ways it is not an unmixed blessing, therefore one is probably not far wrong in saying that those tribes are best off which have as little of it as possible . . .[53]

A similar policy was advocated in 1906 by the new governor of Baḥr al-Ghazāl. He insisted that unnecessary emphasis had been placed on military expeditions :

> . . . Any further patrolling in the Southern districts, except by an inspector and his escort, is undesirable. We want the people to realize that we have ideas beyond the provision of supplies and carriers . . .[54]

Owen, the governor of Mongalla and a former Sudan agent, held quite different views. He favoured active intervention in tribal and intertribal feuds which he was convinced would '. . . make both peoples happy and contented . . .'[55] His suggestion to undertake a punitive expedition against the Beir tribe in 1908 was, however, vetoed by Wingate owing to lack of funds. When Owen renewed his demand two years later, Wingate stated :

L

> . . . Our policy in the Sudan, which I must insist on being understood by all Governors, who, like yourself, have in their provinces a great deal of non-effectively occupied country, must be never to advance into such unoccupied districts unless you fully intend to stay there, and in the present case . . . I am not yet in a position to effectively occupy the Beir Country . . .[56]

In 1911 Wingate was ready to act. During that year the government had undertaken sixteen military expeditions to enforce its authority. Wingate therefore urged Gorst to sanction a punitive expedition against the Beir tribe who were constantly harassing the tax-paying Dinka. '. . . The only alternative would be to abandon all idea of taking taxes from those tribes we cannot effectively protect . . . The moral effect would be disastrous throughout the Sudan . . .'[57] Owing to difficulties of transport and water supply, nearly a year passed before the government was ready to strike. Wingate decided that the concentration of a large military force '. . . affords an opportunity which should not be let slip for undertaking operations against the Anuaks . . .' who were constantly raiding the tribute-paying Nuer tribe.[58] Consequently the largest military operation since the Wad Ḥabūba revolt was set in motion. The expedition against the Beir was reported by Wingate to have been accomplished—

> . . . with a comparatively small loss of life on their side and a minimum of casualties on ours. In all . . . not more than 200 Beirs have been killed, whilst our casualties, including friendlies, were only 41 . . .[59]

The results of the Anuak patrol were regarded as less satisfactory. The intelligence report stated that the Anuak were encountered on 15 March 1912, and that their villages were captured and burnt. However, in the heavy fighting which took place about fifty officers and N.C.O.s lost their lives. The private correspondence between Wingate, Slatin, and Stack indicated that the expedition was a complete failure. The British commander of the expedition underestimated the force of the Anuak, and consequently did not wait for reinforcements but relied on the support of the Nuer 'friendlies' who were reported to be hostile to the Anuak. However, the Nuer were '. . . not sufficiently civilized to appreciate that point of view . . .' and failed to rally to the patrol's support. A special court of enquiry established that the British commander had not only disobeyed his instructions but had nearly caused a political scandal by infringing the Abyssinian border.[60] On 26 March 1912 the government officially declared peace with the Beir tribe, and decided to establish military control over their district. Wingate noted optimistically that the Beir and Anuak were hereditary enemies '. . . and now that the Beirs can be said to have definitely accepted Government authority, we may make some use of them when we take on the Anuaks . . .'[61]

Despite the obvious shortcomings of punitive expeditions Wingate persisted in his view that they were unavoidable. In the years 1913–14, several expeditions were undertaken against the Dinka and the Nuer and only the beginning of the First World War forced the government to call a halt.

In the northern provinces of the Sudan the system of tribal administration followed different lines. Order was maintained by the government posts and military action was only required on the Darfur border. Turbulent tribes were dealt with by ordinary police measures which in most cases proved quite adequate. But the Nuba Mountains, although part of Kordofan, were dealt with on lines similar to those employed in the south. The first major military operation in the Nuba Mountains took place at Talodi in 1906. On 25 May the Arabs near Talodi killed the Egyptian *ma'mūr* and thirty-eight men at a local dance. According to the official report the main reason for the uprising was the Arabs' dissatisfaction with the government's anti-slavery measures. In the ensuing battle, in which the Nuba *makks* of Kadugli, Jabal Iliri, and Jabal Qadīr fought with the government against the Arabs, seven Arab shaykhs and 120 men were killed and 100 prisoners were taken to El Obeid. The government reinforcements, which arrived after the battle was over, killed another 350 Arabs and took 100 additional prisoners.[62] Wingate who inspected Kordofan shortly after the incident, wrote:

> . . . I cannot but feel that with our pin point garrisons at El Obeid Bara, and Talodi, we are really ruling the vast Kordofan country far more by bluff than by anything else . . . "Yeshurun waxed fat and kicked" can well apply to the majority of Kordofan tribes and we ought to be in a position to deal with them if they kick . . .[63]

A major operation against the Nyima mountains of the Nuba district was undertaken in 1908. This group of hills, which had not been under government control during the Turco-Egyptian period and the Mahdia, was captured by an overwhelming force and the inhabitants were punished severely. Justifying the burning of villages and the destroying of crops, the sub-governor of the Nuba Mountains wrote: '. . . Until such a time as we can enforce the Penal Code the punishment must be collective . . .'[64] The Nyima patrol opened a new period in the Nuba Mountains during which the government relied on punitive expeditions to enforce its authority. Action was taken against the Katla Kidu, Tima, Tira, and Dagig hills during the years 1909–1910. The government's method in one of these expeditions was described by Savile, then governor of Kordofan.

> . . . On finding no opposition we only burned the houses and grain and killed all animals . . . after lunch we went on to a few tukls [huts] we had overlooked in the morning and while finishing off those and killing a few more pigs, we saw some of the friendlies coming up and doing a little looting . . .[65]

At one of the mountains Savile met with opposition. The *Makk* of Tagoi refused to accompany him, whereupon Savile ordered his village to be destroyed. In the resulting battle, the government troops were beaten by the Nubas and were forced to retreat. This incident was a direct result of Savile's lack of knowledge of inter-tribal relations. Nevertheless Wingate decided that punishment was essential, and entrusted the expedition to Asser, his adjutant-general. A severe battle took place in which many prisoners were taken. The *Makk* of Tagoi, who succeeded in escaping, was eventually caught and executed in April 1911.[66] Both Slatin and Asser condemned the expedition and blamed the British officer in charge of the Nuba Mountains as being responsible for the unnecessary bloodshed. Asser wrote: '. . . I do not think that such a notoriously bloodthirsty medal hunter as Vickery is the type of man to look after and guide such people as the Nubas . . .'[67] Slatin commented: '. . . The whole Tagoi Expedition is regrettable it was provoked by Bimb. Vickery . . . and could by careful management have been avoided . . .'[68] Nonetheless, similar expeditions were undertaken in the following years. In 1911 five punitive patrols were sent against the Nuba Mountains. Villages and crops were burnt, cattle was confiscated, and many prisoners were taken. A major battle extending for over two months, took place in 1914, when over 5,000 Nubas fought against the government troops before they surrendered. With the outbreak of the First World War Wingate reluctantly decided to postpone further action until the conclusion of hostilities.[69] The only major military action during the War was an expedition against Fiki 'Alī, one of the Nuba *makks*, who rebelled against the government in 1915. By the end of that year the preparations for the conquest of Darfur absorbed all the government's resources, and punitive expeditions against the tribes had to be postponed.[70]

While punitive expeditions were aimed primarily at demonstrating the government's authority and collecting taxes, one of their most disturbing features was the compulsory drafting of prisoners into the army. This was yet another sphere in which the Anglo-Egyptian authorities followed in the footsteps of their Turco-Egyptian and Mahdist predecessors. Or as defined in an article published by the

Anti-Slavery Society in 1902: '. . . it isn't war that they wage in Africa; what is there carried on is nigger hunting . . .'[71]

Following the reconquest many of the old Sudanese soldiers had to be released from the Egyptian army, and were settled in colonies. Despite the mass recruiting which took place both from the ranks of the Mahdist *jihādīya* and from amongst the liberated slaves, there was a constant demand for more recruits. The situation was further aggravated by Wingate's policy of replacing Egyptian units by those composed of Sudanese. Hence provincial governors were instructed to do their utmost to obtain as many recruits as possible.[72] But as volunteers apparently did not supply the required numbers, recruiting became an essential adjunct of the punitive expeditions. One of the major hunting grounds was in the Nuba Mountains where punitive expeditions became very frequent after 1908. Following one of those expeditions, Slatin wrote: '. . . Today arrived over 100 Nuba prisoners; men and boys who were taken from the Kattla and Tirra mountains and will be enlisted as soldiers—all in a pitable [sic] state . . .'[73] It seems that the number of prisoners to be recruited was even taken into account when planning an expedition. Following the patrol against the Beir and Anuak, Asser complained to Wingate: '. . . I find that owing to our expectation of obtaining prisoners from the Annuaks and Beirs not being realized, we are some 3,000 Sudanese short . . .'[74] In 1913 Asser suggested the imposition of a levy of men on some of the southern tribes:

> . . . I see the Nuers and Shilluks have had a scrap. Would it not be a good opportunity to help recruiting by making the Nuers produce a similar number of men to what they killed and hand them over to the Army? It would be a good way of introducing them to the idea of a levy of men . . .[75]

There can be no doubt that these methods of recruiting had a bad effect on the standard of the army as well as on the attitude of the tribes to the idea of voluntary recruiting. Analysing the massive desertion from Sudanese units in 1915, Colonel Drake, the new adjutant-general, wrote that the compulsory recruiting of prisoners and undesirables was largely to blame.[76]

The failure of punitive expeditions was clearly stated by two Anglo-Sudanese officials who served as inspectors during Wingate's governor-generalship. Willis, who became director of intelligence in 1920, defined the government's tribal policy in the south as '. . . administration by raids . . .':

> . . . It is not surprising if the natives could detect but little difference between the old Turkish, the Dervishes, and the Sudan Government.

> They all raided, but the last was not interested in slaves but took cattle only and was possibly more efficient in the methods of getting them . . .

It was only after the First World War that '. . . a return was made to the old plan of peaceful penetration but under circumstances far more difficult . . .'[77] A similar view was taken by Gillan, who had served in Kordofan since 1910: '. . . The success or otherwise of the administration was judged largely in terms of "patrols" and few other questions were asked . . .' He also criticized the use of 'friendlies' in punitive expeditions as '. . . the looting and cruelty committed by undisciplined friendlies usually lead to subsequent recriminations and suspicions which take years to die down . . .' Finally, Gillan warned against the burning of villages and the confiscation of cattle, which punished the innocent but allowed the ringleaders to prepare for the next round.[78]

CHAPTER IX

Land-settlement and Taxation

DURING the later years of the Khalifa's rule the Sudan was struck by continuous famine. Many of the cultivators of the Gezira, the most fertile part of the country, were partially expropriated to make room for the Baqqāra immigrants. Agriculture was not only over taxed, but also ravaged by the ill-disciplined and starving Mahdist soldiers. The immediate resumption of cultivation was essential both economically and politically, and was regarded by the authorities as the best guarantee for peace. To achieve this, cultivators had to be assured that the ownership of their lands would not be challenged by the new authorities. Furthermore, land speculators had to be warned not to purchase land from its previous owners who had fled from the Sudan during the Mahdia and whose claims of ownership could not be acknowledged without evicting the present cultivators. A Khedivial decree was therefore promulgated in April 1897, which provided for the compulsory registration of titles.[1]

Agricultural land-settlement

Following the reconquest, Kitchener proclaimed that no land sales would be recognized without a valid title. This proclamation, which set out to protect the native landowners from foreign speculators, remained one of the guiding principles of the government's land policy. The second principle regarding land-settlement was proclaimed in the *Title to Lands Ordinance 1899*. It ordered that continuous possesssion of lands during the five years preceding the date of claim '. . . shall create an absolute title as against all persons . . .' It further stated that any person who claimed to have been dispossessed of his land during the Mahdia would have to supply ample proof as to his title. Finally, in default of the two previous conditions, '. . . continuous possession since the re-establishment of the civil authority shall create a prima facie title . . .'[2] Thus the government in its desire to resume cultivation and to avoid any further dislocation of the inhabitants recognized the legal validity of titles which were acquired during the Mahdia. In the following years further legislation was undertaken. The *Land Acquisition Ordinance 1903* enabled the government to take possession of any land which was '. . . likely to be needed for any public purpose . . .' Compensation was to be settled by the provincial governors by '. . . a friendly agreement with the person interested . . .' Failing agreement, a commission of three members, two of whom were to be appointed by the governor, was empowered to settle the dispute. Accordingly, in the following years, the government took possession of lands required for development in many towns and rural districts of the Sudan. The land acquisition orders were published in the *Sudan Gazette* and contained the names of the landowners and the size of their respective plots of land.[3]

Until 1905, no mention of government lands was made in any of the ordinances dealing with landownership. '. . . It seems to have been assumed that the Government had an inherent power of disposition over any land in which no private claims had been proved . . .'[4] In 1905 the government promulgated an ordinance for the settlement of rights over waste forest and unoccupied lands. According to this ordinance the government was deemed the legal owner of all lands and forests which were '. . . entirely free from any private rights or that the rights existing . . . do not amount to full ownership . . .' Should the government decide to develop these lands '. . . The Governor-General may compulsorily expropriate all private rights . . . existing in or over such lands . . .'[5] In 1905 further action was taken against the unauthorized sale of lands. Phipps, the civil secretary, warned Wingate that Greek speculators were buying land in the Gezira for as little as P.T.40 a *jad'a*.[6] The government therefore forbade the selling of lands without the written consent of the provincial governors, and declared that all sales to which such consent was not given would be regarded as null and void. Prospective buyers were ordered to apply only to the provincial governors or to the director of agriculture and lands.[7] These orders were slightly modified in the years 1906–8, when the government decided to recognize sales of land in the province of Khartoum which had been concluded prior to the publication of the 1905 order. It also enabled cultivators to sell or mortgage their rights in *buqr* lands without prejudicing the ownership of the government over such lands.[8]

The underlying motive of all these orders was to expand cultivation while safeguarding the inhabitants' rights and encouraging the formation of a Sudanese proprietory class. All lands which were regularly cultivated were regarded as *mulk* and the full rights of their owners were recognized and guaranteed. However, lands which depended for their cultivation on high floods or rains, as well as forests and waste lands, were deemed to belong to the government who could expropriate the cultivators when such lands were required for development. In 1911, Kitchener declared that all the lands in the Sudan were *Kharājīya*, thus aiming to provide the government with yet another safeguard against the alienation of lands.[9] The Sudan government had three major advantages in dealing with land-settlement. It was not hampered by the capitulations which had obstructed land legislation in Egypt and other parts of the Ottoman Empire. Furthermore, most of the cultivable lands were owned by small-holders, and the problems of large estates did not exist. Lastly, *waqf* existed only in a small measure and thus a major difficulty was avoided.

The *Title of Lands Ordinance 1899* provided for the appointment of special commissions in the various provinces and districts in order to determine the ownership of lands within their jurisdiction. These commissions were appointed by the governor-general and consisted of three commissioned officers of the Egyptian army and of two Sudanese notables. Landowners could not appeal to any higher authority against the commission's decisions. However, the commissions were empowered to reconsider a case if a petition was presented within six months of its original decision.[10] The presidents of most of these commissions were British officers and inspectors, and its Sudanese members were generally the shaykhs of the most powerful tribes within its areas of jurisdiction. Parallel to the work of these commissions, a cadastral survey and a registration of title deeds was undertaken in the agricultural districts, while forests and wastelands were treated as a separate category and entrusted to specially appointed 'Settlement Officers'. The work of all these commissions was under the general supervision of the legal secretary who defined their tasks as follows: . . . The settlement of all disputes as to land. The establishment of all titles on a basis of certainty, and the registration of the same. The ascertainment and registration of the rights of the Government to land. Where land is subject to tax the provision of an equitable basis for taxation . . .[11]

In order to achieve these aims the government had to overcome numerous problems which were described by several government officials responsible for land-settlement during that period.[12] In the first few years the settlement officers were concerned primarily with the ownership of *sāqiya* and other lands which were cultivated regularly. Ownership was determined according to continuous cultivation for a period of two to five years, while those who could prove legal ownership but had not cultivated the land during the past few years were compensated with land elsewhere. The ownership of lands that could only be cultivated during the years of exceptional rains or floods was far more difficult to determine. These lands were usually claimed on a tribal basis and there was rarely any documentary evidence to prove ownership. Where valid titles existed they derived from the Funj sultans, the Turco-Egyptian authorities, or the Mahdist state. In the Singa district of the province of Sennar the majority of landownership claims were based on titles acquired during the Funj Sultanate. The tribal leaders who held most of these titles were regarded as the unchallenged owners of these lands, and were duly acknowledged as such first, by the Turco-Egyptians and subsequently by the Mahdist and Anglo-Egyptian authorities. Over the years many of these lands had been subdivided amongst the individual members of the tribe, or were reassigned to other tribes and individual *fakīs*. In the Masalamīya district of the Gezira, titles which were acquired during the Turkiya or the Mahdia had greater weight than those of the Funj Sultanate and were regarded as ample proof when put forward in claiming ownership. In the majority of cases, however, claims were based on oral evidence. In Sennar, the presence of *Makk* 'Adlān, a direct descendant of the Funj Sultans, enabled the government officials to rely on his information. In the Blue Nile province land ownership was based largely on inheritance. In the majority of cases the land inherited was not divided according to the *Sharīʿa*, but was partitioned amongst the heirs by common consent. The registration of titles of inherited land depended on oral evidence as there was generally no documentary proof. Other claims of landownership were based on purchase, dowries, gifts, and continuous cultivation. In cases of dispute the settlement officer '. . . registers the land in the name of the person who appears to be the right owner . . . and directs the other party, if not satisfied with the registration, to petition the Settlement Officer . . .'[13]

A different approach was adopted for uncultivated lands in which native rights were recognized. The settlement officer was ordered to '. . . liquidate those native rights on the spot, and give in land . . . such compensation as he considers desirable, leaving the remainder of the land to be registered to Government free of rights . . .'[14] The inevitable result was that the government commissions were overwhelmed with petitions. In 1906 there were 1,323 petitions dealing with land-settlement in the Shandī district of Berber alone, while many other petitions were directed to the governor-general. Bonham Carter admitted that many of these petitions were the result of mistakes in the early years. He further blamed the many irregular and unrecorded sales which continued despite government orders. Finally he ordered that many of the disputed cases should in future be referred to the *Sharīʿa* Courts and not be left to the sole discretion of the settlement officers.[15]

The area of privately owned land and the size of individual plots varied between the different provinces. Most of the lands in the Kassala province belonged to the government, while lands in the Gezira were mostly privately owned. The average size of individual holdings in the Gezira was 25 feddans, and each plot had to be registered separately. By 1913, the cadastral survey of over 2,300,000 feddans in the Gezira was completed. The ownership of these lands was divided between the government and about 40,000 individual owners.[16] In the province of Khartoum the average size of land-holdings was 15 feddans for *sāqiya* lands and 55 feddans for *buqr* lands. In Dongola and Ḥalfā individual shares in land and date trees were often so small that the governor of Dongola proposed '. . . to compel small shareholders to sell to larger . . .'[17]

In the southern provinces and in the Nuba Mountains land-settlement was not undertaken during this period. Disputes concerning land were adjusted on a tribal basis either by agreement or administrative decision. In Kordofan the only land-settlement undertaken until 1916, was that of El Obeid and Dueim. Nearly all other lands were either owned by tribes or by the government and the few disputes that arose were settled according to local custom. In the district of Bara, where many claims to private land were put forward by members of the riverain tribes, they were recognized whenever supported by valid evidence.

In the years 1907–11 land registration was completed in most of the agricultural districts of the Sudan. Motivated by its desire to increase cultivation and to establish a contented class of small landowners, the government recognized the cultivators as owners and divided tribal lands into individually held plots. By 1912, many of the uncultivated lands which had been given up by their owners owing to the introduction of a progressive land-tax were being reclaimed by their previous owners; '. . . A proof of their increased means of cultivation . . .'[18]

The anti-speculative measures which had been introduced since 1899 were not applied to what the government regarded as reliable capitalist companies which in turn were urged to undertake the development of uncultivated lands. But private enterprise failed to respond; most of the foreign companies who applied lacked the necessary capital, and thus until the end of the First World War, the majority of development projects were undertaken by the government itself.[19] The one notable exception was the Sudan Experimental Plantation Syndicate which was founded by an American, Leigh Hunt, in 1904. The syndicate received a concession of 10,000 feddans at Zeidab, near the confluence of the Atbara with the Nile. It was this company which, under its new name 'The Sudan Plantation Syndicate', undertook the Gezira development project after the First World War.[20]

While capitalist companies failed to respond to the government's appeals, land sales to private speculators flourished despite the government's regulations. There were a number of reasons why the government failed to enforce its policy: firstly, the land in question was in the main privately owned and in many cases sold without government permission; secondly, once the registration of titles was completed the government had no power to stop sales; and lastly, while some of the governors adhered to the regulations, others adopted a more flexible attitude. In 1906 Cromer warned Wingate '. . . that the manufacture of false native claims was going on at a great rate, the Greeks being the instigators . . . We must not allow ourselves to be "done" in the presumed interests of the natives, but in the real interests probably of the Greeks . . .'[21] It was however difficult to stop local landowners from selling, while the sale of government lands was advertised in the *Sudan Gazette* and lands were sold freely to willing bidders.[22] It was not long before some of the Greek merchants commenced buying lands in the Gezira from local landowners. Angello Capato, one of the biggest Greek merchants in the Sudan '. . . purchased about 20,000 feddans in Kamlin mostly from the Habuba family and amongst others from Abd El Kader . . .'[23] Altogether, the resulting alienation of lands did not reach considerable proportions as there was more land for sale than willing purchasers. Moreover, the government refused to register the sold lands. Consequently, when, in 1908, the Sudan was hit by an economic depression, many of the speculators had to sell at a loss, while others, who could not prove their ownership, were declared bankrupt. In the case of Angello Capato, whose liabilities amounted to £E 230,000, Lord Grenfell,[24] chairman of the Bank of Egypt, intervened personally and asked the government to register Capato's lands in the Gezira. This request was turned down by Bonham Carter, on the ground that it was impossible to register purchases of unsurveyed and unsettled land. In a private letter to Wingate, Bonham Carter added that the lands purchased by Capato were '. . . cultivated by permanent tenants . . . and it is doubtful whether it would be advisable to allow these tenancy lands to get into the hands of foreigners . . .'[25]

Aided by the economic depression, the Sudan government succeeded in checking land speculation in the Gezira, which was destined to become the country's major economic asset. In 1914 the government declared that no sales of land in the Gezira which occurred after 1 July 1905 would be recognized as valid. Furthermore, the right to purchase or lease lands in the Gezira was henceforth vested in the government. The government had similar powers to determine prices '. . . without taking into consideration any increase in the value of land . . .'[26] This policy was bitterly criticized by *al-Ahrām* arguing that it was '. . . absurd to deprive the Egyptian of the right to possess land which he watered with his blood . . .'[27] Similar articles appeared in other Egyptian papers. However, the government maintained its policy despite the criticism.

Urban land-settlement

In his annual report for 1899 Cromer wrote that the treatment of urban property presented relatively few problems as compared with landownership in rural districts. Many of the towns had been reduced to ruins during the Mahdia and the reconquest, while others were sparsely populated. Of the major towns only Omdurman and Suakin had a considerable population, whilst Khartoum, Berber, Dongola, and El Obeid were ruined and largely deserted. Legislation for the ownership of town lands was initiated shortly after the reconquest, in all probability prompted by the government's desire to affect rapid urban development. The *Town Lands Ordinance 1899* provided for the '. . . settling of landownership in Khartoum, Berber, and Dongola and for laying out and rebuilding the above towns . . .' It authorized the government to obtain any land it required, either by purchase or by exchange, thus enabling the new towns to be planned without interference from property owners. Landowners were ordered to erect buildings conforming to the '*tanẓīm* regulations', within two years.[28] All lands which were not allotted to private owners, or whose owners failed to comply with the building regulations, were to '. . . become and be the absolute property of the Government . . .'[29] In March 1902, landowners in Khartoum were reminded that the time within which they had to erect buildings on their land expired at the end of 1902. A year later Wingate reported that most of the landowners had complied with the building regulations.[30]

In 1904 the *Towns Lands Ordinance* was extended to Kassala, al-Qaḍārif, Dueim, and El Obeid, where land-settlement commissions had been functioning for some time. The town lands commissions, which were composed of a president, two officers, and two notables, functioned in a similar way to the rural land commissions. The building regulations were henceforth applied to all major towns and in 1907 several landowners lost their lands, having failed to comply with the regulations. In Ḥalfā, landowners who wanted to build had to present a petition to the governor in order to confirm that the land was in fact theirs. In 1909 the 'Town Building Regulations' were announced. They included detailed instructions as to the type of buildings allowed for each class of land and laid down sanitary regulations. Land-holders had to apply to the municipal authorities or to the provincial governor to obtain a building permit.[31] Special ordinances were promulgated for the settlement of town lands in Suakin, Omdurman, and Khartoum North. *The Suakin Land Ordinance* was promulgated in 1904. It provided for the proof of titles by five years consecutive possession and its land-settlement commission consisted of only three members.[32] The lands of Omdurman, unlike those of other towns, were regarded as government property ever since the reconquest. In 1906 the government changed its policy and decided to allocate lands to all genuine claimants who were present at the time of the fall of Omdurman. The sub-governor of Omdurman was ordered to act as commissioner in hearing the cases and in deciding which claims were to be recognized.[33] The *'Hillet Hamid (Khartoum North) Village Lands Ordinance'* was promulgated in 1909. It provided for the appointment of a settlement officer whose decision on claims was to be final, subject only to the approval of the governor-general.[34] The most notable difference between the land ordinance applied to Omdurman and Khartoum North, and those of other towns, was that the inhabitants of the former towns were not represented on the settlement commissions which consisted of a single British official.

Town surveys of Khartoum, Khartoum North, Omdurman, and Port Sudan were begun only in 1906. A year later the *Deeds Registration Ordinance* ordered the registration of '. . . every sale, gift, mortgage or other disposition . . .' The legality of the transaction could be proved by a document signed and sealed in the presence of a witness, or by a *Sharī'a* court.[35] Finally, in 1912 *The Government Town Lands (Native Occupation) Ordinance* was enacted. It enabled governors '. . . to set apart Government land near towns as sites on which natives may squat and erect dwellings . . .' It also provided for compensation in the event of the occupiers being turned out of their sites. The governor was entitled to order the vacation of these sites without stating his reasons, and the compensation of the inhabitants was left to the governor's discretion.[36] In 1913 government lands occupied by the Sudanese in Khartoum, Khartoum North, El Obeid, and Dueim, were declared 'Native Lodging Areas'. Consequently, the labourers who had built Khartoum, and who had lived on the land allotted to them since 1899, became government tenants who could be evicted at a month's notice.[37]

In its desire to effect the rapid development of Khartoum as the country's new capital the government sought the co-operation of private enterprise. Government and private lands were sold freehold '. . . for trifling sums to the Greek traders . . . and much of the most valuable land in the new city, passed thus at once into the hands of a few wealthy capitalists . . .'[38] A similar policy was adopted in other towns, but owing to lack of demand only a few plots of land were sold. It was only in 1905 that the government decided to change its policy, and to stop the sale of government lands in Khartoum. The inevitable result was that prices soared, and land speculators who had bought a plot for £E 30 could now sell it for £E 1000. Wingate explained away the new policy on the grounds that it raised the price of privately owned lands. The governor of Khartoum regarded the increased prices as a good sign for the future development of the city.[39] It is quite clear that the government, which had by that time sold most of its land in Khartoum at very low prices, lost a considerable source of income. In 1906 the government tried to amend its losses by acquiring 1,217 feddans near Khartoum, under the *Land Acquisition Ordinance*. The land was intended for the future expansion of Khartoum and was known as the 'Morgan Scheme'. In 1908 the government abandoned its development. Land prices in Khartoum had decreased considerably as a result of the economic crisis in Egypt, and the scheme had lost its *raison d'être*.[40]

When prospects for the expansion of existing towns and the development of new ones became apparent, the government decided not to sell its lands and adopted the leasehold system. In 1905 all the lands at El Damer were bought by the government '. . . in anticipation of the development of this town, which is situated close to the junction of the Nile–Red Sea Railway . . .' A year later it was reported optimistically that, '. . . the leasehold system adopted at El Damer and Atbara . . . has proved an unqualified success and may well be a forerunner of a general introduction of this anti-speculation method of dealing with town lands . . .'[41] Following the government's decision to establish the Sudan's major port at Shaykh Barghūt (Port Sudan), an investigation was undertaken in order to decide the most suitable land policy for the new town. Wingate, and most of the senior British officials, favoured the leasehold system, which would guarantee the government's ownership of the town's lands. Cromer favoured the outright sale of lands which, he hoped, would provide the necessary funds for the development of Port Sudan. He agreed, however, that the leasehold system be adopted for a trial period of two years.[42] By July 1907 it became clear that the new system had failed. The prospective lessees, of Greek and Egyptian origin, disliked the leasehold system as it prevented them from raising money or speculating. British investors were also reluctant to take leases as they included a clause enabling the government, in case of bankruptcy, to take possession of the lease and all the buildings erected on it without paying compensation.[43] In 1908 Bernard, the financial secretary, suggested abandoning the leasehold system and selling the lands as freehold. Despite the opposition of Wingate and the majority of the senior officials, Gorst ordered that '. . . some plan be devised by which these lands can be bought outright or leased as the public prefer . . .'[44] Thus, what came to be known as 'the combined leasehold-freehold system' came into being. Government lands were offered for sale and the rents procured were lowered considerably. The director of agriculture and lands reported that, owing to the modified terms, eighteen new leases were granted in Port Sudan while not a single plot of land was sold.

> . . . It is clear therefore that there is . . . no public desire to acquire freehold land at Port Sudan . . . except on the part of the speculator . . . The leasehold system is not unpopular with the class of person really wanted at Port Sudan viz. the person who will live and work there . . .[45]

Nonetheless, the new system prevailed and when in 1910 a similar problem arose in Omdurman, the governor-general's council adopted the 'mixed leasehold freehold system' despite strong opposition from many senior British officials. The principal opposers were Currie and Bonham Carter who argued that it was essential that the government should maintain its control over the lands of the major native town in the Sudan. Slatin, however, was against leaseholds, which he regarded as being unpopular amongst the inhabitants. He further argued that any native landowner '. . . is the best and cheapest intelligence agent to the Government . . .' In March 1910, the governor-general's council decided that, '. . . Town lands including market lands should be offered either for sale or lease at the option of the grantee . . .', thereby extending the new system over all the town lands of the Sudan.[46]

The government's land policy, despite the mistakes of the early years, was on the whole successful. By recognizing the rights of private ownership in both rural and urban districts the government effected a rapid increase in cultivation and in urban development. By the end of Wingate's governor-generalship the bulk of the country's land was owned by its inhabitants and by the government. Although speculation and the alienation of lands caused deep concern in the early years, speculators were deterred by the government's policy which was aided by the effects of the economic crisis in Egypt.

Taxation

The principle of light taxation was laid down by Cromer in 1899, when he assured the people of the Sudan that the system of taxation would be similar to that of other Muslim countries. In his first annual report on the Anglo-Egyptian Sudan Cromer elaborated his views:

> . . . On going through the list of the taxes which were collected under the Khalifa's rule, it was found that, although the manner in which they had been levied was cruel and extortiate to the last degree, they were based on principles which are generally recognized in all Moslem countries . . . No radical change of system, was, therefore, necessary . . .[47]

Thus a system of taxation evolved which was largely based on that of the Khalifa, which in turn was not unlike the system of the Turco-Egyptian Sudan. The principle taxes which were levied by the new administration included land-tax, *'ushr*, date tax and herd tax (later animal tax), all of which were imposed on the sedentary population. Nomads paid an annual tribute based upon an approximate assessment of their cattle, and a royalty was imposed on gum, ostrich feathers, and ivory.

One of the first problems to be faced by the new administration was whether a taxpayer belonged to his tribal unit or to the district and province in which he resided. Following Slatin's advice it was decided that '. . . sedentary natives, although from different tribes, belong always to the district in which they are living; nomad Arabs, always to their tribe, although living or grazing in different districts . . .'[48] A second problem was the definition of a nomad tribe. The importance of this definition lay in the fact that nomads paid only tribute, while sedentaries were taxed more heavily. The government's decision in each case depended only partly on the nomadic character of the tribes. Certain tribes in Kordofan, as well as in the southern provinces, paid tribute despite their being partly sedentary. This was done owing to the lack of government officials, who were required in order to impose the more complex sedentary taxes.

The principle of preserving a low rate of taxation was adhered to until 1912. Cromer regarded this as one of the major contributions towards the success of the British administration in the Sudan. Wingate, who was constantly urged to increase taxation, both by the Egyptian press as well as by the mounting financial needs of the Sudan, withstood the pressure largely as a result of Cromer's advice. In 1912 Kitchener decided to withdraw the Egyptian annual subvention which hitherto had enabled Wingate to maintain a low rate of taxation. Consequently taxes had to be raised but, according to Wingate, only by a small margin and '. . . without creating unrest among the inhabitants . . .'[49]

The order promulgating land-tax and date tax was published in May 1899. Land tax was imposed on all irrigable lands the cultivation of which was not dependent upon rainfall. The annual rates of taxation varied between P.T.20–50 per feddan, according to the land's classification and the method of irrigation. The governor-general determined in which districts and provinces the tax was to be levied.[50] In 1899 land-tax was imposed on the province of Dongola and in certain districts of Wādī Ḥalfā and Berber. Khartoum province was brought within the taxation system in 1901–2, and in the following years land-tax was imposed on most of the irrigable lands in the northern provinces. In order to encourage cultivation, landowners erecting irrigation pumps were exempted from land-taxes for the first two years, while those erecting *sāqiyas* were exempted for one year. In 1906 a progressive land-tax was imposed on uncultivated lands in order to induce their owners to commence cultivation. The new tax was to be levied on a quarter of the land after two years, following which the whole plot was to come under taxation within eight to ten years. The progressive land-tax was bitterly resented by most of the cultivators, who failed to understand its logic and many of them abandoned their lands. After a trial period of two years the new tax was therefore abolished.[51]

'Ushr was imposed on all lands depending on rain for their cultivation. It was also levied on irrigable lands which could not be assessed for land-tax owing to lack of detailed information. The assessment and collection of *'ushr* caused a great amount of labour as government officials had to assess the crops before the harvest. Moreover, many of the cultivators preferred to pay their *'ushr* in kind which compelled the government to arrange the required transport. In some of the outlying districts the expenses and labour incurred in transportation exceeded the income derived from *'ushr* and the government decided not to persevere with the tax. Wingate maintained that it was a better policy to accept this loss of revenue rather than embitter the population by demanding payment in money.[52] The preference of the cultivators to pay in kind was probably caused by lack of cash as well as by their fear of being overcharged. The monetary equivalent of *'ushr* was fixed by the government according to the *dhurra* prices at the time of the harvest. However, many cultivators sold their *dhurra* before the harvest to Omdurman merchants at low prices. These merchants were thus in a position to increase the price in the various markets, forcing the cultivators to pay the *'ushr* in prices which were more than double the price paid to them originally. In 1905 it was therefore decided '. . . that no dhurra is to be sold outside a Government market until the assessment of Ushr is completed . . .' By 1908 most of the cultivators were in a position to pay cash, so that the problem was solved without coercion.[53] It was only after 1910 that some of the outlying districts in Kordofan and the Upper Nile provinces were assessed for *'ushr*, while the cultivated lands of the

Baḥr al-Ghazāl and Mongalla were not taxed throughout this period.

While *ʿushr* and a land-tax were promulgated to tax the sedentary population, a herd tax was introduced in 1899 to tax the nomads. Although this tax was supposed to replace the Muslim *zakāh*, (charity tax), which had been levied during the Mahdia, Cromer had his doubts about its efficiency and recommended its early abolition.[54] He was soon to be proved right for the nomad tribes who depended on their herds for their livelihood could only pay the tax by parting with some of their animals. This they refused to do, and instead they withdrew to remote districts, out of reach of government control. Thus the tax, whose principal aim was to tax the nomads, could only be levied on sedentaries who already paid *ʿushr* or land-tax. In August 1901 the herd tax was replaced by two new taxes. Nomads were ordered to pay a yearly tribute which was levied on the tribe as a unit, while sedentaries continued to pay the animal tax. According to the ordinances which were published in the *Sudan-Gazette* both tribute and animal tax had been levied by the Turco-Egyptian authorities and were known as *jizya* and *zakāh,* respectively.[55] The use of the term *jizya*, which was a poll-tax imposed on non-Muslims under Muslim rule, is misleading. Yet it seems that during the Turco-Egyptian rule, *jizya* was levied on the Muslim inhabitants of the Gezira at the rate of P.T. 80 per head.[56] These new taxes, although easier to impose, had their drawbacks. Both the tribute and the animal tax were based on the number of animals as assessed by government officials. But the assessment of nomads' herds was largely based on information supplied by their shaykhs and thus tended to be rather low. The government also feared that nomads would try to evade the tribute and therefore levied it at a lower rate than the animal tax. Finally, tribute was regarded primarily as a political measure and not as a source of income. Inevitably, the result was that the sedentaries attempted to evade the tax by sending their animals to graze with the nomads. Moreover, certain tribes were split between two or more provinces, and while animal tax was levied on one part of the tribe, the other was paying tribute. Consequently, whenever a government inspector came to assess the taxes they crossed the border and joined their fellow tribesmen. A government order published in 1903 tried to overcome this problem by threatening prospective tax evaders with the confiscation of their animals. Evasion, however, continued until an increasing number of tribute-paying tribes were put on to animal tax.[57]

In the southern provinces and the Nuba Mountains only tribute was levied on cattle-owning tribes. The system of assessing the tribute in these inaccessible areas was extremely crude and unreliable. In the Nuba Mountains the amount of tribute levied was, '. . . in inverse ratio to the amount of resistance likely to be incurred in its collection . . . the weak paid and the strong got off free . . .'[58] The same applied to the southern provinces, where tribes like the Nuer or Anuak did not pay any tribute owing to their remoteness from government control, whereas the Shilluk and Dinka had to pay a small tribute from 1902. In 1909, the government decided to impose '. . . a light rain tax, amounting to one-tenth of Government requirements, to be collected from non cattle owning tribes . . .' in the Baḥr al-Ghazāl. Indirect taxation in the southern provinces included an annual requisition of grain for which payment was made below market prices, and a requisition of carriers for government convoys.[59]

While the system of taxation was primarily geared to the agricultural and nomadic population, numerous taxes of lesser importance were imposed on the inhabitants of towns and large villages. A house tax was levied in 1899 at the rate of one-twelfth of the annual rental value. However, very few towns had to pay this tax and even Khartoum and Omdurman were exempt until 1906.[60] It was not until 1913, that a serious effort was made to tax the non-agricultural population probably as a result of the termination of the Egyptian subvention. The *Local Taxation Ordinance 1912* imposed rates on all property owners in the Sudan. Once again the agricultural community was obliged to pay an additional rate amounting to 10% of their *ʿushr* or land tax.[61] Other taxes included a boat tax which was levied according to the boat's carrying capacity. Road tax was levied by provincial governors who exploited the money for road maintenance. Market dues were introduced in 1899. They included fees for the sale of animals, weighing fees, slaughtering fees, and royalties.[62] A trader's tax, introduced by the government in 1913, came under heavy criticism and had to be modified. This was perhaps the first time that the government had to give way under the pressure of public opinion and the local press. As most of the traders concerned were Greeks and Egyptians, the support they received from the Greek-owned *Sudan Herald* was hardly surprising.[63]

The assessment and collection of all taxes was performed mainly by government officials. This was laid down by Kitchener in his instructions to governors and inspectors and was enunciated further in numerous government orders. The system of registering the land tax was copied from Egypt but soon proved too complicated and detailed for the small number of clerks available in each district. Even tribute, which should have been collected without any government assistance was in fact collected with the active participation of Egyptian and British officials.[64] By the end of Wingate's governor-generalship an elaborate system of taxation had evolved, largely based on the system prevailing in other Muslim countries. The agricultural population contributed the larger share of revenue derived from taxation, while nomads and town dwellers continued to be under-taxed.

CHAPTER X

Slavery and Labour

In the early years of the Condominium there was a permanent shortage of labour in the Sudan. This affected development projects as well as agriculture and was intimately connected with the problem of domestic slavery. It was probably this affinity which led the governor-general to entrust both domestic slavery and labour to the intelligence department in Khartoum. Slave raiding and the slave trade were regarded as separate entities. According to the Anglo-Egyptian Slave Trade Convention of August 1877, slave trade from the Sudan was to have stopped by 1880. Owing to the Mahdia, the implementation of this convention in the Sudan had to be deferred until the reconquest. A new convention for the Suppression of Slavery and Slave-Trade, was signed between Great Britain and Egypt in November 1895. Under Article 2 of this convention, Egypt undertook to publish a special law enumerating the penalties to be applied for offences connected with slave trade. Such a law was published by the Egyptian government in January 1896. Shortly after the reconquest, in January 1899, slave trade in the Sudan was declared illegal and its suppression became the duty of the department for the repression of slave trade.

The department for the repression of slave trade

The principles guiding the Sudan government's policy towards slavery were formulated by Lord Cromer in 1899, when he affirmed that domestic slavery would be tolerated by the new administration. This was based on the assumption that the anti-slavery measures undertaken in the Turco-Egyptian Sudan were largely responsible for the Mahdi's success. It is in the light of these beliefs that the subsequent relationship between the Sudan government and the slavery-repression department may be better understood.

The slavery-repression department was under the direction of the Egyptian ministry of the interior until the end of 1910. Its task was to abolish slave raids and to suppress the slave traders. At the time of the reconquest there were not less than 15,000 men employed in the slave trade. The first aim was to stop the exportation of slaves outside the Sudan borders and an order to that effect was published in 1901.[1] Despite the regulations, slave trade continued, especially across the Red Sea to Arabia and through the Abyssinian border. In 1902 a considerable number of Sudanese children and adults were abducted in Dongola and in the Gezira and smuggled to Arabia. Further cases were reported in Suakin and Kassala in 1904. On the Abyssinian border the slave trade was even more difficult to control. The border divided the Anuak tribe between the two countries, and constant raids on the Sudanese section of the tribe provided Abyssinia with an annual supply of slaves. Another source of slaves was the Nuba Mountains where slave raiding was practised both by the Arab tribes and by the Nubas and continued throughout Wingate's governor-generalship.

The main supply of slaves did not come from within the Sudan. Slaves were imported from the French Congo by the *jallāba* who usually stated that they had married the women-slaves whom they imported, or that the slaves were presents from the sultans.[2] The route into the Sudan passed through the western district of Baḥr al-Ghazāl, where vast uninhabited areas made control virtually impossible without considerable forces. Slaves were also smuggled into the Sudan by 'Alī Dīnār's emissaries and were sold in Omdurman market, with Wingate's approval and despite the protests of the department for the repression of slavery.[3] The main route for smuggling slaves was by way of the pilgrimage from Western Africa to Mecca which passed through the Sudan.[4] Owing to the length of the Sudanese borders and the scarcity of border patrols, this movement, which accounted for 90% of all Sudanese pilgrims, could not be controlled. The Fallāta either brought the slaves with them or obtained them in the Sudan, and then took them across to Arabia. Despite all government precautions, the pilgrims could cross the border into Eritrea and thus avoid control. Others sailed to Jedda from Suakin, and were obliged to pay a deposit at the government's quarantine. In the years 1909–1913 over three thousand pilgrims failed to return to the Sudan and many of them were probably sold as slaves.[5]

Thus, in the sphere of slave trade, where the authority of the department for the repression of slavery was unchallenged, it succeeded in reducing the trade but could not stop it. This was partly the result of inadequate means and the vast areas it had to control. However, the main reason for the continuation of slave trade was the demand for slaves in the Arabian peninsula and the high remuneration offered. The department's greater success in suppressing slave raiding was largely due to the extension of administrative control and to the greater risks involved in the raids.

Yet the fact that in 1914 slavery was again on the increase is a clear proof that it was not completely uprooted, and that a more fundamental change in economic and social outlook was necessary in order to overcome it.

The organization of the department for the repression of slave trade was unique in that its headquarters remained in Cairo although its centre of activities was in the Sudan. Moreover, Captain McMurdo, the director of the department until 1910, was not under the supervision of the governor-general of the Sudan. As an official of the Egyptian ministry of the interior he reported to the British consul-general in Egypt. Wingate included comments on slavery in his own yearly memorandum, but no report from the slavery department was printed among the departmental reports of the Sudan government, throughout Wingate's governor-generalship. In some cases Wingate did not receive even a copy of McMurdo's reports. The department appointed its own inspectors who set up posts throughout the country, assisted by their own mounted police and camel corps. They could make arrests and issue warrants without reference to the local authorities. In 1902 the department launched its own stern wheeler 'Liberator', to control slave traffic on the upper reaches of the Nile.[6]

In 1905, the department was reorganized and its police force was divided into three parts with their headquarters at El Obeid, al-Ruṣayriṣ, and Khartoum. Its legal position *vis-à-vis* the Sudan government was defined so as to link it more closely to the Sudan administration and to avoid unnecessary clashes. The department's police force was hence-forward considered part of the Sudan police and its inspectors became ex-officio magistrates of the second class. They were also entitled to give orders to *ma'mūrs* and police officers in connection with slavery cases. On the other hand the provincial governors could make recommendations to the inspectors of the slavery-repression department and represent their views to the department's headquarters at Khartoum. Lastly, all the department's reports had to be forwarded through the governor-general.[7]

Despite these organizational reforms clashes between government officials and the staff of the slavery department were frequent and covered almost every sphere of the department's activities. McMurdo explained the strained relations by the fact that his department functioned as an independent body within the Sudan. He further claimed that owing to Slatin's unique authority over everything connected with slavery: '. . . his [McMurdo's] point of view does not get a fair hearing . . .'[8] Despite a certain element of truth, this was an oversimplification of the issue. Basically, the antagonism was over matters of policy. Wingate regarded the religious and tribal revolts in the Gezira and the Nuba Mountains as a direct result of the slavery department's efforts '. . . to pander to Exeter Hallism in endeavouring to suppress slave hunting and slave trading . . .'[9] As for domestic slavery '. . . any attempt on the part of the slavery department to interfere . . . will provide hundreds of Abdel Kaders before long, and I am afraid that our friend [McMurdo] is about the most injudicious person in Egypt or the Sudan . . .'[10] Wingate regarded it as his duty to convince the British government to follow his policy regarding slavery, rather than McMurdo's '. . . which if persisted in may lose us the Sudan . . .' He concluded that '. . . M. [McMurdo] has no case and if he plays up to Exeter Hall and a Radical Government, the sooner we come to a full and complete understanding, the better . . .'[11] Wingate and Slatin wanted the suppression of slave-trade to be modified according to administrative requirements. An independent department that followed a policy based on a convention between Britain and Egypt, and was not under the control of the Sudan government, was therefore clearly undesirable. It is only in the light of these views that the friction between the Sudan government and the slavery-repression department can be understood.

A suggestion to establish a home for freed slaves in Omdurman was rejected by Wingate on the grounds '. . . that the time has not yet come when we can establish in the Sudan anything in the shape of Government institutions as a refuge for the escaped slaves . . .' This however, did not stop the provincial governors from establishing homes for freed slaves in their provinces under their own supervision.[12] The same attitude prevailed regarding the establishment of stations in the provinces manned by the staff of the slavery department. The Sudan government could not object openly to these stations, but tried to keep them attached to the government posts to allow control by the provincial inspectors. When the department for the repression of slavery suggested that an independent station of its own in south-east Kordofan should be established, Slatin objected saying '. . . I do not like having posts scattered over mountains. Recoment [sic] that inspector and men should stay at Elliri with our own Mamur and Inspector . . .'[13] Again in 1909 when the slavery department wanted to establish a post on the Darfur border, Savile, the governor of Kordofan, objected strongly, despite the fact that slave trade across the borders was a well known fact.[14]

The antagonism between Wingate and Slatin on the one hand, and McMurdo on the other, was of course well known, even to junior inspectors. It was, therefore, hardly surprising that relations at the lower levels of administration were no better than at the top. The following extract from Willis's diary illustrates the situation in Kordofan :

> . . . *19 February 1910* . . . Whithingham . . . has freed various slaves or rather annexed them . . . is full of nonsense about the Homr and slave dealing and is very much down on Ali Gula. He is doing a lot of harm and is putting the country back . . . *28 March 1910* . . . Slatin immensely pleased over my complaint re S.R.D. [slavery repression department] which I put in to Savile on receipt of Ali Gula's complaint about death of a man arrested by Whithingham. Slatin has his knife into him in a lot of other things . . .[15]

The authorities at Khartoum and Kordofan were well aware that 'Alī Julla, the *nāẓir* of the Misīrīya, was deeply involved in the slave trade. Yet they objected to any interference by the slavery department in what they regarded as an internal, tribal affair. Similarly, when, in 1903, Sayyid al-Makkī's son was imprisoned for slave raiding, Wingate wrote, '. . . I think it would be good policy to let the man out on account of his father's services . . .'[16] There seems to have been general confusion as to the exact functions of the department for the repression of slavery. Domestic slaves were outside its sphere of responsibility. But the exchange of slaves within the Sudan's boundaries was regarded by the department as part of the slave trade. The department also objected to the fact that despite the commitment to abolish domestic slavery gradually, new slaves were a common phenomenon. Many of those who were registered as slaves in 1918, were born to free parents after the Condominium Agreement was signed.[17]

Wingate's aim was to remove McMurdo, and to bring his department directly under the governor-general of the Sudan. He wrote to Gorst that should his suggestion be accepted '. . . there would be no further need for the services of a Director . . .' and that in order to induce McMurdo to leave, a '. . . fairly liberal pension . . .' should be offered to him.[18] By November 1910, the ground was prepared. McMurdo had agreed to retire, and Gorst set about the task of convincing the British government to agree to the new status of the department:

> . . . As regards the effect which this change may be expected to have in the battle . . . against this detestable traffic [in slaves] it is obvious that the exclusively British composition of the present Soudan administration affords greater guarantees than have hitherto been obtainable that this branch of their duties will be prosecuted with the utmost vigour . . .[19]

Following Grey's approval, the staff of the slavery department was transferred to the Sudan civil service and Major Ravenscroft was appointed as its new director. The department was financed, as before, by a special grant from the Egyptian government. It was decided to decrease its activities by absorbing its special police force within the ordinary provincial police. When Ravenscroft resigned in 1914, Wingate decided to amalgamate the remaining staff of the department with the provincial administration and wrote that he would '. . . probably do away with the appointment of a Director . . .'[20] Though the department for the repression of slave trade continued to exist, its functions were so limited, and its control by the government so complete, that no further clashes seem to have occurred in the following years.

Domestic slavery

The toleration of domestic slavery was based on the belief that the Sudan's socio-economic structure could not withstand a sudden abolition of slavery, and that it was bound to cause renewed religious upheavals similar to the Mahdist revolt. Hence the government decided:

> . . . whilst making every effort to suppress slave raiding and slave trafficking . . . deal as gently as possible with questions of domestic slavery . . . [hoping to] . . . gradually transform the status of slavery and substitute for it a system of paid labour . . .[21]

The outcome of this policy was that domestic slaves were in fact urged to stay with their owners unless they were maltreated by them. As late as 1915 inspectors were instructed '. . . to induce runaway servants to return to their masters . . .' They were also informed that in order to free a slave the payment of his ransom had to be completed.[22]

Among the measures introduced by the government to prevent the increase of domestic slaves by illegal trade or slave running was an order obliging all governors to register 'Sudanese servants' within their provinces. In the northern provinces registration was started in 1904 and a year later 19,638 Sudanese servants were registered in Dongola.[23] In parts of Kordofan, Wingate objected to the registration as late as 1915, fearing that it might cause disturbances.[24] The very limited effect which registration had in reducing the numbers of domestic slaves was clearly indicated in a memorandum written by Bonham Carter in 1913:

> . . . In some provinces the rules as to the registration of Sudanese . . . have been ignored. It was ordered that a Register of Sudanese should be made and completed as soon as possible. The object was to prevent the future buying or selling of Sudanese and preventing masters from making claims to domestic slaves who were not in their possession at the time the Register was made. In some Mudirias the Register has been kept open, thus defeating the object of the Register. Cases have come to my notice of children who have been born since the reoccupation being entered on such register . . .[25]

It is apparent that there was a vast discrepancy between the official policy and its realization. Slatin, the government's spokesman on slavery, stated that every slave was free to leave his master should he so desire. Yet as an outspoken supporter of slavery, Slatin did everything in his power in order to return runaway slaves to their masters even if they had to be forced.[26] Similarly, the first governor of Kordofan stated in 1903 '. . . personally I am not a great admirer of the black man at his home and am certain that you see him at his best as a slave or soldier . . .'[27] In consequence, government policy was not fully implemented. Bonham Carter stated that '. . . escaped slaves are dealt with on no principle. Decisions are given which are not only contrary to the British policy as regards slavery, but which cannot be justified by Mohammedan Law . . .'[28] In certain cases even free-born men and women, who were enslaved after the reconquest, had to pay ransom before being freed. The governor of Kordofan reported that *Makk Geili*, of the Nuba Mountains, had captured many free people from the Khalifa who now claimed their freedom. '. . . in previous individual cases I have allowed persons claiming their free born relatives to have them on payment of 4–5 rials M., the assumed average price of people after the battle of Omdurman . . .' As for legitimately acquired slaves nobody '. . . should be entitled to claim them unless the owner is willing to take compensation offered . . .'[29]

It is therefore, surprising that the Sudan authorities were not subjected to more pressure by the anti-slavery societies in Britain. *The Aborigines' Friend* and the *Anti-Slavery Reporter*, the respective organs of the two anti-slavery societies, hardly referred to the Anglo-Egyptian Sudan until after the First World War. Whatever criticism these societies made was against the slave trade and slave-raiding. Only in 1919 did the 'Anti-Slavery and Aborigines' Protection Society' prepare a comprehensive memorandum on domestic slavery in the Sudan. Its allegations included the following:

> . . . Fugitive slaves are returned by force to their masters . . . The Arab owners of the slaves take their earnings from them when wages have been paid by the employers . . . There are persistent allegations of cruelty to the slaves . . . Slaves who are subjected to cruelty fear to appeal to the Inspectors . . . Slaves are now being mortgaged under a system the full facts of which are not yet available . . .[30]

Apart from the last complaint, all these allegations could be easily verified. Slaves were not only returned by force to their masters, but in certain cases were even brought to the provincial police station in order to be punished. The practice of keeping wage-earning slaves whose remuneration was forwarded to their masters was also widespread. An official of the Sudan railways wrote,

'. . . sometimes a man will come and ask to work . . . Instead of starting to work himself, he produces a big strapping Sudanese, who he says is his slave and will work for him, which the Sudanese does with a most cheerful spirit . . .'[31]

The criminal tendencies of freed slaves were regarded as a major problem since the reconquest. In 1908 Jackson, governor of Dongola, reported on crime in his province :

> . . . The majority of offenders are Sudanese, men and women, who leave their masters on the slightest provocation . . . Many are reduced to want; after being unable to obtain regular employment take, the men to thieving and the women to prostitution. . .[32]

Similar reports came in from other provinces, whose governors were concerned with the problem of public women. These were segregated and regularly examined by medical officers but the problem could not be solved. One of the governors stated rightly that '. . . until public opinion in these matters is influenced . . . no real control is possible . . .'[33] However, when the Anti-Slavery Society offered its help by opening a home for freed female slaves, Cromer refused on the grounds that there was no problem of female slaves in the Sudan. Cromer was reluctant to admit the society's representatives into the country, and preferred to forego the much-required help in dealing with freed female slaves.[34]

In 1919 the Sudan government sent a confidential circular to all government officials enunciating its policy regarding 'Sudanese Servants'. It defined Sudanese servants as '. . . persons who were in a state of slavery or are considered as such by natives . . .'; further, that '. . . every Sudanese servant not under contract had the right to leave his master if he wishes and may not be compelled or persuaded to return against his will . . .' Yet governors and inspectors were instructed to try to reconcile master and slave as '. . . Sudanese servants who have lived many years with their masters are really happier and better off . . .' Furthermore, as it was feared '. . . that Sudanese should through leaving the homes in which they have been brought up . . . take to thieving or prostitution . . .', governors were ordered to apply the regulations regarding the slaves' right of freedom with great care. The circular instructed all governors to keep the registers of Sudanese servants up to date, thereby implying that new slaves could still be registered. Finally, as slavery was not officially recognized by the government, cases between slaves and masters could not be decided according to Islamic laws but were to be judged according to the rules of trusteeship as between master and servant.[35]

Even in this late circular the ambiguous attitude of the government is quite clear. On the one hand it declared the right of every slave to become free, while on the other hand ensuring that as many slaves as possible should remain with their masters. The reasons for this position are clear; public opinion in England and elsewhere in Europe would not have tolerated the outright legalization of slavery, yet the British administrators of the Sudan were aware of the hazards of the complete abolition of slavery, namely, the disruption of the social and economic life of the country together with an increase in crime.

Labour

The most serious objection to the abolition of slavery was voiced by the governors of provinces whose agricultural cultivation required a great deal of man-power. Hundreds of *sāqiyas* were reported idle in Berber, Dongola, and the Blue Nile provinces, owing to the decrease of slaves. Even the Baqqāra tribes of Kordofan were affected, they being too lazy to cultivate by themselves. By and large the British governors, fearing the decrease in cultivation, sympathized with the landowners and did their utmost to induce slaves and free labourers to remain in their provinces.

> . . . In the interests, therefore, of the cultivators . . . and also of the Sudanese, it appears to be desirable to prevent the emigration of Sudanese without permission . . . The discontent of masters at the constant and increasing loss of their Sudanese servants is growing, and one cannot but sympathize with them . . .

The governors also stressed their belief that '. . . any feeling which may exist against the Government . . . is due to this cause more than to any other . . .'[36] There is no doubt that agriculture suffered greatly through the lack of labour and that extensive areas of arable land remained fallow. In 1908 the revenue derived from agricultural taxation fell for the first time. Analysing the reasons for this, Wingate noted: '. . . the desertion of slaves and the attraction of high pay on public works . . .' Wingate was aware that '. . . until the labouring classes are large enough for the needs of the growing country, it is only natural that the non-technical portion of the insufficient population will select the most profitable and pleasant method of earning a living . . .'[37]

During these early years the government departments were the main employers of labour. The extension of the railway to the Red Sea, the building of Port Sudan, and the opening of new roads required thousands of manual workers. Governors complained that the railway enticed away their agricultural workers by offering higher wages. This situation was exacerbated with the building of Port Sudan which attracted all the casual labourers from the

Khartoum, Berber, and Dongola provinces. By 1907, demand exceeded supply to such a degree that workers arrived from Jedda and the Arabian coast beguiled by the high wages. The government departments did not only fail to consider the needs of agriculture, they also competed against each other for the limited labour market thereby causing a further increase in wages. Finally, the modest beginnings of private enterprise also required labour, and the government, although eager to oblige, could not meet their demands.[38]

This was the situation in all the northern provinces with the exception of Wādī Ḥalfā, whose male population emigrated to Egypt during the winter tourist season to work as domestic servants and dragomans. In the south conditions were different. There were no development schemes or railway extensions. Yet even the very few requirements of labour could not be met locally, as the southern tribes could not be induced to work, and all labourers were imported from the north. The southerners who cleared the roads, built the rest houses or acted as porters for government expeditions, were generally conscripted and forced to work against their will.[39]

The government was quite aware of the situation. As early as 1900 suggestions were made to transport coolies from India to work on the Sudan railways. In 1902 an agreement was reached with the government of India to supply 5,000 Muslim coolies to the Sudan, and the British government agreed to become a partner to the contract.[40] Cromer, however, decided not to continue with this plan. Instead, he ordered Wingate to attempt to recruit the nomad tribes of the northern provinces to undertake the work. It fell to Slatin to organize the recruiting. At a gathering of the shaykhs of the nomad tribes at Kokreb the conditions of work were agreed upon. The head shaykh of the Hadendowa was elected by the shaykhs to organize the work and to represent them in their dealings with the government. By the end of 1903 there were 300 nomads employed on the railways. Wingate reported optimistically that all those experts who had prophesied that nomads were lazy and indolent had been proved wrong.[41] However, this optimism was unwarranted. The nomads did not carry out their agreement. With '. . . the first fall of rains on the mountains, [they] gave up their work, being thoroughly tired of it and longing to get back to their homes . . .'[42] Despite this failure, small groups of nomads continued to be employed on the railway, and by 1908, the Hadendowa had developed into expert bridge builders and were transferred by the railway department to the Khartoum–Shandī section.

Egypt was by far the most obvious labour market on which to draw. Seasonal immigration of Egyptian *fallāḥīn* from Aswān began in the early years of the Condominium. They undertook agricultural work in the Wādī Ḥalfā and Dongola provinces and then returned to Egypt to their own farms. Yet despite repeated efforts to induce Egyptians to settle in the Sudan, only small numbers responded. Wingate concluded that '. . . The Egyptian Fellahin have a rooted objection to coming to the Sudan . . .' and entertained '. . . little hope of success in the future . . .'[43] Efforts were, however, continued and in 1904 Egyptians were contracted to work on the Zeidab plantations. The result, as reported, was that Zeidab became a den of thieves as most of the Egyptians who came were of bad character and left the Sudan the minute they had enough money. In 1905, a plan was devised to settle 3,000 Egyptian families in the Sudan every year, by offering them a subsidy of £E 20 per family, to be paid out of the Egyptian war office budget. The plan though approved by Wingate, apparently met with little success.[44] Though experiments continued, there seems to have been no serious attempt to attract Egyptians to the Sudan by offering them more tempting conditions. When labour on a large scale was again required in the early stages of the Gezira scheme, Kitchener decided to utilize the services of Egyptian convicts rather than recruit more expensive labourers.[45]

In order to overcome the problems created by the shortage of labour and to check the decrease in domestic slaves, it was decided in 1905 to establish a central labour bureau. This bureau was attached to the intelligence department in Khartoum under the supervision of Slatin. Detailed instructions as to the employment of labour were issued and the conditions of labour, including wages, were determined by the labour bureau. The heads of departments were instructed not to recruit labour except through the labour bureau to which they had to submit all their labour requirements at least one month in advance. Employers were further restricted by a maximum daily wage of P.T.3½, which was imposed by the government. Private contractors at Port Sudan were also instructed to recruit their labour only through the central bureau. Wingate, who by inclination opposed any restriction on free enterprise, wrote, '. . . I am aware that in giving effect to the above proposals, some interference with the ordinary principles of supply and demand is involved, but it is contended that the exceptional circumstances . . . warrant the adoption of somewhat exceptional measures . . .'[46] These measures were clearly not implemented and wages continued to rise. In 1909 Wingate commented: '. . . as long as Departments are willing to pay the present "famine wages" the labourers . . . are liable to refuse all offer of lower wages . . .'[47] Departments also continued to compete, one against the other, resulting in the unchecked desertion of agricultural areas. The labour bureau decided to halt this migration by ordering all Sudanese labourers in the provinces to register, and by restricting their movements.[48] In 1910 the labour bureau reported that its statistics proved that the Sudan labour force could meet all the country's requirements. This was confirmed in the following years when the supply of unskilled labour was equal to the demand, and the labour bureau could cope with all the requirements made upon it, from among the 11,443 registered Sudanese labourers. The bulk of this labour force consisted of Sudanese ex-slaves and Fallāta. Of the Arab tribesmen, only a few became regular town workers, while the majority returned to the villages after a short time. The town population expressed their attitude to manual labour when they told Wingate, '. . . "Allah took away our slaves, but sent us the Fallata" . . .'[49]

During the first years of its existence the Sudan government legislated in order to safeguard the interests of employers and employees. In 1901 an order was published obliging all servants to be registered. A special shaykh was appointed to deal with all applications for servants and to be responsible for their misdeeds. All those who employed servants were warned that if servants accompanied them to other provinces they were '. . . responsible for the return of such servants to Khartoum . . .'[50] In 1905 the *Vagabonds Ordinance* was promulgated in order to induce freed slaves to take up permanent employment. A vagabond was defined as a person who can maintain himself partly or fully but refuses to do so; or who begs or gathers alms; or who has no settled home or means of subsistence. On committing an offence a vagabond was liable to more severe punishment than an ordinary citizen who committed a similar offence.[51] Two ordinances safeguarding the rights of workers were published in 1908. The *Workmen Compensation Ordinance* ensured the rights of workers injured or invalided while at work and fixed the amount of compensation. *The Apprenticeship Ordinance* regulated the contracts for the instruction of children in handicrafts. No contracts were allowed without the approval of the governor of the province who had also to give his consent if the apprentice was removed from the Sudan.[52] Until 1908 the only approved apprenticeships were at the Mather Workshops at Gordon College, the government's workshop at Kassala, and the workshops of the railways, steamers, and telegraph departments. Skilled artisans had to be brought mainly from Greece and Italy, thus increasing the costs of many projects. It was to overcome this shortage of skilled labour that the apprentice ordinance was promulgated.[53]

The intimate connection between labour and domestic slavery, and the belief that they should both be controlled from within the same department was stated clearly by Wingate when he wrote to

Gorst: '. . . With regard to the question of Domestic Slavery . . . we are now taking the first step by organizing a Labour Bureau . . .'[54] The establishment of the labour bureau enabled the government to regulate the supply and demand of labour and to control the domestic slaves whose desertion of their masters could have caused a disruption of the socio-economic structure of the Sudan.

Conclusion

THE reconquest of the Sudan presented the Anglo-Egyptian authorities with a number of problems which were not easy to overcome. The vast territory of the Sudan was impoverished through years of internal strife and wars against invaders. The population had decreased as a result of famine, disease and continuous fighting. Agriculture and trade had further suffered both as a result of the dislocation of tribes, and the economic policy of the Khalifa 'Abdallahi.

These were the major internal problems : externally the situation was equally problematic. Following the Fashoda crisis of 1898, which dealt with the claims of France, the British authorities had to secure the southern Sudan against claims by the Congo Free State. These demands were settled only in 1906 as a result of the Anglo-Congolese agreement. Four years later the Lado Enclave reverted to the Anglo-Egyptian Sudan following the death of King Leopold. Another factor which hampered the new administration was that most of the Sudan's borders were inadequately delimitated during these early years. In consequence border incidents were frequent especially in Zandeland along the Congo-Nile watershed and on the Abyssinian border. Finally, the Anglo-Egyptian conquerors came to establish an alien rule in a country which for over a decade had enjoyed independence. British public opinion was persuaded to believe that the Sudan would welcome its liberators with open arms, but in fact the Sudanese fought against the invaders and were only forced to their knees as a result of the Anglo-Egyptian superiority in weapons and organization. It is in the light of these circumstances that one has to assess the policies and the achievements of the Condominium government during its first two decades, a period which coincided with Wingate's governor-generalship of the Anglo-Egyptian Sudan.

The first task undertaken by the new authorities was the pacification of the country. In this they partly succeeded although the methods employed were not always commendable. In the northern Muslim provinces the population was accustomed to obey its rulers. Hence, once the Khalifa's defeat was complete the people accepted the new authorities with little resistance. Although the record of religious upheavals until the First World War is extensive, a close examination reveals that most of them petered out as a result of lack of support. The small units of the Egyptian army which were scattered over a vast territory without sufficient means of communications could not provide an adequate deterrent against an uprising supported by the bulk of the population. The reason why the Muslim north accepted the new regime lay in the economic and religious policies of the conquerors, rather than in their use of military force. A cautious and just land policy, light taxation, the resettlement of tribes and the toleration of slavery, were all geared to associate the new rulers in the minds of the population with economic viability. With the Mahdist regime fresh in their minds, the Sudanese landowners could compare their present prosperity with years of near starvation under the Khalifa. Moreover they knew that their land, their slaves, and their agricultural produce would not be confiscated by the new authorities as long as they abided by the law.

Similarly in the field of religion the government aimed at re-establishing orthodox Islam and at proving that the religious beliefs of the population would be respected. Orthodox Islam received its main impetus through the teachers' and *qāḍīs'* colleges, the establishment of *Sharīʿa* courts under the supervision of the legal secretary, the rebuilding and subsidizing of mosques and the help extended to the pilgrims on their way to the Hejaz. Diversions from what was regarded as orthodox Islam, be they *ṣūfī* beliefs or neo-Mahdist trends, were treated with grave suspicion. Similarly, missionary proselytization in the Muslim provinces was strictly forbidden. The government rightly feared that the activities of European missionaries would be identified in the minds of the local inhabitants with its own policy. Hence, even the limited activities of the missionary societies in the fields of health and education were regarded with grave misgivings by many British officials.

In this way the government succeeded in associating the landowners, the *ʿulamāʾ* and the *qāḍīs* with the new administration. Their economic well-being and their religious beliefs were secured by the government's policy. The result was the loyalty of the bulk of the population to their alien rulers during the First World War. The Ottoman Khalīfa's call for a *Jihād*, as well as Britain's support of the Sharifian revolt, did little to affect the loyalties of the Sudanese one way or another.

There were several important aspects of the government's policy in the northern Sudan which were unrealistic. The complete reliance on the traditional leadership of the old generation to the exclusion of anyone else, was as wrong in the Sudan as it was in Egypt and in other British dependencies. This attitude was most clearly expressed in the government's tribal policy which sought to turn the clock back and to re-establish the structure of tribal society as in pre-Mahdist days. However, this policy failed for two major reasons. Firstly, under the Turco-Egyptian and Mahdist regimes tribal leadership had been disrupted to such an extent that in many cases it was impossible to resuscitate its authority. Secondly, independent tribal leadership, by its very nature, could not exist side by side with a strong centralized government. By entrusting tribal chiefs with administrative duties, and by replacing them whenever they failed, the government changed the status of shaykhs to that of government officials. Hence, their authority was derived from the government and did not reflect their influence with the tribes. The reliance on traditional leadership expressed itself in other ways. The younger generation of Sudanese who had been educated and had matured since the reconquest, was not obsessed by memories of the past. Nationalist ideas, which became current in Egypt during these years, influenced this young educated class which sought to become involved in the country's administration. Instead, they were relegated to posts of minor importance and the British authorities attempted to exclude their ideas from the Sudan. These measures were ineffective and could result only in the alienation of the future leaders of the country on whose co-operation the British authorities ought to have relied.

Again, British policy was unrealistic in its attitude to Sufism and to Neo-Mahdist trends. Believing that the Mahdi's success was largely due to the superstitious beliefs of the majority of Sudanese Muslims, the government did its best to discourage Sufism and to stamp out any deviations from orthodox Islam. However, deep rooted beliefs such as Sufism or Mahdism could not be uprooted overnight. Moreover, while the government discouraged Sufism generally, it extended unofficial aid and preferential treatment to the Khatmīya, the only *ṣūfī ṭarīqa* which had fought against Mahdism. In consequence Sufism continued to have a strong hold over the inhabitants of the Sudan. Many of the tribes who had formerly supported the Mahdi rallied around his posthumous son, Sayyid 'Abd al-Raḥmān al-Mahdī, who lived under the surveillance of the intelligence department. It seems therefore that whilst tribal leaders failed to re-establish their authority, despite government support, *ṣūfī* and other religious leaders, whom the authorities treated with suspicion, emerged as one of the most influential groups within the population. Thus, on the outbreak of the First World War, when the government was seeking widespread support, it was forced to revise its policy in order to gain the confidence of influential *ṣūfī* shaykhs. Similarly, Sayyid 'Abd al-Raḥmān al-Mahdī became *persona grata*, and together with his numerous followers became an outspoken advocate on behalf of the British administration. This was the only case, during Wingate's governor-generalship, in which the government compromised its policy in order to gain the support of an important section of the inhabitants.

Southern administration, by its very nature, required a different approach. The international considerations which effected southern policy have already been commented upon. The main difficulties, however, lay in the lack of communication and funds, both of which were essential in order to establish even a semblance of orderly government in these vast areas.

During the course of the 19th century the north had become accustomed to centralized government while the reverse had been true in the south. Successive waves of invaders, whether slave dealers, Turco-Egyptian government officials, or the Mahdist *anṣār*, had taught the southerners to mistrust foreign domination in any form. The Anglo-Egyptian authorities were no exception and were treated with undisguised hostility. It was clear from the outset that the establishment of orderly government was impossible. However, in face of diverse claims by other European powers the British government had to show the flag. With this aim in view, administrative and punitive patrols were undertaken. The levying of taxes and the extension of codes of justice in the southern provinces were a political by-product of Anglo-Egyptian domination. Their practical value was negligible, but they proved that the south was part of the Anglo-Egyptian Sudan. It was clear to Wingate and to his British subordinates that economic development, education, and the establishment of government in the South, had to wait until the northern Muslim provinces could supply the necessary funds. Hence, the only alternative to government other than direct military rule, was to leave the southern tribes to manage their own affairs. This would probably have been the best solution at the time. But the British government would scarcely have undertaken the conquest of these areas, in face of French and Belgian opposition, only to hand them back to their original inhabitants. It is with this in mind that one has to assess the administrative policies in the south during this period.

Tribal policy was not dissimilar to that in the north, namely to re-establish traditional tribal society and leadership. Despite the break-up of tribal society by previous invasions, many of the southern tribes were in a better position to re-establish their societies than their counterparts in the north. Furthermore, numerous tribal leaders in the south had the authority and the power to rule their tribes without government interference. The most logical step would have been to enlist the accepted leaders of the tribes for the task of administration. This, in fact, was the government's official policy but it was never fully implemented. Tribal leaders who were strong enough resisted the new rulers with all the might they possessed. Once overcome, they were replaced by men of inferior stature, and government officials started to undertake administrative duties with these tribes. This happened with the Shilluk in the Upper Nile province, whose strong chief was deposed and banished to Khartoum. Similarly, in the Azande territory, the powerful Yambio resisted the establishment of alien rule until he was killed in battle. Under the weak leadership of their successors, tribal leadership soon disintegrated. Once again, the only alternative would have been not to set up military posts in these areas, and to leave the tribes to manage their own affairs. Yet political consideration dictated a different course and, as a result, the disruption of tribal society continued. Only those tribes who lived far enough from government posts to defy its authority continued to enjoy their independence for many years. Thus the Beir and the Anuak who lived on the Abyssinian border were brought to heel only in 1912, while the strong Nuer tribe did not submit until the 1930's. Consequently, the first seventeen years of Anglo-Egyptian rule in the south caused a further disintegration of tribal society without being able to replace traditional authority by permanent administration.

While political considerations may be put forward in order to justify tribal policy, the same cannot be said with regard to the government's religious policy. Following the reconquest, the south was opened for missionary activities. Initially the government hoped that the missionary societies would augment its meagre forces in these areas and concentrate their efforts in the spheres of education and medical aid. Furthermore, the British authorities were anxious to keep the missionaries out of the north, where it was believed their presence would cause resentment. The south with its large pagan population presented them with an ideal compromise.

The use of missionary proselytization as an antidote to Islam was probably in the government's mind even in those early days. Already in 1904 the governor of the Baḥr al-Ghazāl was discouraged from opening a government school as it was feared that the teaching of Arabic would encourage Islam. However, an active anti-Muslim policy crystalized only after 1910. The date suggests a connection with the handing over of the Lado Enclave, which for the first time enabled the British authorities to regard the southern problem without undue regard for international complications. In 1910 the British governors of Mongalla and Baḥr al-Ghazāl were instructed unofficially to introduce English in their schools and to begin substituting English for Arabic in their dealings with the inhabitants. At the same time Sunday, which had been the weekly holiday in the Lado Enclave during the Belgian rule, became the official rest day in Mongalla and later in other southern provinces. Finally the Equatorial battalions were organized in order to overcome the Islamizing impact of the Egyptian army. All these measures were undertaken haphazardly without clearly defining the government's aims in these provinces. There is no proof that the separation of the south was contemplated during Wingate's governor-generalship. However, there can be no doubt that the government's religious policy gave rise to separatist notions later and perpetuated the southern problem which had existed prior to the Anglo-Egyptian conquest.

The administrators

The hazards of alien rule are well known and need no further elaboration. However, seen in perspective, the British administrators of the Anglo-Egyptian Sudan were among the best any country under foreign domination could desire.

By virtue of the Anglo-Egyptian agreement absolute powers were vested in the governor-general, and sirdar. Wingate who held these posts for most of this period had imbued them with his personality. He was a strong believer in the direct personal approach both in his relations with his subordinates and his dealings with the Sudanese people. His relations with the British officials were cultivated during his tours of inspection, the annual Cairo gathering, other visits to Khartoum or Dunbar, and a voluminous correspondence, which in many cases went beyond the official relationship of a governor-general and his subordinates. Relations were, nevertheless, not familiar. Wingate's experience and understanding were treated with respect. His relations with the non-British officials were, of course, on a different and more formal level. His attitude to the Sudanese was paternal rather than autocratic. He believed that he was in a better position than they were to know what was best for them. This manifested itself in his attitude to the Mahdia, and to the penetration of Egyptian nationalism into the Sudan, both of which were regarded by him not only as evil but as being contrary to the better aspirations of the Sudanese. In the absence of any free expression of Sudanese public opinion during Wingate's period, it is difficult to assess the popularity of these policies. The attacks launched against them in the Egyptian press can hardly be regarded as an expression of public opinion, as they were motivated primarily by Egyptian political considerations. The only criteria by which the government can be judged, therefore, are the results.

If one were to look for the predominant principle which guided Wingate as sirdar and governor-general, it would be his firm belief in the unity of civil administration and military command in the

Sudan, and his conviction that interference from Egypt, in any form, should be reduced to the utmost minimum. He believed in the unity of civil and military command not only as embodied in his own person but also in the lower echelons of the administration where provincial governors were also the military commanders of their districts. Suggestions to separate these functions made by Cromer, and by senior British officers in the Egyptian army, were rejected by Wingate as absurd. He regarded the insecurity of the Sudan and the fact that most of the higher British officials were army officers as important reasons for maintaining the unity. These reasons, however, are not sufficient. After the first few years of the Condominium, security was never really threatened. The Egyptian army undertook punitive patrols in the southern provinces and occasionally had to suppress religious insurrections which did not, however, endanger security. Moreover, two of the adjutants-general who served in the Egyptian army during that period objected to this unity of command in the provinces which they regarded as detrimental to the army itself. They claimed, with justice, that civil administration took preference over army command and that as a result the army was being neglected. Lastly, Wingate himself devoted most of his time and energy to his work as governor-general, while the running of the Egyptian army was largely entrusted to a handful of British officers. This was probably partly owing to his personal inclination, yet had security conditions really been as bad as he maintained, it is likely that he would have played a more active role in the day-to-day running of the army. Wingate's main reason for opposing the separation was probably his belief that it was bound to increase control from Cairo and to create friction between the military and civil administration. Instead of a unified general supervision exercised by the consul-general over all Sudan affairs, there would have been an additional, purely military control exercised by the General Officer Commanding Egypt and the War Office in London.

Wingate's cherished aim throughout his governor-generalship was to relieve the Sudan of control from Cairo, as exercised by the British consuls-general, and to stop any Egyptian penetration into the Sudan. It was the former of these aims which was the more difficult to achieve. The policies and the administration of the Sudan were controlled by the British consuls-general in Egypt who reported regularly to the Foreign Office. It is difficult to assess accurately the extent of this control. However, it is certain that of the four consuls-general who served during those years it was Cromer's influence on Sudanese affairs which was most decisive. Furthermore, the extent of control from Cairo declined over the years and reached its lowest point under Sir Henry McMahon.

Under the terms of the Condominium agreement, increased supervision over the Sudan necessitated stricter control by the consuls-general, as neither the British nor the Egyptian government was in a position to intervene directly. It seems that the weakening of central control was due to two main factors: the consolidation of the Sudanese administration, and the greater experience of the governor-general as compared with that of his superiors in Cairo. Under these circumstances the freedom of action granted to Wingate in the latter years of his rule was fully justified, and increased intervention would not have improved administrative efficiency.

Wingate's governor-generalship can best be described as government through voluntary consultation. He was not an autocrat by nature and preferred to act on the advice of close colleagues. Moreover, he balked at taking advice from his subordinates merely because they held a particular post. Even after a semblance of constitutional government was introduced in the form of the governor-general's council, he continued to rely on his own confidants rather than on the new body. It was to this aspect of Wingate's rule that Slatin owed his great influence over the administration. Slatin's experience in the Sudan helped the new administration in its early years, but as time progressed, his conservative attitude and pre-Mahdist conceptions about tribal and religious affairs probably hindered the necessary development of a new approach. Most of the British administrators of the Sudan, both civil and military, were honest, hard-working men, who in many cases risked their lives for seemingly inadequate material benefits. The young university graduates soon made their mark on administrative policies and became even more influential after Wingate's departure. The Egyptian officials in the Sudan were never intended to play a significant role in the new administration and had little chance of promotion to higher posts. Hence, it was not surprising that many of those who applied for employment were not of the highest quality. In those spheres of administration where Egyptian supremacy could not be challenged, for want of alternative employees, the standard of the Egyptians was rarely a cause for complaint. This applied to the *Sharīʿa* courts and to education. The government was dilatory in training the Sudanese for administrative posts, and in consequence the rate of progress suffered. Sudanese children who started their education under the Condominium could have graduated from secondary schools by 1910 and filled important administrative posts. Instead they were relegated to minor positions. It was only after 1924 that they achieved some predominance as a result of the rapid removal of the Egyptians which followed the assassination of Sir Lee Stack.

APPENDICES

APPENDIX 1

THE ADMINISTRATIVE STRUCTURE OF THE SUDAN GOVERNMENT (in 1914)*

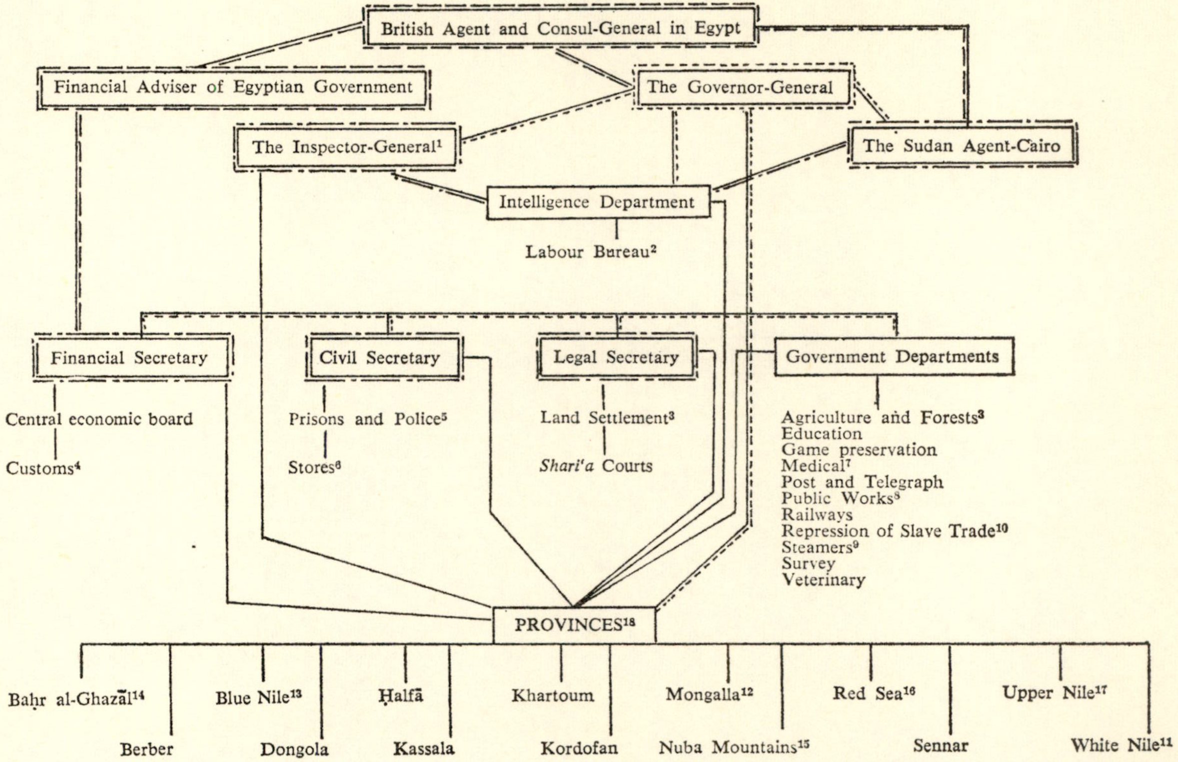

KEY

The control exercised by British officials in Egypt over the Sudan.
The governor-general and his direct control over all departments and provinces.
The high officials of the Sudan government who, apart from the Sudan agent, were *ex-officio* members of the governor-general's council.
Other departments and provinces.

1. The post of inspector-general ceased to exist in 1914, following Slatin's resignation.
2. The Labour Bureau was set up in 1905, *CAO*—241, 18 Jan. 1905.
3. Up to 1910 there was a department for agriculture and lands and a department for woods and forests. In 1910 they were merged, and the lands section became part of the legal department; GGC—1 Nov. 1910, FO/867/1; *SG*—190, 5 Jan. 1911.
4. The customs department was established in 1905 as an independent department and was affiliated to the financial secretary's office in 1914; *CAO*—245, 18 Jan. 1905; Wingate to Clayton, 15 Dec. 1913, SAD/469/5; GGC—3 Mar. 1914, FO/867/5.
5. The prisons and police became part of the civil secretary's office in 1905; see *CAO*—230, 12 Dec. 1904.
6. The stores became part of the civil secretary's department in 1904 when the controller's department was abolished. *CAO*—229, 12 Dec. 1904.
7. Until 1904 it was a military department. The civil department established in 1904 was only in charge of the Northern provinces, while the South remained under the Egyptian army. *GGR*—1904, p. 83.
8. Up to the end of 1906 the Egyptian army works department was responsible for public works. In 1907 a separate public works department was established. *GGR*—1906, p. 59.
9. The steamers department was transferred from the Egyptian army in 1902; *SG*—31, Jan. 1902. Up to 1909 it was called the steamers and boats department, *SG*—147, Jan. 1909.
10. Until 1 Jan. 1910 this department was attached to the Egyptian ministry of Interior. In 1911 it became a central Sudan government department. Wingate to Gorst (secret), 6 Dec. 1910, SAD/298/2.
11. The White Nile province was founded in 1905; *SG*—69, 1 Jan. 1905.
12. Mongalla province was founded in 1906 from the Bor and Mongalla districts of the Upper Nile province; *GGR*—1906, p. 707. In 1910 part of the Lado enclave was annexed to Mongalla.
13. Up to Jan. 1905 it was called the Gezira province; *SG*—69, 1 Jan. 1905; the Gezira province was formed in 1902 out of the southern half of Khartoum province. *CAO*—66, 1 May 1902.
14. The Baḥr al-Ghazāl was under military command until 1902, when it was transferred to the civil administration. *SG*—34, Apr. 1902.
15. The Nuba Mountains province was separated from Kordofan in 1914, *GGR*—1914, p. 60.
16. Suakin was a separate governorate until 10 July 1899, when the Condominium Agreement extended over it. In 1906 its name was changed to the Red Sea province. *GGR*—1905, p. 55.
17. The Upper Nile was called Fashoda district until 1903. *SG*—54, Dec. 1903; the name of the town Fashoda, was changed to Kodok.
18. During the first years of the Condominium there was a distinction between first class and second class provinces (*mudīrīya and muḥafaẓa*). Ḥalfā, Fashoda, and Suakin were second class provinces while all other provinces were first class. *SG*—45, 1 Mar. 1903. This distinction appears to have been discontinued in the later years.

APPENDIX 2

THE ADMINISTRATIVE STRUCTURE OF THE EGYPTIAN ARMY[1]

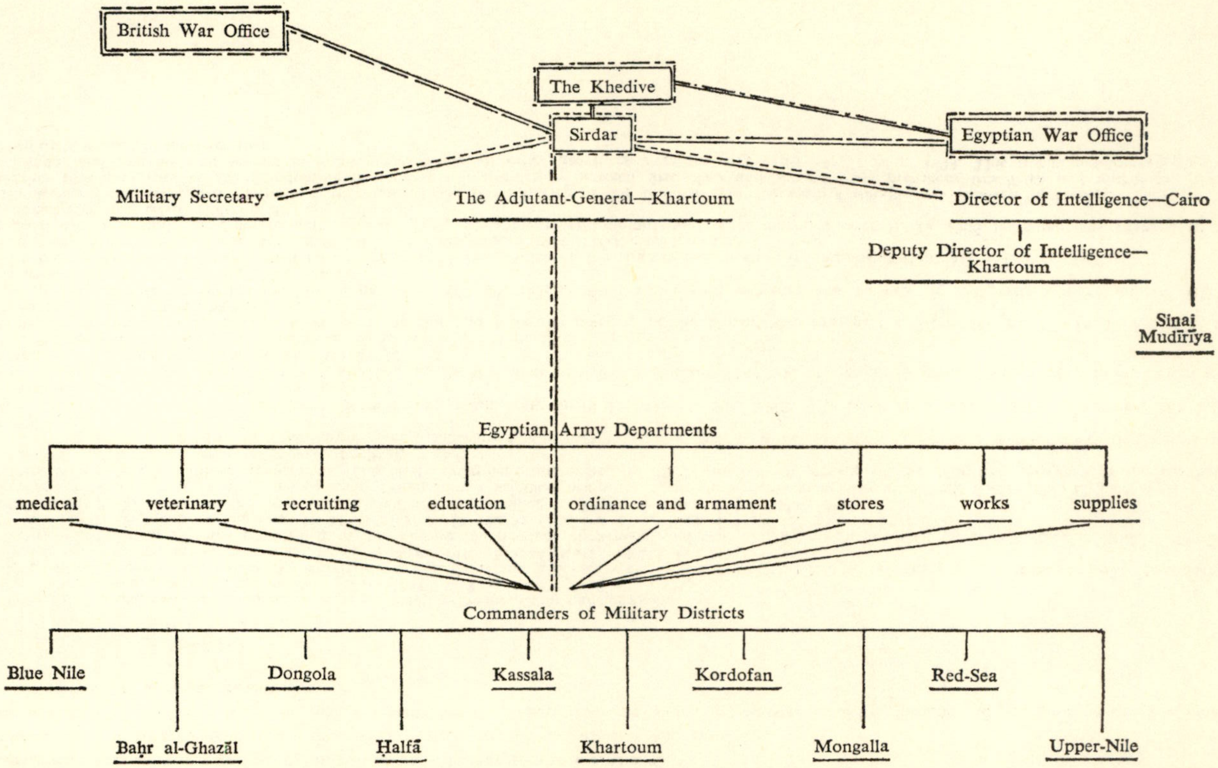

KEY ══════British control; ═ · ═ · ═Egyptian control; ----------control of the British Sirdar

1. *GGR*—1906; see also Asser to Wingate, 16 August 1911, SAD/301/3.

Biographical Notes

Chapter I	*fn.*
Wingate	2
Kitchener	3
Slatin	5
Maxwell	12
Talbot	20
N. Shuqayr	27
Butler	36
Asser	43
Chapter II	
Bernard	4
Cecil	13
Bonham Carter	16
Phipps	22
Clayton	29
Currie	38
Jackson Pasha	68
Owen	82
Stack	85

Chapter III	*fn.*
Symes	8
Savile	11
Willis	14
H. C. Jackson	17
Kerr	65
Chapter IV	
Atiya	6
al-Azharī	7
Chapter VI	
Scott-Moncrieff	46
Chapter VII	
Ryder	16
al-Ṭayyib Hāshim	36
Matthews	43
Chapter IX	
Grenfell	24

Notes

Preface

1. For details see bibliography.

CHAPTER I

The Governors-General, Kitchener and Wingate

1. *SIR*–60, 25 May–31 Dec. 1898.
2. Wingate, General Sir Francis Reginald (1861–1953), joined the Egyptian army in 1883 and was appointed as A.D.C. on the staff of Sir Evelyn Wood, the first sirdar of the post 'Urābī Egyptian army. Following a brief period as assistant military secretary to Sir Francis Grenfell, in 1886–7, he became assistant adjutant-general for intelligence. In 1889 Wingate was appointed director of military intelligence and held this post until he became governor-general of the Sudan in Dec. 1899. For details about Wingate's earlier career, see R. Wingate, *Wingate of the Sudan*, London, 1955, pp. 22–127.
3. Kitchener, Horatio Herbert, 1st Earl of Khartoum and of Broome (1850–1916), joined the Egyptian army in 1882; governor-general of the Red Sea littoral 1886–8; adjutant-general 1888–92; sirdar of the Egyptian army 1892–99; governor-general of the Sudan 1899. For details see P. Magnus, *Kitchener, Portrait of an Imperialist*, Arrow Books, London, 1961.
4. For a detailed account of the diplomatic background of the reconquest see G. N. Sanderson, *England, Europe and the Upper Nile 1882–1899*, Edinburgh, 1965.
5. Slatin Pasha, Sir Rudolf Karl von, Baron (1857–1932). Austrian officer who started his service in the Sudan under Gordon in 1878; 1879–81 governor of Dāra in southern Darfur; 1881–4 general-governor of Darfur; in 1884 he surrendered to the Mahdist army at Dāra and remained in Omdurman for eleven years, first as prisoner and later as one of the Khalifa's private attendants *(mulāzim)*. Following his escape from Omdurman in 1895 he became Wingate's assistant in the intelligence department. For Slatin's earlier career see R. Hill, *Slatin Pasha*, London, 1965, pp. 1–67; see also below pp. 46–58.

6. For a detailed account of the political and diplomatic background of the Condominium Agreement, see Sanderson, op. cit., pp. 332–80; M. Shibeika, *The Independent Sudan*, New York, 1959, pp. 441–59.
7. Salisbury to Cromer, 9 Dec. 1898, FO/633/7.
8. For further details see Shibeika, op. cit., pp. 449–59; see also below pp. 13–15.
9. Salisbury to Cromer, 14 Jan. 1899, FO/407/150. I have not been able to find any evidence that such a declaration was ever made either by Kitchener or Wingate.
10. Cromer to Kitchener, 19 Jan. 1899, FO/633/8.
11. Magnus, op. cit., p. 149, quoting Kitchener to Wingate, 26 Jan. 1899.
12. Maxwell Pasha, General Sir John Grenfell (1859–1929) was first governor of Khartoum 1898–1899; in 1900 he left for South Africa, and returned to Egypt in 1908 as commander of the British troops. *DNBS*, 1922–30, pp. 570–1.
13. *The Times*, 11 Apr. 1900.
14. Inclosure in Cromer to Salisbury, 4 May 1899, FO/78/5023; *Ma'mūr* was the title used by the Egyptian government, for the official in charge of a *ma'mūrīya*, a sub-division of a province. See below pp. 69–74, 78–81, 84–87.
15. *Memorandum to Mudirs*, Inclosure in Cromer to Salisbury, 17 Mar. 1899, FO/78/5022; *Mudīr* was the Egyptian title for a provincial governor. The following details are all from Kitchener's memorandum.
16. Kitchener to Wingate, 26 Jan. 1899, SAD/269/1.
17. Gleichen to Wingate, 24 Oct. 1898. SAD/266/10; Talbot to Wingate [n.d.] Nov. 1898, SAD/266/11.
18. Cromer to Kitchener, 19 Jan. 1899, FO/633/8.
19. Petition to the sirdar [Arabic text n.d. 1898], SAD/430/6.
20. Talbot Pasha, Milo George (1854–1931), joined the Egyptian army in 1897. Following Wingate's appointment as head of the Sudan office in Cairo in 1899, Talbot became assistant DMI, and in 1900–5 was Director of Surveys. He was one of Wingate's closest friends throughout his career, and came to help him during the First World War; Hill, *BD*, p. 355.
21. Talbot to Wingate, 19 Apr. 1898, SAD/266/4.
22. Talbot to Wingate, 1 Apr. 1899, SAD/269/4.
23. Maxwell to Wingate, 19 Jan. 1900, SAD/270/1/2.
24. Kitchener to Cromer, 1 Feb. 1899, FO/407/150; Magnus, op. cit., pp. 135–9.
25. Rodd to Salisbury, 31 Aug. 1899, FO/78/5026. Salisbury's minutes to the letter read: '. . . three or four executions at the very outside . . .'
26. Cromer to Salisbury, 27 Apr. 1900, FO/633/6.
27. Na'ūm Shuqayr (Shoucair) (1863–1922), a Lebanese Christian served in the Egyptian army from 1884 and joined the intelligence department under Wingate in 1890. After the reconquest he remained in the intelligence department in Cairo. During his service he published *Ta'rīkh al-Sūdān al-qadīm wal-ḥadīth wajughrāfiyatuhu*, Cairo

[1903], a major contribution to the history of the Sudan during the Mahdia.

28. Wingate to Kitchener, 7 Feb. 1899, SAD/269/2/1.
29. Wingate to Rodd, 10 Mar. 1899, SAD/269/3.
30. Said Shoucair to Wingate, 27 Jan. 1900, enclosed in Cromer to Salisbury, 7 Feb. 1900, FO/78/5086.
31. *The Times*, 18 Apr. 1900.
32. *al-Ahrām*, 26 Dec. 1899.
33. *The Times*, 18 Apr. 1900.
34. See below pp. 81–84.
35. The following remarks, unless otherwise stated, are based on the Sudan correspondence and Wingate's private letters in the Sudan Archive at Durham.
36. Butler's memoirs, SAD/422/12; Butler, S.S., was seconded to the Egyptian army in 1909 and served in Wad Madanī. In 1910 he was transferred to the Camel Corps in Kordofan and participated in several expeditions against the Nuba. Since April 1911 he served in the intelligence department in Khartoum.
37. *CAO*—38, 16 Feb. 1902; *GGR*—1906, p.6.
38. Cromer to Wingate, 19 May 1905, SAD/234/3.
39. Gwynne to Adeney, 23 Jan. 1902, CMSA/E/03/1902; for details about Bishop Gwynne, see H. C. Jackson, *Pastor on the Nile*, London, 1960; see below pp. 109–115.
40. *A Short History of the Sir Reginald Wingate Lodge*, SAD/292/2.
41. Wingate to Sir Frederick Milner, 21 Jan. 1915, SAD/194/1.
42. Wingate to Clayton, 21 Aug. 1915, SAD/469/10; for further details see below pp. 106–108.
43. Asser Pasha, Sir Joseph John (1867–1944), joined the Egyptian army in 1892 and participated in the reconquest; 1905–14 adjutant-general of Egyptian army; 1910–14 member of governor-general's council. Hill, *BD*, p. 62.

CHAPTER II

The Sudan Egypt and Britain

1. Cromer to Wingate, 25 Jan. 1904, FO/633/8; Gorst to Wingate, 16 Mar. 1910, SAD/469/2/1.
2. Inclosure 2 in No. 65, Cromer to Salisbury, 22 Jan. 1899, FO/407/150. For an extensive analysis of the Sudan finances see John Stone, *The Finance of Government Economics Development in the Sudan 1899–1913*, Sudan Economic Institute Khartoum 1954. (Unpublished.)
3. Financial Regulations to be observed by the Soudan Government, Cairo 6 May 1900, FO/407/157; these regulations were replaced in 1910, following the setting up of the governor-general's council,

by a new set of regulations, signed by Wingate and Harvey. Inclosure 4 in No. 33, FO/407/175.

4. Bernard Pasha, Sir Edgar Edwin (1866–1931), was transferred from the Egyptian army to the Sudan government in 1901; from 1901–1925 he was financial secretary of the Sudan. Hill, *BD*, p. 79.
5. Quoted by Stone op. cit., p. 3; from the 1905 financial department report.
6. Ibid., p. 19; until 1905 the maintenance cost of the Egyptian army did not appear in the Sudan budget. From 1905 this sum was included in Egypt's annual contribution, hence the big increase.
7. There are numerous articles in Egyptian newspapers voicing this criticism. One of the most comprehensive articles was written by Aḥmad Ḥilmī in *al-Liwā'*, 21 Oct. 1907.
8. Wingate to Kitchener, 9 May 1914, SAD/190/2/2.
9. Wingate to Kitchener, (private), 26 Oct. 1911, SAD/301/4.
10. See below pp. 32–39.
11. *SIR*—245, Dec. 1914.
12. Following the declaration of a British protectorate over Egypt on 18 Dec. 1914, the title of the Khedive was changed to Sultan.
13. Lord Edward Herbert Gascoyne Cecil (1867–1918), son of the 3rd Marquess of Salisbury; joined the Egyptian army in 1896 and took part in the reconquest of the Sudan; agent-general of the Sudan government in Cairo 1903–5; under secretary of state in the Egyptian ministry of finance 1905–12; financial advisor 1912–18; DNBS *1912–21*, pp. 101–102.
14. Wingate to Cecil, ('Secret please destroy'.), 13 Jan. 1913, SAD/185/1/1. Najīb 'Azūrī had been employed in the intelligence department at least since 1906 and subsequently became the private secretary of the Egyptian minister of war. I have been unable to establish whether there is any connection between him and Najīb 'Azūrī, founder of the *'Ligue de la Patrie Arabe'*. The latter was suspected of being a French agent. S. G. Haim (ed) *Arab Nationalism*, Los Angeles 1962, pp. 29–30.
15. Memorandum by Clayton on 'procedure regarding Ordinances', 1912, SAD/183/3.
16. Sir Edgar Bonham Carter (1870–1956), joined the Sudan government in 1899 as its first legal secretary, a post he held until 1917, when he was transferred to Iraq.
17. Wingate to Clayton (very private), 27 Mar. 1915, SAD/469/8.
18. See below pp. 89–90, 131–132.
19. Gorst to Wingate, 12 Dec. 1908, SAD/284/15; Memorandum by Khalīl Pasha Ḥamdi Ḥamāda on the history of the Khartoum Mosque [n.d.] FO/141/416.
20. Wingate to Gorst, (private), 22 Dec. 1908, SAD/284/12/3.
21. Wingate to Cromer, 6 Feb. 1906, SAD/278/2.
22. Pownoll Ramsay Phipps (1864–1932), joined the Egyptian army 1899; Wingate's private secretary 1903–4; civil secretary of the Sudan 1905–14. Hill, *BD*, p. 306.
23. Wingate to Phipps, 13 Apr. 1909, SAD/287/1.

24. Clayton to Wingate, 11 Feb. 1914, SAD/469/6/1.
25. Wingate to Cromer, (private), 24 Feb. 1915, SAD/194/2.
26. Channer to Wingate, 10 Aug. 1908, SAD/283/8/2.
27. Wingate to Asser, (private), 29 Aug. 1908, SAD/283/8/4.
28. Wingate to Kitchener, 26 Oct. 1911, SAD/301/4.
29. Clayton to Wingate, 1 Mar. 1910, SAD/290/3/1; General Sir Gilbert Falkingham Clayton (1875–1929), served under Kitchener during the reconquest of the Sudan; joined the Egyptian army in 1900 and was transferred to the Sudan government in 1906; Wingate's private secretary 1908–14; Sudan agent and director of intelligence 1914–17; adviser to the Egyptian ministry of the interior 1919–22; chief secretary in Palestine 1922–5; died in Baghdad in 1929 while British high commissioner for Iraq. *DNBS, 1922–30*, pp. 186–7.
30. Slatin to Wingate, 6 Mar. 1910, SAD/290/3/1.
31. *al-Liwā'*, 4 Feb. 1900; 5 Feb. 1900; 7 Feb. 1900; 3 May 1900; 21 Oct. 1907; 30 May 1908; 15 Nov. 1908.
32. Shoucair to Stack, 24 Jan. 1909, SAD/286/1; see also *al-Muqaṭṭam*, 22 Jan. 1909—article on the Sudan written by Aḥmad Effendi Yūsuf Kandil; and *al-Muqaṭṭam,* 21 Oct. 1908—article signed Ummdurmānī, SAD/234/6.
33. *al-Liwā'*, 19 May 1908; *The Standard*, 31 May 1908; *L'Étendard Égyptien*, 31 May 1908.
34. See below pp. 37–38.
35. Wingate to Cromer, 19 Feb. 1900, FO/141/356; note by R. W. [Wingate] on Omdurman Mutiny, [n.d. Jan. 1900?] SAD/270/1.
36. Wingate to Harvey, 26 Nov. 1907, SAD/281/5; for details see below pp. 117–118.
37. Phipps to Wingate, 7 Sep. 1904, SAD/234/2.
38. Sir James Currie (1868–1937), joined the Sudan civil service in 1900 as director of education and principal of Gordon College. He held these posts until his retirement in 1914; was a member of the governor-general's council in 1910–14. *DNBS 1931–40*, pp. 206–7.
39. Wingate to Clayton (private), 9 Apr. 1916, SAD/470/1. The money came as usual out of the Sudan civil funds.
40. War Office Selected papers—No. 2; British detachment at Khartoum, 1900.
41. War Office to Foreign Office, 9 Nov. 1898, FO/78/5025. The sum involved was £E 29,000.
42 Cheetham to Grey, 10 May 1911; Slade to Mallet, 12 Sep. 1911, FO/371/1113.
43. The Lado Enclave was created by the Franco-Congolese agreement of 1894, and was administered by the Belgians until King Leopold's death in 1910 when it reverted to the Sudan. For details see R. O. Collins, The Transfer of the Lado Enclave to the Anglo-Egyptian Sudan, 1910. *Zaïre*. Vol. XIV, 2. (1960).
44. Gorst to Grey, 12 Mar. 1910, FO/800/47; Gorst to Grey, 20 Mar. 1910, ibid.

45. Wingate to McMahon, 14 Sep. 1915, FO/371/2352; Treasury to FO, 16 Dec. 1915, ibid.
46. *The Times*, 18 Apr. 1900.
47. Wingate to Clayton, 6 Mar. 1910, SAD/469/2/1.
48. Clayton to Wingate, (private), 22 May 1910, SAD/296/2; Wingate to Phipps, 19 Sep. 1910, SAD/297/4.
49. Kitchener to Grey, 10 May 1912, FO/371/1363; Memorandum by E. G. [Grey], 14 May 1912, ibid.
50. For details see A. Gaitskell, *Gezira, a story of development in the Sudan*, (London, 1959), pp. 51–8; see also FO/371/1635 and 1665.
51. Wingate to Hardinge, (private), 1 Mar. 1920, SAD/237/11; Wingate to Curzon, 3 Apr. 1919, SAD/175/4; Wingate to Hardinge, 27 Dec. 1918, ibid.
52. Report of the Milner Mission, pp. 33–4, SAD/107/13/2.
53. Cromer to Revelstoke, 12 Oct. 1910, FO/633/19.
54. Wingate to Clayton, 13 Sep. 1916, SAD/470/3.
55. Cromer to Wingate, 23 Apr. 1915, FO/633/24.
56. Cromer to Wingate, 18 Sep. 1901, SAD/271/9.
57. Cromer to Lansdowne, 4 Mar. 1902, FO/800/124.
58. Cromer to Mallet, (private), 18 Mar. 1909, FO/371/660.
59. See above pp. 13–15.
60. Cromer to Wingate, 25 Jan. 1904, FO/633/8.
61. Cromer to Wingate, 9 Sep. 1905, SAD/234/4.
62. Cecil to Wingate, 14 Sep. 1905, SAD/277/2.
63. Sudan Agent to Findlay, 21 Aug. 1905, FO/141/393.
64. Cromer to Wingate, 8 Apr. 1900, SAD/270/4.
65. Cromer to Wingate, 18 Feb. 1901, SAD/271/1.
66. Cromer to Wingate, 21 Feb. 1905, SAD/276/2.
67. Cromer to Salisbury, 8 June 1900, FO/633/6.
68. Jackson Pasha, Sir Herbert William (1861–1931), was seconded to the Egyptian army in 1888; commanded the Sudanese force at Fashoda in 1898 during the Fashoda incident; became governor of Berber in 1899 and civil secretary in 1900–1; from 1902 until his retirement in 1922, he was governor of Dongola. Hill, *BD*, pp. 188–89.
69. Cromer to Jackson, 2 June 1900, FO/633/8.
70. Cromer to Sanderson, 26 Apr. 1899, FO/78/5026; Cromer to Wingate, 4 Jan. 1907, SAD/103/1; *al-Liwā'*, *al-Mu'ayyad*, *al-Minbār*, *al-Quṭr al-Miṣrī*, *al-Waṭan*, and *Wādī al-Nīl*, were only a few of the newspapers which were stopped by order of the Sudan agent from entering the Sudan.
71. Cromer to Gwynne, 13 Mar. 1903, FO/633/8; for details see below pp. 108–109, 112–115.
72. Cromer to Strachey, 3 Apr. 1906, FO/633/8; Cromer to Kitchener, 30 July 1913, PRO/30/57/No. 44; see also R. Owen, 'The Influence of Lord Cromer's Indian Experience on British Policy in Egypt, 1883–1907'; *St. Antony's papers, Middle Eastern Affairs No. 4 (1965)*, pp. 122–8.
73. Cromer to Wingate, 3 Feb. 1904, SAD/275/2; *Muwallad* (pl. *Muwalladīn*) was the term applied to persons of Egyptian or

partially Egyptian origin, who were born in the Sudan, where they formed an important class, especially in the towns.

74. Currie to Wingate, 25 June 1908, SAD/282/6.
75. Cromer to Salisbury, 8 June 1900, FO/633/3.
76. Cromer to Wingate, 2 July 1905, SAD/234/4.
77. Cromer to Wingate, (private), 21 Feb. 1905, SAD/276/2.
78. Cromer to Grey, (private), 19 Apr. 1907, FO/633/13.
79. Cromer to Revelstoke, 12 Oct. 1910, FO/633/19.
80. Cromer to Grey, (private), 28 Mar. 1907, FO/800/46.
81. Gorst to Grey, (private), 12 Jan. 1908, FO/800/47.
82. Owen to Wingate, (private), 16 May 1908, SAD/282/5. Owen Pasha, Roger Carmichael Robert (1866–1941), was transferred to the Sudan government from the Egyptian army in 1903; director of intelligence and Sudan agent 1905–8; governor of Mongalla 1908–18; Hill, *BD*, p. 300.
83. Wingate to Slatin, (private), 23 Mar. 1910, SAD/431/1/1.
84. Wingate to Slatin, 12 Apr. 1911, SAD/431/1/2.
85. Stack Pasha, Sir Lee Oliver Fitzmaurice (1868–1924), joined the Egyptian army 1899; Wingate's private secretary 1904–8; Sudan agent 1908–14; civil secretary 1914–16; acting sirdar and governor-general 1916–18; sirdar and governor-general 1918–24; assassinated in Cairo 1924. *DNBS 1922–30*, pp. 802–3.
86. Wingate to Stack, (private), 20 May 1911, SAD/300/5/2.
87. See below pp. 74–77.
88. Gorst to Wingate, 13 Jan. 1910, FO/407/175.
89. Currie to Wingate, 7 Mar. 1908, SAD/282/3/1; Harvey to Wingate, 30 Oct. 1907, SAD/281/5; Wingate to Harvey, 26 Nov. 1907, ibid.
90. Wingate to Stack, 31 Mar. 1908, SAD/284/13.
91. Harvey to Gorst, 8 Apr. 1908, FO/141/416.
92. Wingate to Harvey, 16 Apr. 1908, SAD/282/4.
93. Gorst to Harvey, 1 Dec. 1908, FO/141/416; Harvey to Gorst, 2 Dec. 1908, ibid.
94. Gorst to Wingate, 3 Dec. 1908, SAD/284/15.
95. Bernard to Harvey, 17 May 1909; Harvey to Bernard, 2 June 1909, SAD/287/2.
96. Wingate to Clayton, 1 Aug. 1908, SAD/469/1.
97. Gorst to Wingate, (private), 18 Feb. 1909, SAD/286/1.
98. Wingate to Stack, (private), 23 Mar. 1909, SAD/286/3.
99. Wingate to Gorst, 4 Apr. 1909, SAD/287/1.
100. Wingate to Gorst, 14 Mar. 1910, SAD/469/2/1.
101. Gorst to Wingate, 16 Mar. 1910, ibid.
102. Owen to Wingate, 16 Dec. 1907, SAD/281/6.
103. Wingate to Stack, 25 Nov. 1908, SAD/284/13; Wingate to Stack, 20 Dec. 1908, SAD/284/14.
104. Wingate to Clayton, (private), 29 Mar. 1910, SAD/469/2/1.
105. Wingate to Gorst, 27 May 1908, FO/141/416; Gorst to Wingate, 28 May 1908, ibid; Grey to Gorst, 29 May 1908, FO/407/172.
106. Gorst to Grey, (private), 31 May 1908, FO/800/47.

107. Wingate to Gorst, (strictly confidential), 9 Aug. 1908, FO/407/173; Gorst to Grey, 9 Aug. 1908, ibid.
108. Gorst to Grey, (private), 22 June 1908, FO/800/47.
109. Wingate to Gorst, 7 Feb. 1909; Gorst to Wingate, 18 Feb. 1909, SAD/286/2; Gorst to Grey, (private), 12 Feb. 1909, FO/371/659.
110. Wingate to Stack, (private), 3 Jan. 1909, SAD/286/1.
111. Kitchener to Wingate, 25 June 1909, SAD/287/3.
112. Cromer to Strachey, 26 Mar. 1913, FO/633/22.
113. Wingate to Stack, 18 Nov. 1912, SAD/183/2.
114. Stack to Wingate, 6 Apr. 1912; 7 Apr. 1912, SAD/181/1/3.
115. Wingate to Stack, 4 May 1912, SAD/181/2/2.
116. Stack to Wingate, 1 May 1912, ibid.
117. Clayton to Wingate, 3 Nov. 1913, SAD/469/5; Wingate to Clayton, 6 Nov. 1913, ibid.
118. Wingate to Stack, (private), 18 Apr. 1914, SAD/190/1/2.
119. Clayton to Wingate, 3 Nov. 1913, SAD/469/5.
120. Wingate to Stack, (private), 6 May 1913, SAD/108/16.
121. Wingate to Clayton, (very private and personal), 19 Nov. 1914, SAD/469/7.
122. Wingate to Clayton, 9 Jan. 1915, SAD/469/8; following the declaration of British protectorate over Egypt, on 18 Dec. 1914, the British consul-general became high-commissioner, and the British agency was called the residency.
123. Stack to Wingate, (private), 28 Apr. 1915, SAD/195/3; Sir Ronald Storrs was the oriental secretary of the British agency since 1909.
124. Wingate to Kitchener, (private), 2 June 1915, SAD/195/10.
125. Wingate to Parker, (private), 5 July 1915, SAD/201/3.
126. Cecil to Cheetham, 16 Jan. 1915, SAD/194/1.
127. Clayton to Wingate, (private), 11 Mar. 1915, SAD/194/2. The letter was sent by mistake to Clayton, the Sudan agent, together with other correspondence from the residency.
128. Wingate to Cromer, 31 Mar. 1915, FO/633/24.
129. Wingate to Kitchener, 2 June 1915, PRO/30/57/No. 47.
130. Wingate to Clayton, (private), 1 June 1915, SAD/469/9.
131. Wingate to McMahon, (private), 2 June 1915, SAD/195/10. This letter was ostensibly written in order to explain to McMahon, why Egyptian decorations should not be granted to Sudanese.
132. Wingate to Kitchener, (private), 3 Aug. 1915, SAD/196/3.
133. Wingate to Grey, 1 Nov. 1916, SAD/236/5.

CHAPTER III

The Inspector-General, Slatin Pasha

1. For a detailed study of Slatin and of his activities while in the Sudan, see R. Hill, *Slatin Pasha*, London 1965.

2. Ibid., pp. 57–60.
3. Ibid., pp. 63–4.
4. Slatin's diary, 27 Feb. 1900, SAD/441.
5. Ibid., 20 Feb.–20 Mar. 1900.
6. Cromer to Salisbury, 8 June 1900, FO/633/6.
7. Memorandum by Wingate, [n.d. Oct. 1907?], SAD/281/4, Wingate to Asser, 29 Sep. 1909, SAD/288/5.
8. Symes, Sir Stewart, (1882–1963). Joined the Egyptian army in 1906; 1909–12 was A.D.I. Khartoum; 1913–16 was Wingate's private secretary and remained on his staff after he became high commissioner of Egypt in 1917. During the years 1920–34 he served in Egypt, Palestine, Aden, and Tanganyika, and returned to the Sudan as governor-general in the years 1934–40.
9. 'Duties of Inspector-General, Sudan', 4 Apr. 1902, SAD/403/6. The following details are all quoted from this document.
10. Slatin's diary, 1913, SAD/441.
11. Savile, Lieut.-Colonel Robert Vesey; seconded to the Sudan government in 1902; served as inspector in Kassala 1902–6; and Dongola 1906–7; governor of Baḥr al-Ghazāl 1908; governor of Kordofan 1909–1917. *SPS*, p. 11.
12. Refers to the French advance in Wadai, Dār Tama and Masalit.
13. Gelsa *(jalsa)*—meeting, gathering.
14. Willis's diary, Dec. 1910, SAD/210/2. Willis, Charles Armine (b. 1881) graduated from Oxford in 1904, and came to the Sudan in 1905 with one of the first groups of civil-servants. He served in Kordofan 1906–12, first as a junior inspector and following training at the legal department, he became the first legal inspector of Kordofan in 1909; 1913, Senior inspector Red Sea; 1914–15, Dongola; 1915–19, A.D.I.; 1920–6, DMI. *SPS*, p. 19.
15. *Modern Society*, 20 Oct. 1900.
16. Slatin to Wingate, 27 Apr. 1912, SAD/181/1/3, Slatin's diary, Notes 1903, SAD/4611.
17. Slatin to Wingate, 3 Apr. 1913, SAD/186/1/1. H. C. Jackson joined the Sudan government in 1907 and served in the administration for twenty-four years. He should not be confused with Brigadier-General Sir Herbert William Jackson, who was governor of Dongola for twenty years and is referred to as Jackson throughout the book.
18. Slatin to Wingate, 10 Apr. 1913, SAD/186/1/1.
19. Butler's diary, 21 Nov. 1911, SAD/400/10.
20. See below pp. 95–96, 131–132.
21. Slatin to Wingate, 13 Aug. 1901, SAD/271/8.
22. Slatin to Wingate, 1 Sep. 1903, SAD/273/9.
23. Wingate to Stack, [quoting Slatin], 12 May 1908, SAD/284/13; Slatin to Wingate, [n.d. May 1908?], SAD/282/5.
24. Slatin to Wingate, 15 Sep. 1911, SAD/301/3; see below pp. 100–106.
25. See for instance Slatin's diary, 1912, SAD/441, (the list is at the end of the diary).
26. Slatin to Bigge, 6 Sep. 1897, SAD/438/653; the letter was sent in reply to a letter written by Bigge to Prince Francis of Teck on

7 Aug. 1897, ibid.; according to Hill, *Slatin*, pp. 55–6, Bigge's letter was a forgery while Slatin's was written in his own hand.

27. Wingate to Cromer, 11 Dec. 1903, FO/141/378.
28. H. MacMichael, 'Reminiscences of Kordofan in 1906', SAD/294/18.
29. For details see below pp. 170–175.
30. Slatin to Wingate, 2 Dec. 1912, SAD/183/3.
31. For a comprehensive account of the Sultanate of Darfur during that period, see A. B. Theobald, *'Alī Dīnār last Sultan of Darfur 1898–1916,* London 1965.
32. Wingate to Cromer, 3 Mar. 1901, FO/141/364.
33. Mudir Kordofan to Ali Dinar, 25 Sep. 1901, *SIR*—87, Oct. 1901, Appendix 'A'; Theobald, op. cit., pp. 45–50, 126–136.
34. *CAO*—64, 17 Apr. 1902; the following details unless otherwise stated, are based on Slatin's diaries.
35. Tebeldi trees were used for storing water in the arid areas of western Kordofan and Darfur. H. S. Blunt, 'Tebeldis', *SNR*—Vol. 6 (1923), pp. 114–116.
36. Slatin to Wingate, 16 Feb. 1903, SAD/273/2. *Nāẓir* (pl. *nuẓẓār*): inspector in charge of the administration of a tribe.
37. Henry to Wingate, 29 July 1904, SAD/275/5.
38. Slatin to Wingate, 13 Aug. 1908, SAD/283/8/3.
39. Slatin to Wingate, 19 Mar. 1907, SAD/280/3.
40. For details of this concession, which was granted to an American, Leigh Hunt in 1904, see Gaitskell, op. cit., pp. 51–5.
41. *Sakieh (sāqiya)*—a wheel placed alongside the river and driven by oxen in order to lift the water for irrigation.
42. Slatin to Wingate, 17 Aug. 1908, SAD/283/8/4.
43. K. D. D. Henderson, 'Note on the History of the Hamar Tribe of Western Kordofan', 1932, SAD/478/5/2; Hill, *BD*, p. 15; *SIR*—86, Sep. 1901.
44. Ferguson to Wingate, 3 June 1902, SAD/272/4/1.
45. *'Umda* (pl. *'umad*; English form—*'umdas*); village headman, administrative head of a number of villages.
46. Slatin to Wingate, 10 Mar. 1910, SAD/290/3/1.
47. *Kurbāj*, a whip usually made of hippopotamus hide, used for punishing offenders.
48. Slatin to Wingate, 27 Jan. 1903, SAD/273/1.
49. Slatin to Wingate, 14 Apr. 1912, SAD/181/1/3.
50. Slatin to Wingate, 21 Mar. 1913, SAD/185/3/3.
51. Slatin to Wingate, 16 February 1903, SAD/273/2; see below pp. 92–4.
52. Slatin to Wingate, 30 Nov. 1902, SAD/272/8.
53. Wingate to Cromer (secret), 17 Jan. 1902, FO/141/371.
54. Butler's Journal, 1911, SAD/422/12.
55. Interview with Sir H. MacMichael, 6 June 1967.
56. Slatin's diary, 12 Apr. 1910, SAD/441.
57. Slatin to Wingate, 26 Nov. 1900, SAD/270/11.
58. Slatin's diary, 29 Nov. 1911, SAD/441; all the points mentioned by Slatin, were in fact incorporated in the speech.
59. S. Symes, *Tour of Duty*, London 1946, p. 16.

60. Cromer to Lansdowne, 19 Jan. 1902, FO/633/6; for the 'Jackson affair', see Hill, *Slatin Pasha*, p. 79.
61. Gorst to Grey (private), 31 May 1908, FO/800/47.
62. 'Notes on Kassala', Slatin's diary 1909, SAD/441.
63. Slatin to Wingate, 19 Dec. 1908, SAD/284/12/2.
64. Slatin to Wingate, 20 Dec. 1913, SAD/104/6.
65. Kerr, Graham Campbell (1872–1913), joined the Sudan civil service in 1901, with the first group of British civilians recruited from universities. Following eight years service as an inspector in the Red Sea and Sennar provinces, he was appointed in 1909 as governor of the Red Sea province, the first civilian governor in the Anglo-Egyptian Sudan. Hill, *BD*, p. 198.
66. Slatin to Wingate, 20 Mar. 1910, SAD/290/3/1.
67. Slatin to Wingate, 27 Mar. 1910, ibid.
68. Wingate to Slatin, 28 Mar. 1906, SAD/431/11.
69. Slatin to Hakimam [ḥākim 'ām: the Egyptian term for governor-general], 2 June [1908?], SAD/451/124, Wingate to Slatin, 3 June 1908; Slatin to Wingate, 4 June [1908?], ibid.
70. Wingate to Stack, 4 June 1908, SAD/284/13.

CHAPTER IV

Government Departments and Provinces

1. For a table describing the administrative and military structure of the Sudan see pp. 192–194.
2. These circulars were quoted in a confidential report on the Sudan-agency submitted by the Sudan agent to the First Secretary of the Residency in Cairo, 27 Oct. 1925, FO/141/448; I have not been able to locate the original circulars. The following details are all from the confidential report.
3. During Lord Cecil's term of office the Sudan agent was called agent-general, *CAO*—101, 30 Nov. 1903.
4. Channer to Wingate, 10 Aug. 1908, SAD/283/8/2.
5. Owen to Wingate, 7 Apr. 1907, SAD/280/4. I have not been able to locate these reports nor to ascertain whether they were kept.
6. Butler's diary, 13 Oct. 1911, SAD/400/10.
7. Samuel Atiya, a Lebanese, was one of the old employees of the department, and the most experienced of the Khartoum staff. He continued his work in the intelligence department until his retirement in 1928 when his post was given to his nephew Edward Atiyah. E. Atiyah, *An Arab tells his story* (London 1946), pp. 156–9.
8. Ismā'īl Aḥmad al-Azharī (1868–1947), was *muftī* of the Sudan, 1924–32, Ismā'īl al-Azharī, the former President of the Republic of the Sudan, is his grandson. Hill, *BD*, p. 184.
9. Butler's diary, October–November 1911, SAD/400/10.

10. Mahgoub Mohamed Salih, 'The Sudanese Press', *SNR*, Vol. 46 (1965) pp. 1–3.
11. The Sudan agents were: Count Gleichen 1901–3; Lord Edward Cecil 1903–5; Owen 1905–8; Stack 1908–14; Clayton 1914–16. Cecil, Stack, and Clayton were Wingate's private secretaries while Gleichen was one of his closest friends.
12. Wingate to Clayton (private), 13 Sep. 1916, SAD/470/3.
13. The functions of the legal secretary will be discussed below pp. 124–136.
14. See below pp. 74–77.
15. For the Sudan's financial relations with Egypt and Britain see J. Stone, *The Finance of Government Economic Development in the Sudan 1899–1913*, Sudan Economic Institute, Khartoum, 1954 (unpublished); Abdel Wahab Abdel Rahim, *An Economic History of the Sudan 1899–1956*, M.A. thesis, Manchester, 1963; see also above pp. 13–15.
16. Sir Harold MacMichael, *The Anglo-Egyptian Sudan*, London 1934, pp. 78, 90–1, 198.
17. *SG*—5, 2 Oct. 1899, *SG*—6, 2 Nov. 1899.
18. Maxwell to Wingate, 6 Jan. 1900, SAD/270/1/2.
19. *Ṣarrāf*—cashier, money changer; assisted in the collection of taxes.
20. *SG*—10, 1 Apr. 1900.
21. Cromer to Wingate (private), 20 Apr. 1906, [copy sent to Grey], FO/800/46.
22. Gorst to Wingate, 11 Apr. 1908, FO/141/46; see also GGC, 20 Feb. 1912, FO/867/3.
23. Wingate to Cecil, (very private and confidential), 20 Dec. 1912, SAD/183/3. (Wingate later ordered Stack not to deliver this letter.)
24. Wingate to Stack, (private), 25 Apr. 1914, SAD/190/1/2.
25. Phipps to Wingate, 15 July 1907, SAD/288/2.
26. *GGR*—1902, p. 211; *GGR*—1906, p. 240.
27. *GGR*—1902, pp. 156–57. The classification is not clear. The Sudanese were probably southern ex-soldiers of the Egyptian army, while locally enlisted men were mostly town dwellers, and the Arabs were northern Sudanese.
28. *GGR*—1908, p. 308.
29. *GGR*—1902, pp. 142–3; *GGR*—1904, p. 99.
30. See below pp. 104–106.
31. For an extensive survey of the development of transport in the Sudan, see R. Hill, *Sudan Transport*, London, 1965. O. M. Osman Abdu, *The Development of Transport and Economic Growth in the Sudan 1898–1958*, Ph.D. thesis, London 1960.
32. *GGR*—1906, p. 66; Wingate to Stack, 18 Feb. 1911, SAD/300/1.
33. *GGR*—1908, pp. 313–15, 326–31. Kennedy to Wingate, 27 May 1912, SAD/181/2/2.
34. Asser's memorandum, Sep. 1911, SAD/301/3; see also *GGR*—1904, pp. 6, 59–60.
35. For a full account of agricultural development and administration during this period see Arthur Gaitskell, *Gezira, A Story of development in the Sudan*, London, 1959; Abdel Wahab Abdel Rahim is

at present writing a Ph.D. thesis for Manchester University entitled, *An Economic History of the Gezira Scheme, 1900–1950*; J. D. Tothill (ed.), *Agriculture in the Sudan*, London, 1948.

36. *GGR*—1903, p. 154.
37. Wingate to Cromer, 24 Apr. 1905, SAD/276/4; for full details of land policy in the Sudan, see below pp. 155–164.
38. *GGR*—1906, p. 168.
39. Wingate to Gorst, 2 Jan. 1910, SAD/290/1; Wingate to Clayton, 1 Aug. 1910, SAD/297/2, *GGC*, 1 Nov. 1910, FO/867/1.
40. *GGC*—2 Mar. 1915; 7–8 May 1915, FO/867/6.
41. M. O. Beshir, *Educational Development in the Sudan, 1898–1956*, B.Litt. Oxford, 1966; L. M. Sanderson, *Education in the Southern Sudan, 1898–1948*, Ph.D. London, 1966; J. Currie, 'The Educational experiment in the Anglo-Egyptian Sudan', *Journal of the African Society*, Vol. 33, pp. 361–71, 1934; Vol. 34, pp. 41–59, 1935; Bābikr Badrī, *Ta'rīkh Ḥayātī*, Vols, 1–3, Omdurman, 1959–61.
42. H. C. Squire, *The Sudan medical service, an experiment in social medicine*, London, 1958; J. B. Christopherson, *Notes on medicine in the Sudan*, (typescript, n.d.), SAD/407/6.
43. E. R. J. Hussey, 'A fiki's Clinic', *SNR*—Vol. 6, (1923), pp. 35–9; *GGR*—1902, pp. 125–30; *GGR*—1908, pp. 224–5.
44. *Report on the Soudan* by Lieutenant Colonel Stewart, (1883), C.3670.
45. Memorandum presented to Lord Cromer on 4 Apr. 1897, (signed), Sirdar, SAD/266/1/1.
46. This proposal was put forward by Sir E. Palmer, the financial adviser, in a Minute to the Sirdar, 10 Apr. 1897, ibid.
47. Memorandum presented to Lord Cromer, (signed), Sirdar, 10 Apr. 1897, ibid.
48. J. S. R. Duncan, *The Sudan a Record of Achievement*, London, 1952, pp. 64–66.
49. For full details of provincial and district boundaries see *Handbook of the Anglo-Egyptian Sudan*, 1922, pp. 1–2, 171–72, 283–85.
50. *Memorandum to Mudirs*—Inclosure in Cromer to Salisbury, 17 Mar. 1899, FO/78/5022. The following details, unless otherwise stated, are from Kitchener's memorandum.
51. *CAO*—41, 25 Feb. 1902; see also Wingate to Stanton, 24 Aug. 1908, SAD/283/8/4.
52. *CAO*—60, 17 Apr. 1902.
53. *GGR*—1905, pp. 274–6, 279; *GGR*—1908, pp. 699–700.
54. For details see relevant chapters.
55. *GGR*—1903, p. 10, *GGR*—1904, Appendix 'A', pp. 154–7; *GGR*—1905, p. 223.
56. Wingate to Jackson, 25 Nov. 1914, SAD/192/2.
57. E. R. J. Hussey, *Tropical Africa 1908–1944*, London 1947, p. 20.
58. *The Sub-Mamur's Handbook*, pp. 336–37. For lack of other sources, most of the information about non-European officials is derived from the diaries and private letters of European officials. For the duties performed by shaykhs, *'umdas* and *nāzirs* see pp. 142–147.

59. *GGR*—1908, p. 592; see also *GGR*—1907, pp. 119, 122, 132.
60. *GGR*—1914, p. 65.
61. Asser to Wingate, 16 Aug. 1911, SAD/301/3.
62. Clayton to Wingate, 11 Sep. 1911, ibid.
63. This conclusion was reached by assessing Wingate's correspondence during this period. Sir Harold MacMichael, whom I interviewed on 6 June 1967, confirmed my impression and pointed out that Wingate's confidants namely: Slatin, Stack, Clayton, and Symes were all former members of the intelligence department like Wingate himself.
64. Phipps to Wingate, 7 June 1908, SAD/282/6.
65. Wingate to Clayton, 11 Sep. 1909, SAD/469/1.
66. Gorst to Grey, (private), 7 Oct. 1909, FO/800/47.
67. Sir R. Ritchie to Grey, 19 Oct. 1909, FO/800/47.
68. Gorst to Grey, 30 Oct. 1909, FO/800/47.
69. Gorst to Grey, 14 Nov. 1909, FO/371/664.
70. For full text of ordinance see *SG* No. 167, 24 Jan. 1910.
71. Gorst to Wingate, 13 Jan. 1910, FO/867/1.
72. FO/867/1–7.
73. FO/867/1; FO/867/2; Wingate to Gorst, 17 Dec. 1910; Gorst to Wingate, 29 Dec. 1910, SAD/298/3.
74. FO/867/3, pp. 31, 70, 77–8; FO/867/4, pp. 21–2.

CHAPTER V

Government Officials and the Training of Sudanese

1. Report by the Inspector-General of the Overseas Forces of an inspection of the Soudan, 1913 (Secret), FO/371/1639.
2. Symes, op. cit., p. 13.
3. *Reports of His Majesty's Agent and Consul General on the Finances, Administration and Condition of Egypt and the Soudan, 1899*, C.D.95. (short reference is *SAR*.)
4. Inclosures 1 and 2 in Cromer to Salisbury, 11 May 1900, FO/78/5087.
5. Conditions of service of British Officers in the Egyptian army, War Office, Cairo, 17 Nov. 1900, FO/78/5088.
6. Cromer to Lansdowne, 2 Jan. 1902, FO/407/157; War Office to Cromer 3 Mar. 1902; Lansdowne to Cromer, 17 Oct. 1902, ibid.
7. War Office to Grey, 31 Jan. 1914, FO/371/1966; Kitchener to Grey, 1 Mar. 1914, ibid.
8. Crowe to Secretary Army Council, 26 Mar. 1914, ibid.; War Office to Grey, 25 May 1914, ibid.
9. Wingate to Clayton, 29 Mar. 1914, SAD/469/6/1; see also Wingate to Kitchener, 29 Mar. 1914, FO/371/1966.
10. MacMichael, *The Anglo-Egyptian Sudan*, Appendix to Chapter 6.

11. Willis to O., 29 Dec. 1908, SAD/209/1.
12. *The Times*, Financial and Business Supplement, 22 July 1907.
13. Cromer to Salisbury, 8 June 1900, FO/633/6.
14. Lansdowne to Cromer, 29 Jan. 1902, FO/800/123; Cromer to Lansdowne, 9 Feb. 1902, ibid.
15. Cromer to Wingate, 25 Nov. 1905, SAD/234/3; Wingate to Cromer, 30 Nov. 1905, SAD/277/5.
16. Wilfred Cummings to Wingate, Karachi, Christmas 1904, SAD/275/1. These letters are preserved in the Wingate papers at the Sudan Archive in Durham, and are not the official letters of reference, which were required from every candidate.
17. Wingate to Phipps, 6 July 1912, SAD/182/1/2.
18. Egyptian and Sudanese Civil Services, Information to Candidates, June 1913, SAD/152/7/7.
19. Wingate to Cromer, 1 Aug. 1913, SAD/187/2/3. Pease was appointed and served in the Sudan until 1911. In his letter Wingate asked Cromer to use his influence in order to get a post for Pease at the new School of Oriental Studies at London University.
20. Hussey, op. cit., p. 1; R. Davies, *The Camel's Back*, London 1957, pp. 8–14, 23–5; H. C. Jackson, *Sudan Days and Ways*, London 1954. The following information is based on the above sources, unless otherwise stated.
21. *SPS*, pp. 17–37.
22. Bonham Carter to Wingate, 30 June 1910, SAD/469/2/1.
23. Wingate to Clayton, 2 July 1910, SAD/469/2/2.
24. Clayton to Wingate, (private), 8 Apr. 1914, SAD/469/6/2; Wingate to Clayton, (private), 16 Apr. 1914, ibid.
25. *Memoirs of Ryder, 1905–1916*, (typescript), SAD/400/8, p. 66.
26. Cromer to Wingate, 10 Apr. 1905, SAD/234/3.
27. Wingate to Cromer, 24 Apr. 1905, SAD/276/4.
28. Stack's minutes to an application for post of private secretary by Mr. Alfred W. Allsworth, 10 Oct. 1905, SAD/234/4.
29. Wingate to Kitchener, 7 Feb. 1899, SAD/269/2/1; Talbot to Wingate, 10 Feb. 1899, ibid; Buṭrus Ghālī to Cromer, 25 May 1899, FO/407/151; Cromer to Salisbury, 8 Jan. 1900, FO/407/151; Cromer to Salisbury, 8 Jan. 1900, FO/78/5086.
30. Notes on Civil Administration in the Sudan n.d. [1897?] SAD/266/1/3; Cromer to Salisbury, 4 Dec. 1898, FO/407/147.
31. Wingate to Phipps, 5 Apr. 1913, SAD/186/1/2.
32. Currie to Wingate, 6 Sep. 1907, SAD/281/3.
33. Bonham Carter to Wingate, 25 May 1909, SAD/287/3; Nason to Wingate, 8 Aug. 1902, SAD/272/6; Willis's diary, 27 Sep. 1910, SAD/210/2; *GGR*—1907, p. 185, *GGR*—1908, p. 687.
34. Wingate to Cromer, 9 May 1906, SAD/278/5.
35. Wingate to Savile (private), 19 Apr. 1915, SAD/195/2.
36. 'Gordon College—Proposed reorganization of the Upper School', [n.d. July 1915?], SAD/196/5.
37. Wingate to Kitchener (private), 3 Aug. 1915, (26th Anniversary of the Battle of Toski), SAD/196/3.

38. *GGR*—1902, p. 16.
39. *CAO*—21, 7 Mar. 1903; *CAO*—[?], 25 Jan. 1905; *CAO*—401, 15 Mar. 1906; *GGR*—1908, pp. 261–3; see below pp. 129–132.
40. *GGR*—1908, p. 156.
41. Wingate to Cromer, 13 Apr. 1903, SAD/273/4.
42. Syrian Community to Wingate, 29 Nov. 1914, SAD/192/2 (signed), Juredini (editor of the *Sudan Times*).
43. Lord Cromer's Speech at Khartoum, 28 Jan. 1903, FO/633/25.
44. *GGR*—1902, p. 114; *SG*—61, Apr. 1904. The monthly subsidy paid to teachers was £E 3. The Sudanese *kuttābs* were traditionally known as *khalwas*. However, in all the official documents, the term *kuttāb* is used for the Qur'ān schools.
45. W. Scott Hill, Memoir, 'Ten Years in the Sudan', [n.d.], SAD/466/4/4.
46. *GGR*—1908, pp. 224–5, 628.
47. *SAR*—1900, p. 76; see also J. Currie, 'The Educational Experiment in the Anglo-Egyptian Sudan', *Journal of the African Society*, Vol. 33, (1934), p. 364.
49. *GGR*—1905, pp. 50–1, 224–6, *GGR*—1906, pp. 216–7.
48. *GGR*—1908, pp. 149–50, 167–8, 572.
50. *GGR*—1908, p. 154.
51. Bonham Carter to Wingate, 16 Jan. 1907, SAD/280/1; Wingate to Bonham Carter, (private), 28 Sep. 1916, SAD/201/8.
52. *GGR*—1905, p. 55.
53. *GGR*—1903, p. 18; *GGR*—1904, p. 59; see also 'Historical Records Military School, Khartoum' (Sudan), n.d., SAD/106/4.
54. Wingate to Phipps, 21 May 1912, SAD/181/2/2.
55. Asser to Wingate, 15 Sep. 1912, SAD/182/3/2.
56. List of the family of the Mahdi, the Khalifa, and of leading Mahdist Amirs, their place of residence and employment [n.d. 1914?], SAD/106/2.
57. Currie to Wingate, 24 June 1914, SAD/190/3/2; Wingate to Currie, 1 July 1914, ibid.
58. 'Memorandum on the Future Status of the Sudan', Major-General Sir L. Stack to Field Marshal Viscount Allenby, 25 May 1924, SAD/248/37.
59. 'Memorandum by Wingate on interview with Mudassir Ibrahim (late kateb of the Khalifa)', Inclosure in Cromer to Salisbury, 11 Apr. 1899, FO/407/151; *GGR*—1902, p. 317; *GGR*—1903, pp. 74, 96; *GGR*—1904, p. 105; *GGR*—1906, p. 702.
60. *GGR*—1903, App. 'D'.
61. *GGR*—1906, pp. 223–4, 265–7; Bābikr Badrī, *Ta'rīkh Ḥayātī*, Vol. II, Omdurman 1960, pp. 64–6.
62. *SG*—44, Feb. 1903.
63. See below pp. 146–147.
64. For the relation of Wingate and Slatin with Egyptian and Sudanese officials, see above pp. 10–12, 19–21, 52–55.
65. Balfour to Lady F. Balfour [his mother], 30 Apr. 1907, SAD/303/6.

66. *Fakī*—a colloquial contraction of *faqīh*, 'student of law', was applied in the Sudan indiscriminately to men of religion.
67. Hussey, op. cit., pp. 3, 7.
68. Willis's diary, SAD/210/2.
69. Atiyah, op. cit., pp. 137–40.
70. Badrī, op. cit., pp. 53–4, 65–8.
71. 'Note on the Political State of the Sudan', 17 Jan. 1916, SAD/236/4.

CHAPTER VI

Religious Policy, Islam and Christianity

1. Viscount Cromer's speech to the Sheikhs and Notables of the Soudan at Omdurman, 4 Jan. 1899, FO/633/25.
2. *Memorandum to Mudirs,* Inclosure in Cromer to Salisbury, 17 Mar. 1899, FO/78/5022.
3. Cromer to Salisbury, 11 Oct. 1898, FO/407/147.
4. Blyth to Cromer, 21 Feb. 1900, FO/407/155; see below pp.
5. For a comprehensive study of Islam in the Sudan, see J. S. Trimingham, *Islam in the Sudan*, London 1965.
6. The term orthodox Islam, was used by the British authorities in the Sudan in order to distinguish the Islam they supported from Sufism and Mahdism. I have used the same terminology without trying to determine whether this Islam was really orthodox.
7. Adeney to Baylis, 21 Jan. 1902, CMSA/E/03/1902. The proclamation was published in the Egyptian *Journal Officiel*, 14 Nov. 1901.
8. Wingate to Cromer, 13 June, 1901, SAD/271/6.
9. Willis to Slatin, 15 Mar. 1921, SAD/438/653.
10. These mosques, which included *ṣūfī zāwiyas*, were referred to as 'private mosques', in all the Sudan government reports, whilst the mosques subsidized by the government were defined as public. I have followed this terminology for reasons of clarity although this distinction does not exist in Islam.
11. *GGR*—1904, p. 81.
12. *GGR*—1904, p. 78; *GGR*—1905, p. 114; *GGR*—1906, p. 702.
13. P. M. Holt, *Holy families and Islam in the Sudan*, Princeton Near East Papers, No. 4 (1967) see also below p. 130.
14. Rodd to Cromer, 29 Aug. 1900, FO/78/5088.
15. *GGR*—1908, pp. 627–8.
16. Note by Said Shoucair on cost of pilgrimage [n.d.], SAD/493/3.
17. *SIR*—245, Dec. 1914; *SIR*—247, Feb. 1915; *SIR*—252 July 1915.
18. C. A. Willis, *Report on Slavery and the Pilgrimage* (1926), SAD/212/2; see also Wingate to Harvey, 20 Oct. 1910, SAD/284/10/1.
19. Trimingham, *Islam*, p. 234.
20. Wingate to Said Ali, 28 May 1912, SAD/101/17/4.
21. Wingate to Cecil, 5 July 1916, SAD/201/2.
22. Slatin to Wingate, 12 Apr. 1913, SAD/186/1/1.

23. C. P. Browne, Writings (typescript n.d.), SAD/422/14.
24. Butler's Journal, 1911, SAD/422/12.
25. Butler's diary, Oct.–Nov. 1911, SAD/400/10.
26. Wingate to Cromer, 24 Feb. 1901, SAD/271/2.
27. Wingate to Cromer, 1 Mar. 1900, FO/141/356.
28. *SIR*—84, July, 1901; Gleichen to Wingate, 25 July 1901, SAD/271/7; Slatin to Wingate, 13 Aug. 1901, SAD/271/8.
29. *SIR*—85, Aug. 1901.
30. Nason to Wingate, 18 Aug. [1903?], SAD/273/8; Nason to Wingate, 3 Sep. 1903, SAD/273/9; Wingate to Nason, 11 Sep. 1903, ibid.
31. Wingate to Cromer, 11 Oct. 1903, Inclosure in Cromer to Lansdowne, 17 Oct. 1903, FO/403/334.
32. *GGR*—1904, pp. 9–10; *SIR*—121, Aug. 1904; Henry to Findlay, 16 Aug. 1904; Findlay to Henry, 17 Aug. 1904, FO/141/386; Wingate to Henry, 4 Sep. 1904, SAD/275/7.
33. *GGR*—1905, p. 14.
34. *SIR*—143, June 1906; *SIR*—150, Jan. 1907.
35. *SIR*—166, May 1908, Appendix D.
36. Grey to Gorst, 30 May 1908, FO/141/416.
37. Currie to Slatin, 4 July 1908, SAD/431/50.
38. Article in *al-Liwā'*, 28 May 1908, quoted in Graham to Grey, 8 Aug. 1908, FO/407/172; see also above pp. 20–21.
39. Wingate to Stack, (private), 12 May 1908, SAD/284/13.
40. *SIR*—167, June 1908.
41. Proclamation by Wingate, 26 May 1908, Inclosure 2 in Graham to Grey, 6 Sep. 1908, FO/407/172.
42. Wingate to Maxwell (private), 12 May 1908, SAD/110/8.
43. *GGR*—1908, p. 200; Memorandum by Sir R. Wingate, 9 Aug. 1908, (Strictly Confidential), FO/407/173, see above pp.
44. *SIR*—167, June 1908; *GGR*—1908, p. 590; Asser to Wingate, 9 Aug. 1908; Slatin to Wingate, 9 Aug. 1908, SAD/283/8/4; this rumour was caused by a seasonal movement of nomad tribes.
45. *GGR*—1908, pp. 49–52.
46. Scott-Moncrieff, the British inspector who was killed, had joined the Sudan civil service in 1906, having graduated from Oxford a year earlier. His father, Sir Colin Scott-Moncrieff had been in charge of Egyptian irrigation since 1883. As early as 1902 another British inspector by the name of Scott-Barbour was murdered by the Aggar Dinka. However, an uprising by a southern tribe which had not yet been brought under government control and was regarded as savage, was not viewed in the same light as the Wad Ḥabūba revolt. See below pp. ???
47. Wingate to Stack (private), 3 Jan. 1909, SAD/286/1; Channer to Wingate, 13 Sep. 1909, SAD/288/5.
48. Phipps to Wingate, 14 July 1910; Wingate to Phipps, 28 July 1910, SAD/297/1. The arrested *fakīs* had the Mahdi's *rātib* in their possession; *SIR*—192, July 1910.
49. *GGR*—1910, pp. 66–7; the *fakī* later died of his wounds, *SIR*—190, May 1910.

50. *SIR*—193, Aug. 1910; *SIR*—195, Oct. 1910; the sentence of one of the sons was later commuted to life imprisonment.
51. S. Bibaku and Muhammad Al-Tajj, 'The Sudanese Mahdiyya and the Niger-Chad region', in I. M. Lewis (ed.), *Islam in Tropical Africa*, London, 1966, pp. 425–37; see also *The immigration and distribution of West Africans in the Sudan*, Sudan Government Memorandum [n.d.], (short reference: *West Africans*).
52. Wingate to Gorst, 19 Nov. 1910, SAD/298/2; *SIR*—196, Nov. 1910; *SIR*—246, Jan. 1915.
53. *West Africans.*
54. *GGR*—1912, p. 9; Wingate to Wilson, 13 May 1912; SAD/181/2/2; Butler to Wingate, 12 June 1912, SAD/181/3; the date suggests a possible connection with the Italian conquest of Tripoli and Cyrenaica and its possible repercussions in the Sudan which greatly concerned Wingate; see Wingate to Kitchener, 9 Nov. 1911, SAD/301/5.
55. Wingate to Phipps, 20 Mar. 1908, SAD/282/3/2; Slatin to Wingate, 2 Apr. 1908, ibid; see also Hasan Dafalla, 'A note on the political prisoners of Wadi Halfa', *SNR*—47 (1966), pp. 148–50. Mr. Dafalla's claim that the prisoners were moved owing to the pressure of British liberals and of the Egyptian press is not accurate.
56. Wingate to Gorst, 26 Dec. 1909, FO/141/423; *SIR*—215, June 1912.
57. Minutes by F. G. Vansittart on a Parliamentary question by Mr. Ponsonby M.P., 6 Feb. 1913, FO/371/1637.
58. List of the Family of the Mahdi, The Khalifa, & c. with place of residence and employment [n.d.], SAD/106/2.
59. Owen to Wingate, 3 June 1915, SAD/195/3.
60. Wingate to Cromer, 8 May 1906, FO/141/402.
61. *SG*—266, 16 Nov. 1914; *GGR*—1914, p. 43; *SIR*—247, Feb. 1915; *SIR*—260, Mar. 1916.
62. *SIR*—249, Apr. 1915.
63. 'H. E. Governor-General's Speech to the Ulema at Khartoum,' 8 Nov. 1914, *SIR*—244, Nov. 1914. Wingate's speech included a passage referring to the rulers of Turkey as a '. . . syndicate of Jews, financiers and low born intriguers . . .' The speech was published in *The Times* 29 Dec. 1914, and caused an immediate protest by Anglo-Jewry. The editor of *The Jewish Chronicle*, on 1 Jan. 1915, demanded that '. . . this incendiary document should be recalled without delay . . .' The foreign office which had endorsed Wingate's speech in Nov. and had marked the passage '. . . This Syndicate of Jews . . .' as 'quite nice' (signed) L. O. [Oliphant], (Minute to *SIR*—Nov. 1914, FO/371/2349,) suddenly inquired whether Wingate had in fact made these remarks (Crowe to Cheetham, 7 Jan. 1915, SAD/194/1). Wingate rendered apologies to the *Jewish Chronicle*, through Symes, (Symes to Editor of *The Jewish Chronicle*, 23 Mar. 1915, SAD/194/3/2).
64. Wingate to Cromer, 27 Nov. 1914, FO/633/23.
65. *GGR*—1914, pp. 11–12; The Cultivators of Zeidab to Wingate, [n.d. Feb. 1915], SAD/194/3/3.

66. Balfour to Lady Balfour, 21 July 1915, SAD/303/6; Wingate to Clayton, 25 Mar. 1915, SAD/469/8.
67. Pearson to Wingate, 26 May 1915, SAD/195/6; Wingate to Savile, 19 June 1915, SAD/195/10; Balfour to Wingate, 20 Aug. 1915, SAD/196/3; *SIR*—251, June 1915.
68. *SIR*—175, Feb. 1909. Wingate to Grey (private), 8 Oct. 1916, SAD/202/1.
69. Wingate to Jackson, (private and confidential), 21 Sep. 1915, SAD/196/5.
70. Wingate to Clayton, (private), 24 Apr. 1915, SAD/469/9.
71. *Sudan Times*, 14 Aug. 1915; see also Juredini [editor of the *Sudan Times*] to Wingate, 20 Aug. 1915, SAD/196/3.
72. *The Times*, 28 June 1916, quoting Lord Cromer's speech. See also speeches by Lord Grenfell and Viscount Bryce in praise of Wingate, ibid.
73. 'Note on the Political State of The Sudan', 17 Jan. 1916, SAD/236/4.
74. 'Alī al-Mīrghanī to Wingate, 25 Apr. [1915?], SAD/194/3/3; Wingate to McMahon, 15 May 1915, SAD/195/6.
75. Stack to Wingate, 3 July 1919, SAD/237/11.
76. For a biography of Bishop Llewellyn Gwynne see H. C. Jackson, *Pastor on the Nile*, London 1960.
77. Cromer to Blyth, 26 Oct. 1902, FO/633/8; Gwynne to Rev. Gelsthorpe, 5 Apr. 1947, SAD/419.
78. Gorst to Wingate (private), 22 Dec. 1910; Wingate to Gorst, 29 Dec. 1910, SAD/298/3; Blyth to Wingate, 28 Jan. 1911, SAD/300/1; Blyth to Bishop Wilkinson, 11 Feb. 1911, SAD/420/2.
79. Blyth to Gwynne, 3 Jan, 1912; Blyth to Wingate, 10 Jan. 1912, SAD/420/3.
80. Report on Interview with Lord Cromer and Sir Herbert Kitchener, 11 Oct. 1898, CMSA/E/03/1898/no. 51; see also Memorandum of interview accorded by Lord Kitchener to the Rev. F. Baylis and Dr. F. J. Harpur, 18 July 1899, CMSA/E/03/1899.
81. Adeney to General Committee CMS, 12 Dec. 1899, and Minutes of the General Committee instructing Gwynne and Harpur to remain in Omdurman and not to proceed to Fashoda, CMSA/Egypt/1899/125; Gwynne and Harpur to Adeney, 22 Dec. 1899, CMSA/E/03/1899.
82. Maxwell to Wingate, 19 Jan. 1900, SAD/270/1/2.
83. CMS Headquarters minutes, 31 July 1900, CMSA/Egypt/1900/78; Cromer to Salisbury, 9 Nov. 1900, FO/78/5088.
84. Cromer to Lansdowne, 9 Mar. 1900, FO/633/8; Cromer to Salisbury, 27 Apr. 1900, FO/407/155.
85. Baylis to Harpur, 31 July 1900, CMSA/Egypt/Vol. 2; Baylis to Gwynne, 25 Oct. 1901, ibid.
86. MacInnes to Baylis, 13 May 1905, CMSA/Eg/03/1905; see also Baylis to Gwynne, 7 Apr. 1905, CMSA/Eg/Vol. 3; Wingate to Baylis, 11 May 1905, CMSA/Eg/03/1905; Wingate to Cromer, 19 Apr. 1905, FO/141/393.
87. Baylis to Gwynne, 17 Nov. 1905, CMSA/Sudan/Vol. 1.

88. Wingate to Gwynne, 22 Mar. 1910, SAD/290/3; Wingate to Gwynne, 27 Feb. 1913, FO/371/1638.
89. Blyth to Gwynne, 23 Jan. 1912; Wingate to Blyth, 1 Feb. 1912, SAD/420/3; Wingate to Kitchener, 11 Feb. 1912, SAD/180/2/2.
90. Wingate to Clayton, 14 Feb. 1914, SAD/469/6/1.
91. Wingate to Clayton, (private), 7 Mar. 1914, ibid.
92. Blyth to Archbishop Davidson, 17 Mar. 1906, SAD/420/2.
93. Gwynne to Wingate, 19 Nov. 1911, SAD/301/5.
94. *Khartoum Cathedral*, [n.d.], SAD/103/3.
95. MacInnes to Baylis, 13 May 1905, CMSA/E/03/1905.
96. *The Times*, 28 Sep. 1911; Wingate to Gwynne, 9 Oct. 1911, SAD/301/4.
97. Wingate to Kitchener, (private, please destroy), 11 Feb. 1912, SAD/180/2/2; Wingate to Kitchener, 28 Nov. 1911, SAD/301/5; Circular Memorandum No. 244, Port Sudan, 19 Mar. 1910, SAD/402/12; the reason for introducing Sunday as weekly holiday in Port Sudan was probably because it was a new town with a very cosmopolitan population. In 1906 there were 2,725 foreigners in Port Sudan, out of a total population of 4,289, *GGR*—1906, p. 720. For Sunday observance in the south, see below pp. 121–122.
98. J. S. Trimingham, *The Christian Approach to Islam in the Sudan*, London, 1949, pp. 12–21; R. Gray, *A History of the Southern Sudan, 1839–1889*, London, 1961, pp. 23–6.
99. See below pp. 118–123.
100. J. K. Giffen, *The Egyptian Sudan*, New York, 1905, pp. 60–8.
101. Minutes of CMS Managing Committee, 31 July 1900, CMSA/EG/3/1900; Adeney, Harpur, and Hall to CMS, 18 Apr. 1901, ibid, 1901.
102. Gwynne to Adeney, 16 Apr. 1901, CMSA/E/03/1901.
103. Gwynne to Baylis, 12 Nov. 1902, CMSA/E/03/1902.
104. Baylis to Gwynne, 23 May 1903, CMSA/EG/Vol. 2. Gwynne's report to the Egyptian Missionary Conference, 20 May 1903, CMSA/E/03/1903.
105. Spence to Secretary of Foreign Department, CMS, 15 Sep. 1903, CMSA/E/03/1903.
106. MacInnes, Report on the Sudan, Nov.–Dec. 1903, CMSA/E/03/1904. Gwynne to Baylis, 24 Feb. 1903, CMSA/E/03/1903.
107. *Al-Mu'ayyad*, 17 Dec. 1906.
108. Gwynne to Wingate, 29 Dec. 1906, SAD/103/6.
109. *GGR*—1906, pp. 39–43; Confidential Report on Missionary Schools in the Northern Sudan, 2 Dec. 1906, (signed), Sterry, Currie, Bonus, SAD/103/6.
110. Phipps to Wingate, 19 Jan. 1907, SAD/103/6.
111. Cromer to Wingate, 6 Feb. 1907, FO/141/409; Wingate to Cromer, 19 Mar. 1907, SAD/103/7/1.
112. *GGR*—1912, pp. 289–90; see below p. 121.
113. 'Instructions as to the procedure to be carried out by individuals or societies desirous of opening schools in the Sudan', (signed) R. Wingate, 31 Jan. 1912, CMSA/Sudan/1; The instructions applied to all private schools, except *kuttābs*.

114. Giffen, op. cit., p. 57.
115. H. C. Jackson, *Pastor on the Nile*, pp. 27, 47, 193–4. Dr. Lloyd's Journal, Apr. 1908, SAD/203/9/12; Giffen, op. cit., pp. 53–4.
116. *Jallāb*: trader; the *Jallāba* were traders mainly from the riverain tribes of the Sudan. During the Turco-Egyptian period many of them acted as intermediaries in the slave trade and some of them continued this practice during the early years of the Condominium.
117. Wingate to Gwynne, (private), 4 Dec. 1910, SAD/298/3.
118. Boulnois to Currie, Jan. 1904; Currie to Boulnois, Jan. 1904, SAD/103/7/2.
119. Wingate to Boulnois (private), 3 Feb. 1904, SAD/103/7/2.
120. Hill to Civil Secretary, 19 Dec. 1906; Currie to Civil Secretary, 2 Feb. 1907, SAD/103/7/2; *GGR*—1907, pp. 183–4; *GGR*—1908, p. 466.
121. Stack to Wingate, 25 Mar. 1912, SAD/180/3.
122. Gwynne to Wingate, 29 Aug. 1911, SAD/301/2; Wingate to Gwynne, 9 Oct. 1911, SAD/301/4.
123. Wingate to Gorst, (private), 1 Mar. 1911, SAD/300/3.
124. Conditions of Service, Equatorial Battalion, 27 Feb. 1912, SAD/106/4; *SIR*—220, Nov. 1912; *SIR*—236, Mar. 1914.
125. Wingate to Phipps, 6 Sep. 1911, SAD/301/3; Asser to Wingate, 15 Sep. 1912, SAD/182/3/2.
126. Wingate to Feilden, 28 Mar. 1914, SAD/189/3.
127. Wingate to Balfour, 2 Nov. 1915, SAD/197/2/2; 'Historical Records Nuba Territorial Company', SAD/106/5.
128. Hall to Adeney, 12 Mar. 1901, CMSA/E/03/1901; *GGR*—1904, p. 37.
129. Gwynne to Blyth, 10 Oct. 1913, SAD/420/3.
130. Wingate to Kitchener, 20 Mar. 1912, SAD/180/3; Wingate to Sir Andrew Wingate, 25 July 1913, SAD/187/1/1.
131. Wingate to Wilson, 3 July, 1913, SAD/420/3; *SIR*—261, Apr. 1916.
132. Regulations and conditions under which missionary work is permitted in the Sudan (signed) R. Wingate, 31 Jan. 1912, CMSA/S/01/1912; see also *GGR*—1905, pp. 151–2.
133. Gwynne to Parent Committee, 16 Aug. 1906, CMSA/S/01/1906; Owen to Thornton, 12 June 1907, SAD/208/6.
134. Wingate to Phipps, 3 Aug. 1908, SAD/283/8/3.
135. Wingate to Phipps, 18 Nov. 1912, SAD/183/2; Wingate to Phipps, 19 Nov. 1912, SAD/183/1.
136. Instructions of the Committee to Missionaries proceeding to the Gordon Memorial Soudan Mission, 5 Oct. 1905, CMSA/Sudan/Vol. 1.
137. Baylis to Cook, 27 Oct. 1905, CMSA/Sudan/Vol. 1. Hadow to Baylis, 15 Jan. 1907, 30 May 1907, CMSA/S/01/1907.
138. Hadow to Parent Committee, 1 Dec. 1906, CMSA/S/01/1906. Hadow to Baylis 15 Jan. 1907, 30 May 1907, CMSA/S/01/1907.
139. Gwynne to Wingate, 20 Apr. 1908, SAD/282/4; Baylis to Gwynne, 10 Apr. 1908, CMSA/Sudan/Vol. 1.
140. Wingate to Feilden, (private), 27 May 1912, SAD/181/2/2.

141. Report on Missionaries in the Upper Nile, (signed) Willis [n.d.], SAD/212/9.
142. Hill to Wingate, 30 Mar. 1907, SAD/103/7/2.
143. Wingate to Feilden (private), 27 Dec. 1910, SAD/103/7/2.
144. C. H. Stigand, *Equatoria, the Lado Enclave*, London, 1923, pp. 201–2.
145. *The Times*, 26 Apr. 1907, Parliamentary Question by Mr. J. M. Robertson, M.P.

CHAPTER VII

The Administration of Justice

1. Agreement between Her Britannic Majesty's Government and the Government of His Highness the Khedive of Egypt, relative to the future administration of the Soudan, J. C. Hurewitz, *Diplomacy in the Near Middle East*, Vol. I, Princeton, 1956, pp. 216–8.
2. J. N. D. Anderson, 'The modernization of Islamic Law in the Sudan', *The Sudan Law Journal and Reports*, 1960; *The Sub Mamur's Handbook*, Khartoum, 1926.
3. *SG*—86, 1 Jan. 1906; a year later the Codes were enforced in the Baḥr al-Ghazāl; *SG*—107, 7 Feb. 1907.
4. Wingate to Mitchell Innes, 7 Aug. 1919, SAD/297/3.
5. *GGR*—1905, p. 79; *CAO*—104, 30 Nov. 1903.
6. *SG*—73, 1 Mar. 1905.
7. *GGR*—1903, p. 29.
8. *GGR*—1907, p. 86; *GGR*—1908, p. 193; For details see below pp. 127–128.
9. *GGR*—1904, p. 57.
10. *GGR*—1906, p. 351.
11. Wasey Sterry, 'Some notes on the administration of justice in Africa', *Reale Accademia D'Italia*—VIII Convegno 'Volta'. (Roma 4–11 Ottobre 1938) p. 4.
12. *CAO*—133, Feb. 1904; as to lands, five years continuous possession was regarded as proof of ownership. See below pp. 155–159.
13. Wingate to Stack (private), 10 May 1912, SAD/181/2/2; Wingate to Stack (private), 19 May 1912, ibid.
14. Hussey, op. cit., pp. 45–6.
15. Balfour to Lady F. Balfour, 25 Nov. 1906, SAD/303/6.
16. 'Memoirs of Ryder, 1905–1916', SAD/400/8, p. 66; Ryder started his career in the Sudan in 1905 as a surveyor. In 1906 he was appointed land settlement officer in Berber, and from 1908–12 he became judicial inspector of Berber province.
17. Findlay (acting consul-general) to Grey, 29 Aug. 1906, FO/407/167. Findlay quoted from a letter he received from Wingate; 'Proceedings of Court Martial held at Talodi', 28–29 July 1906; enclosed in Cromer to Grey, 25 Oct. 1906, ibid.

18. Bonham Carter to Wingate, 5 Oct. 1906, SAD/279/4; Bonham Carter to Wingate, 27 Aug. 1906, SAD/279/2.
19. Cromer to Wingate, 9 Sep. 1906, SAD/279/3.
20. Cromer to Grey, 25 Oct. 1906, FO/407/167.
21. Wingate to Wilson, 30 Sep. 1915, SAD/196/6.
22. *Report on the Soudan*, by Lieutenant-Colonel Stewart, 1883, C. 3670.
23. P. M. Holt, *The Mahdist State in the Sudan 1881–1898*, London 1958, pp. 115–16, 243.
24. *SG*—35, May 1902.
25. *SG*—284, 31 Aug. 1915.
26. J. N. D. Anderson, 'The Modernization of Islamic Law in the Sudan', *The Sudan Law Journal and Reports* (1960), pp. 295–96; J. N. D. Anderson, *Islamic Law in Africa*, London, 1954, pp. 312–13. (reprinted by Frank Cass & Co. Ltd. 1970.)
27. *SG*—76, 1 May 1905; see also *CAO*—43, 21 May 1903, which allowed *qāḍīs* to send summonses to persons residing in another *ma'mūrīya.*
28. *SG*—98, 1 July 1906.
29. *SG*—227, 28 Dec. 1912; *Ma'dhūn*—official authorized by the *qāḍī* to perform and register marriages and divorces.
30. *SG*—19, 1 Jan. 1901.
31. Wingate to Gorst, (private), 22 Dec. 1908, SAD/284/15; see above p. 18.
32. *GGR*—1911, p. 141.
33. *GGR*—1903, p. 79.
34. *GGR*—1904, p. 60.
35. *GGR*—1905, p. 88.
36. Al-Ṭayyib Aḥmad Hāshim (*c.* 1857–1924) was born at Berber of Ja'alī origin, studied in the *khalwa* of Shaykh Muḥammad al-Khayr Khūjalī and was a clerk in the *Sharī'a* court at Berber when the Mahdists took over. During the Mahdia he became secretary to the Khalifa's brother and tutor to his son al-Sayyid Muḥammad 'Abdallāhi. After the reconquest he became the first judge at the *Sharī'a* court of Khartoum. From 1900–1924, he was *muftī* of the Sudan. Hill, *BD*, p. 354.
37. Quoted by Cromer from a confidential report by the grand *qāḍī*; see Cromer to Wingate, 11 Feb. 1907, SAD/280/2.
38. *GGR*—1908, p. 148; al-Marāghī later became rector of al-Azhar and supported the 1936 law which modernized the teachings of that institute. 'Sheikh Maraghi as I knew him', by Bishop Gwynne, (n.d.), SAD/466/9/8.
39. *GGR*—1908, p. 203; *GGR*—1912, pp. 360–1; *SG*—208, 28 Dec. 1911, 'Circuit of Kadis of Mohammedan Law Courts, During 1912'.
40. Wingate to Sutherland, 28 Feb. 1907, SAD/280/2; *CAO*—345, 20 Sep. 1905.
41. Bonham Carter to Wingate, 15 Aug. 1904, SAD/275/6.
42. *Handbook Series, Kordofan and the region to the west of the White Nile*, Dec. 1912, pp. 108–9.
43. Matthews Pasha, Godfrey Escourt (1866–1917), was seconded to the

Egyptian army in 1896 and took part in the Nile campaigns. After one year as assistant civil secretary, he headed an expedition in 1901, to clear the *sadd* on the White Nile. In 1902–3, he was administrator of Fashoda district and in 1904–10, governor of the Upper Nile province which included Fashoda (later renamed Kodok); in 1911–13 he commanded the military district of Khartoum. Hill, *BD*, p. 235.

44. *GGR*—1904, p. 132.
45. *GGR*—1908, p. 663.
46. *GGR*—1903, pp. 9–10; see below pp. 142–147.
47. *GGR*—1908, p. 463.
48. Cameron to Wilson, 9 May 1905, in *SIR*—130, May 1905. Dengkur was part of Sennar province until 1906, when it became part of Mongalla.
49. *SIR*—138, Jan. 1906; *SIR*—139, Feb. 1906, Appendix A.
50. *SIR*—170, Sep. 1908; *SIR*—179, June 1909, Appendix A, 'Mongalla province diary' by R. C. R. Owen.
51. *Handbook Series, The Bahr El Ghazal province*, Dec. 1911, p. 44.
52. *SIR*—179, June 1909.
53. J. W. Sagar, 'Notes on the History, Religion and Customs of the Nuba', *SIR*—186, Jan. 1910, Appendix A; these notes were published as an article in *SNR*—Vol. 5 (1922), pp. 137–156; *SIR*—226, May 1913.
54. H. C. Jackson, 'The Nuer of the Upper Nile province', *SNR*—Vol. 6 (1923), p. 91.
55. Wingate to Owen, 21 June 1915, SAD/195/11.
56. *GGR*—1906, p. 743.
57. E. S. Hartland to Russel Rea, 29 Jan. 1908, SAD/282/1. This letter was written after Hartland had read the code of Dinka laws prepared by Captain O'Sullivan, a Sudan government inspector.

CHAPTER VIII

Tribal Policy

1. *SIR*—60, 25 May–31 Dec. 1898.
2. For an English version of these letters, signed Kitchener, 28 June 1897, and the replies of their recipients see SAD/101/1.
3. *Memorandum to Mudirs,* Inclosure in Cromer to Salisbury, 17 Mar. 1899, FO/78/5022.
4. Maxwell to Wingate, 17 Jan. 1899, SAD/269/1.
5. Cromer to Salisbury, 11 Dec. 1899, FO/78/5024.
6. Lansdowne to Cromer, 3 Oct. 1902, FO/403/323; Inclosure [signed: Sparkes and Gleichen] in Cromer to Lansdowne, 14 Oct. 1902, ibid.
7. *SIR*—93, Apr. 1902.
8. Gwynne to Wingate, 29 Aug. 1911, SAD/301/2.

9. Wingate to Cromer, 24 Apr. 1902, SAD/272/2.
10. *SIR*—171, Oct. 1908.
11. Asser to Wingate, (private), 15 July 1909, SAD/288/1.
12. Wingate to Kitchener, 20 Mar. 1912, SAD/190/3; *GGR*—1914, p. 61, see below pp. 147–154.
13. *SIR*—225, Apr. 1913.
14. *SG*—105, 8 Jan. 1907, *Ordinance for regulating the import of ammunition*; *SG*—123, 1 Jan. 1908, *Arms Ordinance 1907*; *SG*—128, 1 Mar. 1908, *The Sudan explosives Ordinance*.
15. *Jihādīya*—regular troops who were recruited by the Egyptians from slaves obtained in the Sudan. The *jihādīya* was maintained as a special force during the Mahdia.
16. *SIR*—171, Oct. 1908.
17. Cromer to Wingate, 11 Feb. 1902, SAD/272/1.
18. *SG*—49, July 1903.
19. *SG*—129, Mar. 1908; *SG*—115, July 1907.
20. Wingate to Phipps, 25 Aug. 1912, SAD/182/2/1.
21. *SG*—110, 1 Apr. 1907; *SG*—9, Feb. 1900; *SG*—26, Aug. 1901; *SG*—31, Jan. 1902.
22. *SIR*—71, 9 June–8 July, 1900; *SIR*—75, 8 Oct.–8 Nov. 1900.
23. *The Times*, 30 Mar. 1900.
24. *GGR*—1902, p. 305; *GGR*—1905, p. 121; *GGR*—1908, p. 695.
25. *Sub-Mamur's Handbook*, p. 336.
26. *CAO*—7, 18 Jan. 1902.
27. *GGR*—1902, p. 242; *GGR*—1905, pp. 14–15, 26.
28. *GGR*—1906, p. 710.
29. Willis's diary, 12 Nov. 1911, SAD/210/2.
30. K. D. D. Henderson, 'Some notes on the history of the tribes living south of the Wadi el Ghala', (typescript), pp. 9–11; SAD/478/5; I. Cunnison, *Baggara Arabs, power and lineage in a Sudanese nomad tribe*, London, 1966, pp. 108–9.
31. *Some aspects of Nuba administration*, Sudan Government Memorandum, No. 1, Nov. 1931, By J. A. Gillan, *Strictly Confidential.*
32. *GGR*—1903, pp. 9–10.
33. Matthews to Wingate, 19 July 1903, SAD/273/7.
34. Davies, op. cit., pp. 59–62, 181–2, 187–9.
35. *SIR*—184, Nov. 1909; Willis's diary, 22 Oct., 22 Nov. 1909, SAD/210/2; *SIR*—191, June 1910; Interview with Sir Harold MacMichael, 6 June 1967.
36. Savile's diary, 4 Jan. 1916, SAD/427/7.
37. D. Newbold, 'The Beja Tribes of the Red Sea Hinterland', in J. A. de C. Hamilton, (ed.) *The Anglo-Egyptian Sudan from within*, London, 1935, p. 160.
38. Colonel R. V. Savile, Diary of a tribute collecting tour in northern Kassala, 7–14 Apr. 1903, SAD/427/3.
39. *GGR*—1903, p. 80; *CAO*—3, 17 Jan. 1900; *CAO*—28, 16 Feb. 1902.
40. *CAO*—28, 16 Feb. 1902; *CAO*—46, May, 1903; *CAO*—92, 25 Oct. 1903.
41. Wingate to Clayton, 13 Feb. 1911, SAD/469/3; C. E. Lyall, 'Rights

dues and customs prevailing among Arab tribes in the White Nile Province', *SNR*—Vol. 4 (1921), pp. 199–203.

42. Willis's diary, 6 Nov. 1911, SAD/210/2.
43. H. C. Jackson, *Sudan Days and Ways*, p. 45.
44. C. C. Reining, *The Zande Scheme*, Illinois, 1966, p. 35.
45. Wingate's diary, 2 Mar. 1902, SAD/272/8; *SIR*—88, Nov. 1901; *GGR*—1902, p. 229.
46. Ibid, p. 226.
47. *SIR*—94, May 1902; *SIR*—93, Apr. 1902.
48. *GGR*—1902, p. 346.
49. Reining, op. cit., pp. 17–20.
50. *GGR*—1904, p. 133.
51. Matthews to Wingate, 12 Apr. 1904, SAD/275/3.
52. *GGR*—1905, pp. 16, 150.
53. *GGR*—1908, p. 655.
54. *GGR*—1906, p. 552.
55. Owen to Wingate, 16 Aug. 1908, SAD/283/8/3.
56. Wingate to Owen, 14 Jan. 1910, SAD/290/1.
57. Wingate to Gorst, 1 Mar. 1911, SAD/300/3; Wingate to Grey, 20 Aug. 1911, SAD/301/2.
58. Wingate to Kitchener, 7 Dec. 1911, SAD/301/6/2; *SIR*—211, Feb. 1912.
59. Wingate to Stack, 12 Apr. 1912, SAD/181/1/3; Minutes—No. 13908, 2 Apr. 1912, FO/371/1362, (signed) R. P. M.
60. Wingate to Stack, (private), 20 Apr. 1912, SAD/181/1: Wingate wrote that none of these points would be mentioned in the official report; Wingate to Stack, 9 May 1912, SAD/181/2/2; Stack to Wingate, 20 May 1912, ibid.
61. Wingate to Stack, 12 Apr. 1912, SAD/181/1/3.
62. *GGR*—1906, p. 7; *SIR*—143, June 1906.
63. Wingate to Cromer, 12 Dec. 1906, SAD/279/6.
64. *GGR*—1908, p. 590; Wingate to Gorst, 29 Dec. 1908, FO/371/659.
65. Savile's diary, 1 Feb. 1910, SAD/427/7.
66. Wingate to Asser, 12 Sep. 1910, SAD/297/3; Wingate to Gorst, 22 Sep. 1910, ibid; *SIR*—189, Apr. 1910; *GGR*—1911, p. 8.
67. Asser to Wingate, 12 Oct. 1910, SAD/298/1.
68. Slatin's diary, 6 Nov. 1910, SAD/441.
69. *GGR*—1911, p. 8; *GGR*—1914, pp. 5–6; *SIR*—240, July 1914.
70. Wingate to Balfour, 20 Dec. 1915, SAD/197/3/2; for details see Theobald, *'Alī Dīnār,* pp. 154–161.
71. H. R. Fox Bourne, 'Punitive Expeditions in Africa', *The Aborigines' Friend*, Vol. 6 (Apr. 1902), p. 3.
72. *CAO*—66, 28 May 1901.
73. Slatin's diary, 29 Dec. 1910, SAD/441.
74. Asser to Wingate, 12 Aug. 1912, SAD/182/2/1.
75. Asser to Wingate, 4 Apr. 1913, SAD/186/1/2; Stack who was then Sudan agent came forward with the idea of exchanging cattle for recruits; Stack to Wingate, 7 Sep. 1913, SAD/187/3/1.
76. Drake to Wingate, 26 May 1915, SAD/195/5.

77. *Survey of the policy of the Sudan Government in the Upper Nile*, [n.d.1926?], SAD/212/10/1.
78. Gillan, op. cit., pp. 5, 53–5.

CHAPTER IX

Land-settlement and Taxation

1. S. R. Simpson, 'Land Law and Registration in the Sudan', *Journal of African Administration*, Vol. VII, No. 1. (1955), p. 11.
2. *SG*—2, 27 May 1899; *SG*—1, 7 Mar. 1899; *SG*—10, 1 Apr. 1900.
3. *SG*—45, Mar. 1903; *GGR*—1903, p. 80.
4. Simpson, op. cit., p. 12.
5. *SG*—80, 24 Aug. 1905.
6. Phipps to Wingate, 12 June 1905, SAD/276/6; according to Phipps a *jadʿa* consisted of $5^{1}/8$ feddans and was the measurement used for taxation.
7. *SG*—78, July 1905, 'Disposal of land by natives'; *SG*—79, Aug. 1905, 'Sale or lease of lands'.
8. *SG*—96, 23 May 1906; *SG*—113, June 1907; *SG*—123, Jan. 1908. *Buqr* or *Karu* were the lands lying behind the river banks which were only cultivable in years of exceptionally high floods.
9. Kitchener to Wingate, 5 Apr. 1912, SAD/181/1/3; *Kharājīya* lands which originally did not amount to full ownership, had since 1891 been regarded as equal to *mulk*. Thus Kitchener's declaration seems to have had no legal significance; see G. Baer, *A history of landownership in modern Egypt 1800–1950*, London, 1962, pp. 8–12.
10. *SG*—2, May 1899. *SG*—45, Mar. 1903, amending the *Title of Lands Ordinance 1899*.
11. *GGR*—1908, The Legal Secretary's Report, p. 197.
12. The most comprehensive work in this field is by H. St. G. Peacock, *A Report on the Land Settlement of the Gezira, Messelemia District*, London, 1913. Peacock was a judge of the Sudan civil court and was in charge of the Gezira land-settlement in the years 1906–10. A second report was written by J. G. Matthew, inspector in the Sennar province 1905–9, and president of the land-settlement commission for Singa district. 'Land Customs and Tenure in Singa District', *SNR*, Vol. 4, (1921), pp. 1–19. The third report was about land-settlement in the province of Berber and was written by Ryder, who became land-settlement officer in 1906. 'Memoirs of Ryder 1905–16', (typescript), SAD/400/8. The following, unless otherwise stated, is based on these reports.
13. Peacock, op. cit., p. 35.
14. Corbyn (Settlement Officer Kamlin) to Legal Secretary, 28 Feb. 1910, SAD/290/2/2, inclosure in Wingate to Gorst, 29 Mar. 1910, SAD/290/3/1.

15. *GGR*—1906, pp. 6, 351–2; *GGR*—1908, pp. 197–9.
16. Pearson [director of survey] to Wingate, 25 Apr. 1913, SAD/108/16.
17. *GGR*—1906, pp. 519, 614, 639.
18. *GGR*—1912, p. 102. For the introduction and the effects of the progressive land-tax, see below p. 166.
19. *GGR*—1904, pp. 45–50; Gaitskell, op. cit., pp. 46–50.
20. ibid., pp. 51–73.
21. Cromer to Wingate, 2 Feb. 1906, SAD/278/2.
22. *GGR*—1902, pp. 242, 282; *GGR*—1906, pp. 570, 636.
23. Bonham Carter to Wingate, 25 May 1909, SAD/287/3.
24. Grenfell, Francis Wallace, 1st Baron (1841–1925), sirdar of the Egyptian army 1888–1892; commanded the Egyptian army in the Battle of Tūshkī in 1889; in 1902 he was raised to the peerage; was made field marshal in 1909; *DNBS*, 1922–1930, pp. 362–4.
25. Bonham Carter to Wingate (private), 22 June 1909, SAD/287/4.
26. *SG*—247, Feb. 1914.
27. *Al-Ahrām*, 5 July 1914; the quotation is from a letter to the editor signed by a former Sudan government official. It was written following an article in *al-Ahrām*, 1 July 1914, which criticized the Sudan government's attitude to foreigners and its land policy. The article and the letter were translated by the intelligence department, SAD/191/1/2.
28. *SG*—2, 27 May 1899. The *tanẓīm* regulations set down the standard of buildings which had to be erected according to the classification of the land.
29. W. H. McLeon, 'The Planning of Khartoum and Omdurman', Paper read at the R.I.B.A. Town Planning Conference (London 10–15 Oct. 1910), SAD/235/1. According to *The Times*, 11 Apr. 1900, the two years regulation was imposed in order to induce the inhabitants of Omdurman who owned land in Khartoum to move to the new town.
30. *SG*—33, Mar. 1902. *GGR*—1903, p. 63.
31. *SG*—206, 2 Nov. 1909; the only town where municipal authorities existed during that period was Khartoum.
32. *SG*—63, June 1904.
33. *GGR*—1906, p. 660; *SG*—103, Dec. 1906.
34. Inclosure in Asser to Gorst, 2 Oct. 1909, FO/141/423.
35. *SG*—117, Sep. 1907.
36. *GGR*—1912, pp. 92–3; *SG*—225, 23 Nov. 1912.
37. *SG*—232, 20 Mar. 1913; *SG*—238, 30 June 1913; A. J. V. Arthur, 'Slum Clearance in Khartoum', *Journal of African Administration*, Vol. 6, No. 2 (1954), p. 73.
38. *The Times*, 11 Apr. 1900.
39. *GGR*—1905, pp. 72, 93–4.
40. *GGR*—1906, p. 183; *GGR*—1908, p. 316; Slatin to Wingate, 15 Mar. 1906, SAD/278/3.
41. *GGR*—1906, p. 83; *GGR*—1905, p. 7.
42. Bonus to Wingate, 17 Nov. 1906, inclosure in Wingate to Cromer,

17 Nov. 1906, FO/141/402; Corbett to Cromer, 26 Nov. 1906, ibid., *SG*—100, Sep. 1906.

43. Amery to Wingate, 20 July 1907, SAD/281/1; *The Times*, 15 May 1908; *SG*—100, Sep. 1906.
44. Bonus to Wingate, 12 Apr. 1908; Wingate to Gorst, 28 Mar. 1908; Harvey to Gorst, 8 Apr. 1908; Gorst to Wingate, 11 Apr. 1908, FO/141/416.
45. *GGR*—1908, pp. 12–14.
46. GGC, 22 Jan.–10 Feb. 1910, FO/867/3; 28 Feb.–14 Mar. 1910, FO/867/1.
47. *SAR*—1899, p. 47.
48. *GGR*—1902, p. 114.
49. Wingate to Kitchener (private), 7 Apr. 1912, SAD/181/1/3.
50. *SG*—2, 27 May 1899.
51. *GGR*—1905, p. 69; *GGR*—1908, p. 21.
52. *GGR*—1906, p. 502; *GGR*—1907, p. 75.
53. *GGR*—1905, p. 133; Phipps to Wingate, 27 Aug. 1905, SAD/277/2; *GGR*—1908, p. 391.
54. *SG*—7, 2 Dec. 1899; *SAR*—1899, p. 49.
55. *SG*—26, 1 Aug. 1901, *The Tribute Ordinance* 1901, *The Taxation of Animals Ordinance* 1901.
56. Peacock, op. cit., p. 16; see also Holt, op. cit., p. 34, who quotes a proclamation of the Mahdi stating that the Turks imposed *jizya* on the Muslim inhabitants of the Sudan.
57. Wilkinson to Wingate, 27 Dec. 1903, SAD/273/12; *CAO*—51, 21 May 1903; *SG*—48, 1 June 1903; *GGR*—1906, p. 758; *GGR*—1908, p. 672; *GGR*—1909, p. 118.
58. Gillan, op. cit., p. 40.
59. *GGR*—1909, p. 118; *Handbook Bahr El Ghazal*, pp. 44–5.
60. *SG*—3, 31 July 1899; this tax was amended in 1905; *SG*—73, Mar. 1905; *SG*—86, Jan. 1906.
61. 'The Local Taxation Ordinance 1912', *SG*—225, 23 Nov. 1912.
62. *SG*—3, 31 July 1899; *GGR*—1904, p. 212, *Sub-Mamur's Handbook*, pp. 337–9.
63. *SG*—232, 20 Mar. 1913; Wingate to Slatin, 21 Apr. 1914, SAD/104/6; Wingate to Bernard, 6 May 1913, SAD/186/2/1.
64. See above pp. 72–74, 145–147.

CHAPTER X

Slavery and Labour

1. P. F. Martin, *The Sudan in Evolution*, London, 1921, p. 216. *CAO*—133, 5 Dec. 1901; this order was superseded by more detailed instructions; *SG*—63, 1 June 1904.
2. *GGR*—1906, p. 558.

3. Talbot to Wingate, 20 June 1903, SAD/234/1; Wingate to Cromer, 11 Dec. 1903, FO/141/378.
4. The following details, unless otherwise stated, are taken from C. A. Willis, *Report on Slavery and the Pilgrimage*, (1926), SAD/212/2; the report was based on the data collected by the Sudan intelligence department of which Willis was the director since 1920.
5. The figures quoted by Willis do not agree with those given in the *Sudan Intelligence Reports* for those years; *SIR*—174–233, Jan. 1909–Dec. 1913.
6. *SG*—30, 1 Dec. 1901; *GGR*—1902, p. 304; *GGR*—1903, p. 51.
7. Henry to Wingate, 18 July 1904, SAD/275/5; *CAO*—268, 'Repression of Slavery Department', Khartoum, 12 Mar. 1905; *GGR*—1905, pp. 56–7.
8. Stack to Wingate, 20 May 1908, SAD/284/14/1; quoting a discussion he had with McMurdo. For Slatin's views on slavery, see above pp.
9. Wingate to Gorst, 19 Nov. 1908, SAD/284/15; Exeter Hall in London was a centre of anti-slavery activities in Britain, and Wingate believed that McMurdo was taking his orders from the Anti-Slavery Society. See Wingate to Stack, 31 May 1908, SAD/284/13; R. Hill, 'The Period of Egyptian Occupation, 1820–1881', *SNR*—Vol. 39 (1958), pp. 101–2.
10. Wingate to Stack, (private), 12 May 1908, SAD/284/13; 'Abd al-Qādir Wad Ḥabūba was the leader of the Gezira rebellion in 1908; see above pp. 101–103.
11. Wingate to Stack, 31 May 1908, SAD/284/13.
12. McMurdo to Wingate, 5 Dec. 1906; Wingate to McMurdo, 16 Dec. 1906, SAD/279/6; *GGR*—1902, p. 332.
13. McMurdo to Stack, 18 Mar. 1907, SAD/280/3; Slatin to Wingate, 20 Mar. 1907, ibid.
14. Willis's diary, 16 May 1909, 6 Nov. 1909, SAD/210/2.
15. Willis's diary, Feb.–Mar. 1910, SAD/210/2. Whithingham was one of the senior inspectors of the slavery department. Wingate's and Slatin's mistrust for him was a well known fact.
16. Wingate to Nason, 4 Aug. 1903, SAD/273/8.
17. For details see below pp. 175–178.
18. Wingate to Gorst, 13 Apr. 1910, SAD/431/11.
19. Gorst to Grey, 5 Nov. 1910, FO/371/895.
20. Wingate to Ravenscroft, (private), 1 July 1914, SAD/191/1/2.
21. *GGR*—1904, p. 36.
22. J. Matthew (acting governor Red Sea) to all Inspectors, 26 Jan. 1915, Anti-Slavery Archive, G/282.
23. *GGR*—1905, p. 51; Domestic slaves were always referred to as servants in official communications.
24. Wingate to Savile, 17 May 1915, SAD/195/6.
25. Bonham Carter to Wingate, 28 Dec. 1913, SAD/188/3/1.
26. Slatin to Wingate, 31 July 1909, SAD/288/1; Slatin's diary, 1902, SAD/44; see above pp. 50–51.
27. *SIR*—104, Mar. 1903, Appendix 'E'.
28. Bonham Carter to Wingate, 28 Dec. 1913, SAD/188/3.

29. *SIR*—130, May 1905.
30. Memorandum from the Anti-Slavery and Aboringines' Protection Society upon the Existence of Slavery in the Sudan, 24 Nov. 1919. Anti-Slavery Archive, G/282; although this memorandum was written after Wingate's governor-generalship, most details concern the period under discussion.
31. *Storrar's Letterbooks*, 25 June 1905, SAD/549; W. E. Law to Director of Department for the Repression of Slave Trade, 16 Dec. 1918, Anti-Slavery Archive, G/282.
32. *GGR*—1908, p. 515.
33. *GGR*—1907, p. 231; see also *GGR*—1906, pp. 600, 728.
34. Travers Buxton to Wilkinson, 13 June 1901; Cromer to Travers Buxton, 26 June 1901; in *The Anti-Slavery Reporter*, Vol. 22, (1901), pp. 53–4.
35. Sudan Government—Confidential Circular Memorandum No. 33, *Regulations as to Sudanese Servants.* (signed) R. M. Feilden Lewa, Civil Secretary, 1 May 1919. Anti-Slavery Archive, G/282.
36. *GGR*—1907, p. 236; *GGR*—1908, p. 488.
37. *GGR*—1908, pp. 21, 177.
38. Phipps to Wingate, 1 June 1905, SAD/276/6; A. C. Parker, 'Memoirs of the early days', SAD/294/10; *GGR*—1906, pp. 565, 663, 720; *GGR*—1907, p. 126.
39. *Handbook, Bahr El Ghazal*, pp. 72–3; Slatin's Diary 1913, 'Notes Gedaref', SAD/441.
40. 'Report on the Soudan Railway', by G. B. Macauley, Director of Soudan Railways, 2 Dec. 1900, FO/403/312; Government of India to Lord Hamilton, India Office, 4 Aug. 1902, FO/403/323; Lansdowne to Cromer, 22 Oct. 1902, ibidC9?a
41. *GGR*—1903, pp. 22–4, 61–2, Appendix 'B'; 'Report by Slatin Pasha on the "Kokreb" meeting with Sheikhs of Nomad tribes to arrange the work on the Red Sea railway'.
42. *GGR*—1904, p. 14.
43. *GGR*—1903, p. 23; *GGR*—1902, p. 280.
44. Cecil to Wingate, 25 July 1905, SAD/277/1; Wingate to Cecil, 10 Aug. 1905, SAD/277/2. *GGR*—1905, pp. 13–14.
45. Clayton to Wingate, 17 Dec. 1913, SAD/469/5.
46. *GGR*—1905, pp. 29, 30, 160–61, Appendix 'A', Instructions as to the Employment of Labour.
47. *GGR*—1909, p. 55.
48. ibid, pp. 53–4.
49. *GGR*—1909, p. 55; *GGR*—1914, p. 10.
50. *SG*—61, 1 Apr. 1904; *SG*—19, Jan. 1901.
51. *SG*—80, 24 Aug. 1905; *GGR*—1905, p. 90.
52. *SG*—129, 29 Mar. 1908; *SG*—138, 21 June 1908.
53. *GGR*—1905, pp. 31–2.
54. Wingate to Gorst, 19 Nov. 1908, SAD/284/15.

Bibliography

I. UNPUBLISHED SOURCES

(*a*) Anti-Slavery Society Archive, Rhodes House, Oxford.
This archive contains the papers of the Aborigines' Protection Society and the Anti-Slavery Society which were founded in the 1830s. The material relevant to slavery in the Sudan in the years 1898–1916 is in Box G–282.

(*b*) Church Missionary Society Archive, London.
The archive contains the correspondence between the CMS missionaries in the Sudan and their headquarters in Egypt and London. Until Nov. 1905, the Sudan belonged to Group No. 3 in Egypt and the material relevant to the Sudan is classified together with Egypt. From 1905 there are separate boxes and precis books containing the Sudan correspondence.

(*c*) Foreign Office Archive at the Public Record Office, London.
FO/78 Turkey Egypt, Political 1898–1905.
FO/141 Egypt, agency and consular archives, 1900–1909, 1924. There are special letter books containing the correspondence between the British consul-general in Egypt and the governor-general of the Sudan.
FO/371 Egypt political 1906–1916. This series replaced FO/78 which was discontinued since Dec. 1905. Apart from correspondence between the consul-general and the foreign office, it also contains the *Sudan intelligence reports*.
FO/403 Confidential prints, North East Africa and the Soudan. This series was discontinued in 1904.
FO/407 Confidential prints, Egypt and the Soudan 1898–1916. The original letters and memoranda printed in these series are in FO/78 and FO/371.

II. PRIVATE PAPERS

(*a*) At the Public Record Office, London.
1. The Cromer papers, FO/633/5–24.
2. The Grey papers, FO/800/46–8.
3. The Kitchener papers, PRO/30/57, 10–48.
4. The Lansdowne papers, FO/800/123–4.

(*b*) At the Sudan Archive, School of Oriental Studies, University of Durham.
This archive is made up of numerous collections of private papers

Q

belonging to British and other officials who served in the Sudan. The major collections are those of Sir Reginald Wingate, governor-general of the Sudan, 1899–1916, and Sir Rudolf von Slatin Pasha, inspector-general of the Sudan, 1900–1914.

1. The Wingate papers contain his private correspondence since 1878 and his correspondence regarding the Sudan from 1883–1916. However, many letters relevant to the Sudan are in the private correspondence. Special boxes contain Wingate's diaries and memoirs, and the manuscripts of *Mahdiism and the Egyptian Sudan*, and *Ten years' captivity in the Mahdi's camp*.
2. The Slatin papers contain his correspondence from 1895–1932 (the correspondence between Wingate and Slatin is arranged in special boxes). The English and German manuscripts of *Fire and Sword in the Sudan*, are in boxes 443–5. Slatin's diaries for the years 1896–1916 were of particular value, they are written partly in German and partly in English and contain Slatin's impressions during his tours of inspection as well as his recommendations regarding administrative policy.

Of the numerous other collections which have been used in writing this book, the following are the most important:

3. The private letters of Lieutenant-Colonel Frank C. Balfour, who started his service in the public works department at Port Sudan and later became inspector in the Nuba Mountains.
4. The diaries and memoirs of Major-General Stephen S. Butler contain his memoirs on the Egyptian army and his diaries for the years 1911–1912 while serving in the intelligence department.
5. The correspondence of Sir Gilbert F. Clayton Pasha with Wingate during his period as Wingate's private secretary 1908–1914, and as Sudan agent 1914–1916.
6. The private papers of Bishop Llewellyn Henry Gwynne are split between the Sudan archive in Durham and the CMS archive in London, both of which have been used extensively.
7. The letters and the manuscripts of several articles by K. D. D. Henderson (boxes 448; 478–9).
8. The Journals of Reverend F. B. Hadow and Dr. E. Lloyd of the CMS, for the years 1905–8 (box 203). Hadow and Lloyd arrived in the Sudan in 1905 with the first group of CMS missionaries who opened the station at Melut in the Upper Nile province.
9. A memoir written by Colonel C. F. Ryder (box 400/8) was of particular value for the chapter dealing with land-settlement in the Sudan.
10. The diaries of Lieut.-Colonel Robert V. Savile (box 427) were of considerable interest with regard to tribal administration and taxation in Kassala (1902–6) and Kordofan (1909–17).
11. The papers of Na'ūm Shuqayr (Shoucair) contain very little of his private correspondence (box 101/20). More important are his notes on the history of the Majdhūbīya order (box 195), and his work in connection with Ismā'īl 'Abd al-Qādir's biography of the Mahdi (box 260/2).

12. The private papers of Sa'īd Shuqayr (Shoucair) cover the years 1909–1934. They are classified according to subjects and deal with the Sudan, Palestine, and Syria (boxes 493–4).
13. The correspondence and diaries of Charles Armine Willis (boxes 209–212) are of great interest. As a junior inspector in Kordofan since 1905, Willis kept a regular diary of events which contain many details regarding religious and tribal policy. His later diaries and memoranda afford a critical view of the government's policy as seen by a director of the intelligence department.

III. UNPUBLISHED AND CONFIDENTIAL REPORTS

(a) British.

1. *General Military Report on the Egyptian Sudan 1891*, compiled from statements made by Father Ohrwalder, War Office, London 1892.
2. *General Report on the Egyptian Soudan, March 1895*, compiled from statements made by Slatin Pasha.
3. *Sudan Intelligence Reports*, 60–269, 1898–1916. War Office library, London.

(b) Sudan Government.

All these reports are in the Sudan Archive, Durham, unless otherwise mentioned.

1. *A Note on Government policy towards the native population*. [n.d.]
2. *Governor-General's Council, minutes of, 1910–1916*, FO/867/1–7, (Public Record Office).
3. *Regulations as to Sudanese Servants*, Sudan Government Confidential Circular memorandum, No. 33, 1 May 1919 by Lewa R. M. Feilden, Civil Secretary. (Anti-Slavery Archive, Rhodes House, Oxford.)
4. *Slavery and the Pilgrimage, 1926*, report by C. A. Willis, O.B.E.
5. *Some aspects of Nuba administration*, Sudan Government Memorandum No. 1, Nov. 1931, by J. A. Gillan, Strictly Confidential.
6. J. Stone, *The finance of Government economic development in the Sudan 1899–1913*, Sudan Economic Institute, Khartoum 1954.
7. *Survey of the policy of the Sudan Government in the Upper Nile.* [n.d., probably written by C. A. Willis.]
8. *The immigration and distribution of West Africans in the Sudan*, Sudan Government Memorandum, [n.d.].

IV. UNPUBLISHED THESES

1. A. W. Abdel Rahim. *An economic history of the Sudan 1899–1956*, M.A. thesis, Manchester, 1963.
2. A. W. Abdel Rahim. *An economic history of the Gezira Scheme 1900–1950*, Ph.D. thesis, Manchester, (in preparation).
3. M. Abdel Rahim. *The constitutional development of the Sudan, 1899–1956*, Ph.D. thesis, Manchester, 1964.

4. O. M. O. Abdu. *The development of transport and economic growth in the Sudan, 1898–1958*, Ph.D. thesis, London, 1960.
5. G. M. A. Bakhit. *British administration and Sudanese Nationalism, 1919–1939*, Ph.D. thesis, Cambridge, 1965.
6. M. O. Beshir. *Educational development in the Sudan 1898–1956.* B.Litt. thesis, Oxford, 1966.
7. P. M. Holt. *The personal rule of the Khalifa ʿAbdallahi al-Taʿaishi.* Ph.D. thesis, Oxford, 1954.
8. S. M. Nur. *A critical edition of the memoirs of Yūsuf Mikhāʾīl*, Ph.D. thesis, London, 1963.
9. M. K. Osman. *Education and social change in the Sudan, 1900–1958.* M.A. thesis, London, 1965.
10. L. M. Sanderson. *A history of education in the Sudan with special reference to girls' schools.* M.A. thesis, London, 1962.
11. L. M. Sanderson. *Education in the southern Sudan, 1898–1948.* Ph.D. thesis, London, 1966.

V. OFFICIAL PUBLICATIONS

(a) British.
1. C.3670. *Report on the Soudan* by Lieutenant-Colonel Stewart, 1883.
2. *Reports by His Majesty's Agent and Consul-General on the Finances, Administration, and Condition of Egypt and the Soudan:* 1898—C.9231; 1899—CD.95; 1900—CD.441; 1901—CD.1012; 1902—CD.1529; 1903—CD.1951; 1904—CD.2409; 1905—CD.2817; 1906—CD.3394; 1907—CD.3966; 1908—CD.4580; 1909—CD.5121; 1910—CD.5633; 1911—CD.6149; 1912—CD.6682; 1913—CD.7358; 1914–19—CMD.957.

(b) Egyptian.
1. *Journal officiel.*

(c) Sudanese.
1. *Civil Administration Orders* 1900–1908.
2. *Handbook Series.* The Sudan government handbooks were compiled in the intelligence department in Khartoum. Those used in this book are:
   The Bahr El Ghazal Province, Dec. 1911.
   Kordofan and the region to the west of the White Nile, Dec. 1912.
   Handbook of the Anglo-Egyptian Sudan, 1922, I.D.1218.
   The Sub-Mamur's handbook, Khartoum, 1926.
3. *Reports on the Finances, Administration, and Condition of the Sudan.* Confidential. The reports are divided into four parts. A report by the consul-general in Egypt; a memorandum by the governor-general of the Sudan; reports of the central government departments; and reports by the provincial governors. The reports for the years 1902–1914 are in the School of Oriental Studies, Durham and in the library of the Foreign Office. I have not been able to locate the reports for the years 1899–1901.
4. *Sudan Gazette* 1899–1916. In the British Museum.

5. *Sudan Political Service 1899–1929*. Civil Secretary's Office, Sudan Government 1930.
6. *The Sudan a record of progress 1898–1947*, published by the Sudan Government. [n.d.]

VI. NEWSPAPERS AND PERIODICALS

(a) Daily and weekly newspapers.
al-Ahrām, Cairo.
L'Étendard Égyptien, Cairo.
The Jewish Chronicle, London.
al-Liwā', Cairo.
al-Mu'ayyad, Cairo.
al-Muqaṭṭam, Cairo.
Neue Freie Presse, Vienna.
The Standard, Cairo.
The Sudan Herald, Khartoum.
The Sudan Times, Khartoum.
The Times, London.
al-Waṭan, Cairo.

(b) Periodicals.
The Aborigines' Friend, London.
Anti-Slavery Reporter, London.
Journal of African Administration, London.
Journal of African History, London.
Journal of African Society, London.
Middle Eastern Studies, London.
Sudan Notes and Records, Khartoum.
Zaïre—Belgian African Revue, Brussels.

VII. BOOKS AND ARTICLES

1. M. Abdel Rahim. 'Early Sudanese Nationalism, 1900–1938', *SNR*, Vol. 47, (1966).
2. M. Abdel Rahim. 'The development of British policy in the Southern Sudan, 1899–1947', *Middle Eastern Studies*, Vol. 2, No. 3, (1966).
3. J. N. D. Anderson. *Islamic law in Africa*, London, 1954, reprinted by Frank Cass & Co. Ltd. 1970.
4. J. N. D. Anderson. 'The modernization of Islamic Law in the Sudan', *The Sudan Law Journal and Reports*, (1960).
5. A. J. V. Arthur. 'Slum clearance in Khartoum', *Journal of African Administration*, Vol. 6, No. 2, (1954).
6. E. Atiyah. *An Arab tells his story*, London, 1946.
7. Bābikr Badrī. *Ta'rīkh Ḥayātī*, Vols. 1–3, Omdurman, 1959–61.
8. G. Baer. *A history of landownership in modern Egypt 1800–1950*, London, 1962.
9. W. S. Blunt. *My diaries, being a personal narrative of events 1888–1914*, (Single volume edition), London, 1932.

10. J. B. Christopherson. 'Notes on medicine in the Sudan', (typescript n.d. SAD/407/6).
11. R. O. Collins. *The Southern Sudan 1883–1896*, Yale, 1962.
12. R. O. Collins. 'The Sudan: link to the north', *The transformation of East Africa*, (editors) S. Diamond & F. G. Burke, New York, 1966.
13. R. O. Collins. 'The transfer of the Lado Enclave to the Anglo-Egyptian Sudan, 1910', *Zaïre*, Vol. 14, No. 2, (1960).
14. Cromer, Earl of. *Modern Egypt*, 2 vols., London, 1908.
15. I. Cunnison. *Baggara Arabs, power and lineage in a Sudanese nomad tribe*, London, 1966.
16. J. Currie. 'The educational experiment in the Anglo-Egyptian Sudan', *Journal of the African Society*, Vols. 33–4, (1934–5).
17. R. Davies. *The camel's back*, London, 1957.
18. E. E. Evans-Pritchard. 'An ethnological survey of the Sudan', in Hamilton (no. 23).
19. E. E. Evans-Pritchard. *The Nuer*, London, 1940.
20. A. Gaitskell. *Gezira, a story of development in the Sudan*, London, 1959.
21. J. K. Giffen. *The Egyptian Sudan*, New York, 1905.
22. R. Gray. *A history of the Southern Sudan 1839–1889*, London, 1961.
23. J. A. de C. Hamilton (editor). *The Anglo-Egyptian Sudan from within*, London, 1935.
24. J. A. de C. Hamilton. 'Devolutionary principles in native administration', in Hamilton (no. 23).
25. Hasan Dafalla. 'A note on the political prisoners of Wadi Halfa', *SNR*, Vol. 47, (1966).
26. K. D. D. Henderson. 'Some notes on the history of the tribes living south of the Wadi el Ghala', (typescript, n.d., SAD/478/5).
27. R. Hill. *A Biographical dictionary of the Sudan*, (2nd edition), reprinted by Frank Cass & Co. Ltd., 1967.
28. R. Hill. *Egypt in the Sudan 1820–1881*, London, 1959.
29. R. Hill. 'Government and Christian Missions in the Anglo-Egyptian Sudan, 1899–1914', *Middle Eastern Studies*, Vol. 1, No. 2, (1965).
30. R. Hill. *Slatin Pasha*, London, 1965.
31. R. Hill. *Sudan Transport*, London, 1965.
32. S. Hillelson. 'Religion in the Sudan', in Hamilton (no. 23).
33. P. M. Holt. *A modern history of the Sudan*, (2nd edition), London, 1963.
34. P. M. Holt. *Egypt and the Fertile Crescent 1516–1922*, London, 1966.
35. P. M. Holt. *Holy families and Islam in the Sudan*, Princeton Near East Papers, No. 4, (1967).
36. P. M. Holt. *The Mahdist state in the Sudan 1881–1898*, London, 1958.
37. E. R. J. Hussey. 'A Fiki's clinic', *SNR*, Vol. 6, (1923).
38. E. R. J. Hussey. *Tropical Africa 1908–1944*, (published for private circulation), London, 1947.
39. H. C. Jackson. *Pastor on the Nile*, London, 1960.
40. H. C. Jackson. *Sudan days and ways*, London, 1954.
41. H. C. Jackson. 'The Nuer of the Upper Nile Province', *SNR*, Vol. 6, (1923).

42. P. D. Kauczor. 'The Afitti Nuba of Gebel Dair and their relation to the Nuba proper', *SNR*, Vol. 6, (1923).
43. E. F. Knight. *Letter from the Sudan*, London, 1897.
44. G. D. Lampen. 'The Baggara tribes', in Hamilton, (no. 23).
45. C. E. Lyall. 'Rights dues and customs prevailing among the Arab tribes in the White Nile province', *SNR*, Vol. 4, (1921).
46. H. A. MacMichael. *A history of the Arabs in the Sudan*, 2 vols, (2nd impression), reprinted by Frank Cass & Co. Ltd., 1967.
47. H. A. MacMichael. 'Reminiscences of Kordofan in 1906', (typescript, n.d., SAD/294/18).
48. H. A. MacMichael. *The Anglo-Egyptian Sudan*, London, 1934.
49. H. A. MacMichael. 'The Kheiran', *SNR*, Vol. 3, (1920).
50. P. Magnus. *Kitchener, portrait of an imperialist*, (Grey Arrow edition), London, 1961.
51. Mahgoub Mohamed Salih. 'The Sudanese press', *SNR*, Vol. 46, (1965).
52. P. F. Martin. *The Sudan in evolution*, London, 1921.
53. J. G. Matthew. 'Land customs and tenure in Singa district', *SNR*, Vol. 4, (1921).
54. K. Meinhof. *Eine studienfahrt nach Kordofan*, Hamburg, 1916.
55. L. F. Nalder. 'The two Sudans: some aspects of the South', in Hamilton, (no. 23).
56. D. Newbold. 'The Beja tribes of the Red Sea Hinterland', in Hamilton, (no. 23).
57. A. Paul. *A history of the Beja tribes of the Sudan*, Cambridge, 1954. [to be reprinted by Frank Cass & Co. Ltd.]
58. H. St. G. Peacock. *A report on the land settlement of the Gezira, Messelemia district*, London, 1913.
59. C. C. Reining. *The Zande Scheme*, Illinois, 1966.
60. Saburi Biobaku and Muhammad Al-Hagg. 'The Sudanese Mahdiyya and the Niger-Chad Region', in I. M. Lewis (ed.) *Islam in Tropical Africa*, London, 1966, pp. 425–441.
61. J. W. Sagar. 'Notes on the history, religion, and customs of the Nuba', *SNR*, Vol. 5, (1922).
62. G. N. Sanderson. *England Europe and the Upper Nile 1882–1899*, Edinburgh, 1965.
63. L. M. Sanderson. 'Educational development and administrative control in the Nuba region of the Sudan', *Journal of African History*, Vol. 4, (1963).
64. L. M. Sanderson. 'Educational development in the Southern Sudan', *SNR*, Vol. 43, (1962).
65. M. Shibeika. *The independent Sudan*, New York, 1959.
66. N. Shuqayr (Shoucair). *Ta'rīkh al-Sūdān al-qadīm wa'l-ḥadīth wa jughrāfiyatuhu*, Cairo, n.d. [1903].
67. R. C. Slatin Pasha. *Fire and Sword in the Sudan . . .1879–1895*, London, 1896.
68. H. C. Squires. *The Sudan medical service, an experiment in social medicine*, London, 1958.
69. W. Sterry. 'Some notes on the administration of justice in Africa',

Reale Accademia D'Italia VIII Convegno 'Volta', (Roma 4–11 Ottobre, 1938).

70. C. H. Stigand. *Equatoria, the Lado Enclave*, London, 1923, reprinted by Frank Cass & Co. Ltd., 1968.
71. S. Symes. *Tour of Duty*, London, 1946.
72. A. B. Theobald. *'Alī Dīnār, last Sultan of Darfur 1898–1916*, London 1965.
73. A. B. Theobald. *The Mahdīya, a history of the Anglo-Egyptian Sudan 1881–1899*, London, 1951.
74. R. L. Tignor. *Modernization and British colonial rule in Egypt 1882–1914*, Princeton, 1966.
75. J. D. Tothill (editor). *Agriculture in the Sudan*, London, 1948.
76. J. S. Trimingham. *Islam in the Sudan*, reprinted by Frank Cass & Co. Ltd., 1965.
77. J. S. Trimingham. *The Christian approach to Islam in the Sudan*, London, 1949.
78. C. A. Willis. 'Religious confraternities of the Sudan', *SNR*, Vol. 4, (1921).
79. F. R. Wingate. *Mahdiism and the Egyptian Sudan*, (2nd edition), reprinted by Frank Cass & Co. Ltd., 1968.
80. F. R. Wingate. *Ten years' captivity in the Mahdi's camp 1882–1892 . . . From the original manuscripts of Father Joseph Ohrwalder*, London, 1892.
81. R. Wingate. *Wingate of the Sudan*, London, 1955.

Index